FRIEND OF
SCIENCE
FRIEND OF
FAITH

Listening to God in His Works and Word

FRIEND OF SCIENCE FRIEND OF FAITH

Listening to God in His Works and Word

GREGG DAVIDSON

Kregel
Academic

Friend of Science, Friend of Faith: Listening to God in His Works and Word
© 2019 by Gregg Davidson

Published by Kregel Academic, an imprint of Kregel Publications, 2450 Oak Industrial Dr. NE, Grand Rapids, MI 49505-6020.

All Scripture quotations, unless otherwise indicated, are from the New American Standard Bible® (NASB). Copyright © 1960, 1962, 1963, 1968, 1971, 1972, 1973, 1975, 1977, 1995 by The Lockman Foundation. Used by permission. www.Lockman.org

Scripture quotations marked ESV are from The Holy Bible, English Standard Version® (ESV®), copyright © 2001 by Crossway, a publishing ministry of Good News Publishers. Used by permission. All rights reserved.

Scripture quotations marked KJV are from the King James Version.

Scripture quotations marked NIV are from the Holy Bible, New International Version®, NIV®. Copyright © 1973, 1978, 1984, 2011 by Biblica, Inc.™ Used by permission of Zondervan. All rights reserved worldwide. www.zondervan.com

All additional italicized portions of Scripture are the author's emphasis.

The Greek font GraecaU and the Hebrew font New JerusalemU are both available from www.linguistsoftware.com/lgku.htm, +1-425-775-1130.

Figures 1–3, 5–16, 18–20, 23, 28, 31, 34–41 are illustrated by Hayden Lambert, Le'Herman Payton, Paul Mitchel, and D'Marius Madkins. Used by permission of Gregg Davidson.

The following figures were used by permission: Figure 21 (archeopteryx skeleton) adapted from D. R. Prothero, *Evolution: What the Fossils Say and Why It Matters*, 2007, Columbia University Press, 277, by Gregg Davidson; Figure 21 (dove skeleton) adapted from Wikipedia page by Gregg Davidson; Figure 22 adapted from Robert L. Carroll, *Vertebrate Paleontology and Evolution*, 340; Figure 24 from D. R. Prothero, *Evolution: What the Fossils Say and Why It Matters*, 2007, Columbia University Press. Reprinted with permission of the publisher; Figures 25–26 adapted from multiple sources by Gregg Davidson; Figure 27 by Roman Yevseyev; Figures 32, 33, *The Fossil Trail*, 2nd ed., by Tattersall Copyright © 2009, by permission of Oxford University Press, USA; Figure 42 adapted from Davidson and Wolgemuth (2018) *Perspectives on Science and Christian Faith, 70*(2):75–89 by Gregg Davidson. The full original article is available at https://network.asa3.org/page/PSCF?.; Figures 4, 17, 21, 29, 30, 43 are public domain (pre-1923).

ISBN 978-0-8254-4541-5

Printed in the United States of America

19 20 21 22 23 / 5 4 3 2 1

To my parents, Paul & Ruth,
who first instilled in me
a desire to understand,
and to my wife, Kristin,
who has made the
journey a delight.

CONTENTS

ACKNOWLEDGMENTS

This work has benefited from a great number of teachers, colleagues, and friends over many years. My early investigations as a student were inspired by Gerald Haddock, a devoted Christian and geology professor long ago at Wheaton College. Davis Young was influential in my thinking, first through his seminal book *Christianity and the Age of the Earth*, and later as a friend and collaborator. His more recent book, *The Bible, Rocks and Time*, coauthored with my friend Ralph Stearley, is a wonderful reference for anyone interested in the history and defense of modern geological science from a Christian perspective. Ken Wolgemuth, a ministry partner for more than a decade (whose enthusiasm is unquenchable), encouraged and supported this work in too many ways to list. The descriptions and arguments contained in *Friend of Science, Friend of Faith* reflect input (intentional or otherwise) from a wide array of scientists, theologians, friends, and acquaintances representing a variety of viewpoints, including those whose opinions differ greatly from my own. Early drafts benefited significantly from spirited e-mail exchanges with Nathaniel Morgan (the friendly opposition). I am indebted to Dale Ralph Davis for listening to and commenting on theological arguments. Richard Potts graciously granted an interview at the Smithsonian Institution to bring me up to speed on the nuances of human ancestry. Reviews by Robert Kroeger and Arend Poelarends on cosmology, Gabriel Wrobel on anthropology, Steve Threlkeld and Joel Duff on biology, Ryan Bebej on paleontology, Dennis Venema on genetics, David Wilcox on human evolution, and Neil Manson on Intelligent Design, helped ferret out mistakes derived from my limited understanding in each discipline (any remaining mistakes are entirely my own). Many others made contributions through discussions, encouragement, and proofreading; a hopelessly incomplete alphabetical list (without reference to where they fall in the origins debate) includes Kathryn Applegate, Marie Barnard, Brad Bertelsen, David Campbell, Matthew Campbell, Paul Davidson, Lee Dearing, Darrel Falk, Jonathan Grimes, Carol Hill, Erik Hom, Ken Keathley, Keith Long, Melvin Manickavasagam, Richard Mercer, Keith Miller, Steve Moshier, Kent Ratajeski, David Rice, Marcus Ross, Joshua Swamidass, Ken Turner, David Vaughn, Pete Waller, Ray Williams, and

Lance Yarbrough. I also have a great appreciation for the inquisitive students at the University of Mississippi who have interacted with me in the classroom and joined animated after-hour discussions on Scripture and the history of life. To bring the book to final fruition, I am indebted to the staff at Kregel Publications: Shawn Vander Lugt, for shepherding the book through its multiple revisions; Laura Bartlett, for insightful comments and book design; Deborah Helmers, for extraordinary work catching potentially embarrassing typos and factual errors, and Dennis Hillman, for seeing value in the project at its start. Finally, nothing would have been possible without the encouragement, support, and grounding of my wife, Kristin Davidson, my soulmate of thirty years—and counting.

PREFACE

F*riend of Science, Friend of Faith* is a deep revision of an earlier book called *When Faith and Science Collide*. The decision to amend the title was driven, in part, from hearing someone once explaining the premise of the book as being "not really about conflict, but about reconciliation." The old title inadvertently drew more attention to the apparent clashes between science and Christian faith than on their resolution. The new title better reflects the nature of the work.

Why the need for a revision? For one, a great deal of new material was published in the last ten years that is pertinent to the conversation, from both scientific and religious perspectives. It is an exciting time to live, with new discoveries and insights coming out almost daily. On the scientific side, advances in DNA sequencing, for species ranging from whales to Neanderthals, is opening a whole new world of inquiry into the history of life. New fossils are rewriting popular understandings of how modern organisms are tied to those in the past, and evolutionary hypotheses are even being put to the test in benchtop experiments. On the religious side, significant contributions have been made by theologians and Christian scientists wrestling with how new scientific findings comport or challenge traditional understandings of the Bible. Some are encouraging, and some troubling.

A second reason is a maturation of my own understanding of the issues and conflicting voices at the intersection of science and the Bible. Chapters addressing the intelligent design and young-earth movements have been expanded, with more attention given to foundational assumptions, methods of argument, and the resulting impact on the mission of the church. More attention has also been given to the subject of biblical inerrancy.

Finally, with the benefit of readers and critics of the original book, I have tossed out some material that did not have the desired effect, reorganized the content into five parts to make the logical flow easier to follow, and added more than twenty new figures.

PART 1

CONFLICTS NEW AND OLD

1

SETTING THE STAGE—CRISIS OF FAITH

Riley sat alone in her dorm room feeling as though her world was getting turned upside down. She had come to college two years earlier, full of dreams and aspirations of a career in the sciences. With a love for the outdoors and uncertain which field of science to pursue, she had tested the waters with introductory classes in both biology and geology. She had known her faith would be tested. Her parents and youth minister had forewarned her about the humanistic worldview pervasive in American universities. Full of the energy and confidence of a young bird launching from the nest, she was ready for the challenge. She believed what the Bible taught and had answers to challenge the flimsy presuppositions employed in support of evolution and millions of years.

But she did not encounter what she expected. She had anticipated arguments based largely on wishful humanistic thinking, with theories built on untestable assumptions that could not even reasonably be called science. As she plunged into her studies, she was increasingly confronted by both the breadth and depth of evidence for views she had previously dismissed. To make matters worse, the evidence was not just being preached by proselytizing atheists. Yes, there had been a few professors and fellow students who mocked all forms of religious belief, especially Christian belief, but the larger number seemed to be normal people honestly striving to understand how nature worked.

At a small group Bible study, she sat in silent upheaval as a fellow student spoke derisively of the supposed absence of transitional fossils to support evolution. Riley kept her mouth shut about the wealth of transitional fossils now known, ranging from feathered dinosaurs to whales with legs. Afterward, she caught up with Doug, a campus-ministry intern who was leading the study. She asked him if being a Christian required belief in a literal six-day creation in the recent past. For Doug, there was a simple answer to this simple question. If God truly inspired the writing of the Scriptures, a literal, or "plain sense" reading of the Genesis account must be true. Any other reading would challenge its veracity and authority.

The next day, Doug called Riley from the lobby of the dorm to tell her he had brought her a book. She was genuinely appreciative of the effort, though less certain about the gift itself. The book was written by a prominent young-earth creationist. Back in her room, Riley opened the book at random to the second chapter, one of several devoted to debunking old-earth science and biological evolution. The chapter was filled with examples of "incontrovertible facts" documenting the impossibility of scientific claims. She read one, squinting and reading again, sure she had misunderstood. She read another and was equally confounded. She read the entire chapter, dumbfounded at the number of misconceptions and false assertions about fossils, scientific laws, and even the definition of terms.

She shook her head at the audacity of one in particular, that uniformitarian geologists assume that the rates of natural processes observed today were always the same in the past. She marveled that the writer could say such a thing, knowing that her "uniformitarian" professors taught that competing views for the demise of the dinosaurs included a giant meteorite impact and massive volcanic eruptions. No professor had *ever* taught her that rates in the past were constant, nor that they were all slow.

If the veracity of the Bible was linked with the purported truthfulness of the book she had been given, she could not fathom how the Bible could be considered the legitimate Word of God, at least not a God who valued logic, reason, and truth. Her disquiet began to turn to resentment as she contemplated the possibility that her family and church had unwittingly indoctrinated her with fairy tales. Though it would be months before she could bring herself to tell her parents, her Bible found itself that evening sitting in her waste bin, waiting for its new home in the county landfill.

There is a growing population of young adults, raised up in Christian churches, who could read this opening story and reasonably believe I was telling *their* story. In its general description, it is neither unique to one person's experience nor infrequent in occurrence. Many tentative seekers could also readily identify with Riley's experience, differing only in detail. For a time, they considered the possible truth of Christianity, until encountering the stumbling block of a recent creation and finding it insurmountable.

The underlying cause of these spiritual shipwrecks is hotly contested in the church today. For some Christians, it is the inevitable result of clashes between biblical and humanistic worldviews. Their primary sympathies lie with Doug, grateful for his faithful effort to reach out with a defense for the gospel and saddened by hearts hardened against truth. An implicit assumption is made that the stumbling block to faith is not really scientific evidence, but a basic unwillingness to take God at his word. If people would simply *believe* the Bible, they would *see* that science actually supports a young earth.

Other Christians argue, with equal conviction, that the battle lines have been drawn not just in the wrong spot, but entirely on the wrong field. Our imperfect interpretation of the Bible has been conflated with the Bible itself, a flawed theological foundation leading to the construction of an equally flawed scientific house of cards. It is the young-earth position that does not take God truly at his word, imposing human ideas on the biblical text. Doug, in this view, has erected a needless barrier in the path to faith—a well-intentioned builder of stumbling blocks!

Which view is correct? There is no shortage of websites, books, articles, blogs, and videos that claim to answer this question. Some are quite good, though very few back up to ask the more basic question of *how* to approach Scripture and science when they seem to conflict. History should teach us that this is not just a matter of "believing the Bible." Seventeenth-century believers taking this simplistic approach unjustly condemned Copernicus and Galileo for undermining the "plain meaning" of Scripture that the sun orbits the earth. The Bible was not wrong, but many were too quick to assume that the traditional understanding of what the Bible taught was what the writers intended.

With history in mind, the objectives of this book are twofold. The first is to develop a general approach for addressing apparent conflicts whenever they may arise, in a way that honors Scripture and honestly engages science. It will not start with an assumption that science is right. Science, as the study of God's natural creation, will simply be allowed to raise questions that will drive us back to Scripture, with the humility to recognize that human understanding of God's perfect Word is not as equally perfect. While new questions may lead occasionally to new scriptural insights, none will challenge the truth of the Bible nor any core Christian doctrine.[1] Rather, where multiple interpretations *could* be true for a particular passage, new insights may simply serve to dust away never-intended meanings that cloud our view, allowing the true message, one that was there all along, to shine more brightly.

The second objective of the book is to apply the approach to the current discord on origins to see what may be learned. In the pages that follow, we'll first look to see how believers in the past wrestled with apparent conflicts between science and biblical understanding to help us develop our approach for looking forward. As we apply this method to the subject of origins, science will be permitted to prompt a return to Scripture, looking with fresh eyes for what Scripture can tell us about itself on each question raised. Part of this exercise will require, and benefit from, an assessment of how our own culture influences the way we define terms like *truth* and *inerrancy*. Only after a thorough reckoning of the written Word (three chapters worth) will we dive into the strength of evidence offered up by those who study the material world.

My conviction is not only that modern science fails to contradict an accurate understanding of the Bible, but that the simplicity and elegance with which God's natural revelation illustrates his special revelation is breathtaking. My hope is that this book will not end with the last word of the final chapter, but that Doug will finish the opening story with a more edifying visit to Riley.

---

1. For example, the doctrines expressed in the Nicene and Apostles' Creeds.

2

HISTORICAL CONTEXT—HELIOCENTRISM VS. SCRIPTURE

"The sun rises and the sun sets...." (Eccl. 1:5)

The year was 1633. Galileo Galilei stood before the ecclesiastical court for the final time under the demand that he recant his heresy that the earth was not the center of the universe. It was a confrontation more than 100 years in the making. Heliocentrism, the theory that the sun, rather than the earth, resides at the center of our solar system, was suggested as far back as the early Greeks and Romans, but was not taken seriously again until similar arguments were made by Copernicus in a handwritten book called the *Little Commentary* in 1514.[1] A century later, Galileo had amassed a sizable body of scientific evidence demonstrating that the sun—not the earth—was indeed the center of our local system. The Vatican, and many professing Christians at the time, vigorously opposed the idea on the grounds that it challenged the authority of the Bible. God inspired the words recorded in Ecclesiastes 1:5 and Psalm 19:6 saying that "the sun rises and the sun sets," and that the sun's "rising is from one end of the heavens, and its circuit to the other end." Two additional Psalms proclaim that the earth is "firmly established" and "will not be moved"

---

1. Copernicus published a more expansive work in 1543 called *De Revolutionibus Orbium Coelestium* (*On the Revolutions of the Celestial Orbs*); Broderick, *Galileo: The Man, His Work, His Misfortunes*, 18.

(Pss. 93:1; 104:5), and the history of Israel's battles includes an account of a miraculous event when the sun stood still in the sky (Josh. 10:13). Because of these verses, it was strongly believed that Galileo's measurements and conclusions were not only erroneous, but heretical.

Modern Protestant believers are tempted to dismiss this science-church conflict as a Catholic mistake, but such an assertion is unwarranted. The Catholic Church is the focus of the historical account only because of the legal injunctions eventually levied against Galileo by the Vatican and its political authority to act on its indictments. The possibility that heliocentrism might be inherently in conflict with Scripture was a Christian concern, not just a Catholic one. Following the publication of the *Little Commentary*, Martin Luther, the father of the Protestant movement, spoke of the foolishness of heliocentric notions and cited Joshua 10:13 as effectively settling the matter.[2] John Calvin was another prominent Protestant who took issue with heliocentrism. A little more than a decade after the publication of *Revolutions*, Calvin wrote,

> We will see some who are so deranged, not only in religion but who in all things reveal their monstrous nature, that they will say that the sun does not move, and that it is the earth which shifts and turns. When we see such minds we must indeed confess that the devil possesses them.[3]

Though it is not possible to know the condition of Galileo's heart four centuries removed, his writings suggest that he never felt that he was challenging Scripture or the Christian faith. Galileo did not suggest that the Bible was flawed. Rather he argued that the traditional interpretation of these verses was flawed:

> The holy scriptures cannot err and the decrees therein contained are absolutely true and inviolable. But...its expounders and interpreters are liable to err in many ways; and one error in particular would be most grave and frequent, if we always stopped short at the literal signification of the words.[4]

---

2. *Luther's Works, Table Talk*, 358–59. *Table Talk* was published twenty years after Luther's death. If it does not accurately reflect Luther's views, as some claim, it nonetheless represents the thinking of the Protestant Christian recalling the conversation.
3. White, "Calvin and Copernicus: The problem reconsidered," 236. Calvin was not anti-science, nor did he support an overly literalistic view of Scripture, but he did write against heliocentrism.
4. Broderick, *Galileo*, 76.

Galileo argued that the interpretation of God's special revelation (Scripture) should be consistent with and illuminated by God's natural revelation (science). When faced with excommunication by the church and possible corporal punishment, Galileo signed a written abjuration confessing his sin and promising to cease his heretical teachings. For Galileo, however, the evidence for a sun-centered celestial system was so convincing that a true denial was a denial of reason itself. These sentiments were best recorded in an earlier, now frequently quoted statement,

> I do not think it necessary to believe that the same God who gave us our senses, our speech, our intellect, would have put aside the use of these.[5]

The infallibility and authority of Scripture remain central tenets of Christianity, yet few Christians today hold that the earth is the center of the universe. Somewhere during the last four centuries, the church at large transitioned from a strictly literal interpretation of the verses in Ecclesiastes, Psalms, and Joshua, to an interpretation deemed more accurate even though less literal. It is still believed from Scripture that a miraculous event took place during Joshua's battle and that it is God who establishes the order of the universe, but Christians no longer argue that the intent of these Scriptures was to describe the physical movement of the sun and planets.

To avoid confusion over terminology, we need to be clear about what is meant here by the word *literal*. Some conservative Bible scholars define the word *literal* as the intended meaning taken within the context.[6] In this sense, *literal* is essentially synonymous with *literary*, where forms of literature, figures of speech, context, and the author's intent are all taken into consideration to arrive at the appropriate interpretation. While I concur with this approach to understanding Scripture, I find the definition of the term unfortunate, serving to confuse more than clarify. By this definition biblical poetry and allegory are correctly interpreted in a *literal* fashion, which means to interpret them *figuratively*. Meanwhile, among folks sitting in the pews, *literal* means nearly the opposite. A literal understanding is one that accepts the words to mean exactly what they say. A passage of Scripture is *either* literal *or* it is figurative.

Confusion on this subject has led some to speak instead of the "straightforward reading" or the "plain sense" meaning of the text. This turns out to

---

5. Broderick, *Galileo*, 78.
6. *Chicago Statement on Biblical Hermeneutics*, Article XV.

be of questionable help, for there are many places in Scripture where one could argue that the "plain sense" reading is a figurative reading (think of the dragon of Revelation 12). With common folks in mind, I have chosen to use the more vernacular definition of *literal*, where a literal interpretation is one that accepts the words in question to mean just what the words say.

Returning to our historical account, fast-forward three centuries from the time of Galileo to Darwin, Hutton, and other scientists who presented scientific theories that again appeared to be in conflict with Scripture. Initially, one must ask if these modern conflicts are of the same essence as the conflict championed by Galileo, or if they are wholly different. Many Christian writers today argue with considerable conviction that they are indeed wholly different. The conflict arising from Galileo's assertions altered our interpretation of expressions in the "Wisdom Literature" of Ecclesiastes and the poetry of Psalms, and simply brought to our attention that in Joshua descriptions are often made from the perspective of the viewer rather than from some fixed point in space. As an example, today we still insist that we can accurately predict the time of a "sunrise" even though we know the sun is not rising in a literal sense. In contrast, evolution and billions of years of earth history are said to challenge the very foundation of Scripture. If the opening words of Scripture cannot be taken literally, what can be? If a nonliteral interpretation of the creation story is accepted, are we not stepping out onto the proverbial slippery slope where ultimately nothing in Scripture can be taken at face value?

Though it is argued that the challenges to Scripture presented by Galileo and Darwin are quite different, it is not likely that church leaders (Protestant or Catholic) of the seventeenth century would have agreed.[7] Placing ourselves in their shoes, if it was conceded that the sun does not revolve around the earth, then a portion of Scripture that was interpreted literally for thousands of years must now be interpreted nonliterally. If the sun did not actually stop its revolution around the earth during Joshua's battle, did a miraculous event really take place at all? Could we even believe with confidence that there was a God-ordained conquest of Canaan, a Davidic kingdom, or real prophets? Is the entire Bible mere allegory? Either science is right, or Scripture is right. Scientific theories are continually in flux and not all stand the test of time. Scripture, on the other hand, is God-breathed and immutable. Therefore, when science and Scripture clash, science must yield to Scripture!

---

7. Davis and Chmielewski, "Galileo and the Garden of Eden: Historical reflections on creationist hermeneutics," 449–76.

The idea that science might be used to help interpret Scripture was also problematic. To allow the use of telescopes and mathematical calculations to arrive at an altered understanding of a biblical passage suggests that the Scriptures are not really accessible to the common person. And why would God allow his people to believe something false for millennia only to reveal the truth through secular scientists? Are scientists to be our new high priests and Nature our new revealed Word?

The *perceived* challenge was no different in the time of Galileo than it is today. Those who opposed heliocentrism on biblical grounds did so as passionately as people today oppose evolution and deep time.[8] So what is to be done? No one consciously wishes to repeat the mistakes of the past, but neither do we desire to make new mistakes in an effort to avoid old ones. How do we know when we should hold fast to a traditional interpretation of Scripture in the face of all opposition, and when we should welcome new discoveries to aid our understanding? Must traditional interpretations of Scripture make way for science every time a new theory comes along? Surely not, but how do we make these assessments?

Reliance on God's Spirit to provide illumination is a necessity. Having said this, we must acknowledge the human propensity for "relying" on the Spirit to reach conclusions determined before ever really seeking truth. The vast number of Christian denominations in existence is a testament to how often people reach different conclusions while all claiming reliance on the Spirit. God's Spirit does not lie or mislead, but our sensitivity to his working is imperfect. This book was written on the conviction that God, who created both the universe and the Bible, has given us both his Spirit and the ability to reason through a series of logical questions to address this issue.

ASSESSING APPARENT SCIENCE-BIBLE TENSIONS

Here are three questions that can be asked when a scientific theory appears to conflict with Scripture:

1. Does the infallibility of Scripture rest on a literal interpretation of the verses in question?
2. Does the science conflict with the intended message of Scripture?
3. Is the science credible?

---

8. *Deep time* is a term used to refer to natural history going back millions or billions of years.

The questions do not start with science. Question 1 is not some form of, "Well, how strong is the physical evidence?" The questions address the scientific evidence only after the scriptural questions have been answered. Science initially serves only as the impetus for driving us back to the Bible for another look.

Seventeenth Century Revisited

Consider heliocentrism in this context. Prior to Copernicus, there was no reason to doubt the traditional interpretations of Ecclesiastes or related verses regarding the cosmos, for there was no evidence to call them into question. Christians and atheists alike held the words of Scripture to be true when describing the rising and setting of the sun, for this seemed to be self-evident. A reevaluation of these Scriptures was not necessary until Copernicus, and later Galileo, provided reasons to begin asking the questions above. Though the church was initially slow to ask these questions, they were all eventually addressed (though perhaps not consciously in the order suggested).

Question 1: Does the infallibility of Scripture rest on a literal interpretation of the verses in question?

We can approach the relevant verses today in much the same fashion as they would have been approached in the days of Galileo. Passages such as Solomon's description of the sun rising and setting[9] and Joshua's reference to the sun standing have two possible interpretations that would not call into question the infallibility of Scripture. The phenomena described could have happened exactly as recorded (sun orbits earth), or the phenomena could have happened as witnessed from the reference point of the human observer. In other words, the passages accurately describe what Solomon and Joshua *saw*, just as we may accurately describe the beauty of a "sunset" rather than an "earthroll."

References to the immovability of the earth in the Psalms could likewise be interpreted in two ways. The literal, "plain sense" reading is that the earth is stationary. But by allowing Galileo's work to prompt us to take a deeper look, we may discover that the expression "will not be moved" does not always mean "assigned to a fixed point in space." Using Scripture to interpret Scripture, we find the same phrase (same Hebrew words) in Psalm 16:8 where David says, "I have set the LORD always before me: because he is at my right hand, I shall not be moved" (KJV).[10] David obviously was not referring to his

---

9. Though generally attributed to Solomon, the author of Ecclesiastes is not known with certainty.
10. Hebrew: בַּל אֶמּוֹט (*'emowt-bal*), "be moved, not"; NASB translates as "not be shaken."

geographical location, suggesting he was now fixed in one position, no longer able to step forward or back, left or right. He was speaking of the firm establishment of his own welfare in the providence of God. The same may be said for the earth. The planet is firmly in the providential care of the Creator, and it will not be removed before its time.

These observations illustrate that Bible-honoring, nonliteral interpretations are *possible* for these passages without assessing which is more accurate. This brings us to the next question.

Question 2: Does the science conflict with the intended message of Scripture?

It is clear to us today that the central message of these texts was never celestial mechanics. Solomon's message was not instruction on solar migration, but about the futility of human efforts. Joshua's message was intended to relate to future generations that God is master of his creation, intervening in a marvelous and incredible way on behalf of his people. A lesson in orbital dynamics would have only confused ancient readers and distracted from the power of the intended message.

When considering the Psalms, even independently of the scientific evidence, what message is of greater significance: the motion of the planet, or the fact that it was made, set into place, and protected by the Lord God? Of course, Scripture does not have to be limited to a single meaning. The Psalms could speak of *both* the immobility of the earth and God's provision for it, but nothing is ultimately lost from Scripture if it becomes evident that the Bible was not written with instruction on the orbit of planets in mind. In fact, brushing away the unintended understanding serves to allow the true message to fully capture our easily distracted attention.

These observations bring us to the recognition that Galileo's science presents no threat to Scripture. The only remaining question, then, addresses the *quality* of the science.

Question 3: Is the science credible?

We take the credibility of Galileo's observations much for granted today. Of course the earth revolves around the sun. But consider the seventeenth-century farmer or store clerk pondering the unbelievable assertion that the sun stands still while the earth hurtles through space at breathtaking speed. Could Galileo bring his observations into the laboratory and test them? Could he contrive a way in which he could physically see the earth's motion? If the earth continually spins toward the east at 1,000 miles per hour, surely the wind would always blow to the west as an unrelenting super-hurricane. Nothing could remain standing!

Galileo could not physically see the earth in motion, nor were his hypotheses fully testable in the laboratory. Most of his conclusions derived from calculations based on observations of the time and position of planets millions of miles away. There was already a scientifically based explanation for the position of planets that left the earth at the center. Ptolemy had a system of equations that allowed the path of each planet to be predicted as it traveled around the earth. So why trade in Ptolemy's universe for Galileo's?

The trouble with the Ptolemaic system was at least twofold. First, from a human perspective, the planets periodically appear to reverse direction for a time, requiring each to travel along a mini-orbit, called an *epicycle*, as it traversed its much larger orbit around the earth (Fig. 1). A heliocentric model accounted for planetary motion with simple orbits, without the need of epicycles. Second, the planets continually drifted from the predicted Ptolemaic path, requiring periodic corrections. The heliocentric model required fewer adjustments over time (especially with Kepler's discovery that the orbits were elliptical rather than circular).

A third problem, unknown to Galileo and his contemporaries, would not be understood until Isaac Newton's formulation of gravity a half century later.

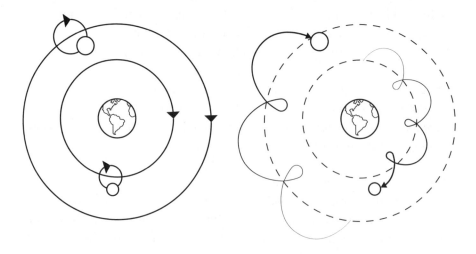

Figure 1—Geocentric model showing orbits and epicycles of two planets traveling around the earth. The looping arrows on the right show the expected pathway combining the orbits and epicycles on the left.

Gravity provided a logical mechanism for the orbits of the planets around the much more massive sun. No physical mechanism could account for the orbits or epicycles of the geocentric system.

It was further appreciated that not all legitimate science is done in a laboratory. Hypotheses may be drawn and tested using both historical and distant observations of natural phenomena. We will dive more deeply into this subject in Chapter 8.

WHY DIDN'T THEY SEE IT?

The scriptural conclusions drawn above seem obvious to many Christians today, so it is worth considering why they were not viewed as obvious in the days of Copernicus and Galileo. We benefit today from a long history of acceptance of the current interpretations of Ecclesiastes 1:5; Joshua 10:13; and Psalms 19:6; 93:1; and 104:5 by theologians and preachers we trust. At the time when theologians were first grappling with heliocentrism and its scriptural implications, there was no history of acceptance. Every believer who decided that the Bible was not teaching about planetary movement did so without the explicit support of the current and ancient church body. It is far easier for us to believe as we do today with more than three centuries of belief by Christians who paved the way before us.

The idea of reevaluating long-standing scriptural interpretation because of scientific evidence was unsettling to seventeenth-century Christians, and it continues to be unsettling today, often because of a sense that any reevaluation driven by science is "giving up ground." There are at least two underlying reasons for this feeling.

Problem 1: Failure to Recognize That Nature Reflects Its Author

We tend to think of the Bible as being a self-contained document requiring no other source than God's illumination for understanding. At one level, this is true. The central message intended for all times and all believers must be understandable apart from scientific observations only available after the Renaissance or the nuclear age. But what of unintended meanings that we may have unconsciously added to Scripture? Seventeenth-century Christians believed that the intention of Ecclesiastes 1:5 was to teach both on the condition of humanity *and* on the movement of planets. The twenty-first-century Christian believes the intent was only instruction on the condition of humanity. The central message remains unchanged and independent of knowledge of modern scientific discovery. Knowledge of science served only to cast off an unintended, secondary message.

Even this makes us uneasy, though, because of a sense that science should not play *any* role in understanding Scripture. We forget that God repeatedly uses his natural creation, even within the pages of Scripture, to illuminate his message. Indeed, Romans 1:20 tells us, "For since the creation of the world His invisible attributes, His eternal power and divine nature, have been clearly seen, being understood through what has been made...." Scripture repeatedly draws analogies from the natural world to convey spiritual realities.[11] If nature reflects its Author, we should expect then that a thorough study of nature will occasionally give us previously unrecognized insights into the Scriptures themselves.

Far from giving up ground, these new insights can be thought of as freshly plowed soil that unearths problematic rocks to discard. The rich theological soil was there all the time, but our understanding is improved by removal of a few infertile interpretational rocks. In this sense, it is *gained* ground.

Problem 2: Failure to Differentiate Scripture and the Interpretation of Scripture

The second and perhaps more important reason reevaluation of Scripture is unsettling comes back to our tendency to conflate God's Word with our interpretation of his Word. God's Word is immutable and true; our interpretation is not always so. Failure to recognize this has the potential to cause tremendous personal upheaval. If the weight of evidence begins to accumulate that my interpretation is in error, but I am unable to differentiate my interpretation from Scripture itself, I will begin to retreat into a world of contradictions where some truths must be ignored in order to cling to others.

This can be illustrated using a variation of the familiar parable of houses built on rock and those built on sand. In this reformulated parable, Scripture is the foundation and our interpretation is the house built upon it. Two builders both recognize the inferiority of sand and build their houses on rock. When small storms pass, both houses are damaged, but still stand. One builder recognizes defects, not in the foundation, but in the design of the house built upon it. He modifies the construction to anchor it more effectively on the undamaged foundation and weathers the next storm with few ill effects.

---

11. Examples of nature used to illustrate theological principles: industry of ants (Prov. 6:6), responsiveness of sheep (John 10:3), security of rock deer (2 Sam. 22:34), sinners compared to weeds/tares (Matt. 13:24–43), kingdom of God compared to seeds and leaven (Matt. 13:3–23, 33–35).

The second builder, unable to see the difference between structure and foundation, refuses to see damage as weakness and builds a second story with the same faulty construction. Living on the newly built second floor, the builder remains confident because the foundation is sure. Unrepaired and weakened by the weight of additional floors, the house eventually falls. Conditioned by years of belief in his own work, the builder's last thought is that the *foundation* has failed him.

In this light, consider the plight of a group of eighteenth-century Christians still convinced that the now widely accepted theory of heliocentrism directly contradicts Scripture. Unable to distinguish between their understanding of Scripture and Scripture itself, they hold fast to belief in an earth-centered universe. As the evidence continues to build for heliocentrism, the group finds various ways of coping with the assault on their faith.

- Some come to believe that scientists throughout the Western world have conspired to maintain the longest-running hoax in human history.

- Others, unable to conceive of a conspiracy of such immense proportions, believe that scientists are accurately reporting what they see, but that God's natural creation does not reflect the way it was actually made. The universe was created with the *appearance* of heliocentrism, perhaps to test believers, or to mislead the godless who are unwilling to have faith in God's eyewitness account.

- A third subset argues that nature accurately demonstrates geocentrism if one has a biblical worldview. Ministries are established pointing out the ever-changing nature of science versus the immutable Word of God, piling up "evidence" against the biblically compromising position of heliocentrism, and linking the degradation of societal morals to the disregard of God's clear teaching.[12]

- A final portion responds by simply insulating themselves from the discussion and believing what they wish without having to wrestle with difficult evidence.

---

12. These are not just hypothetical. Some geocentric ministries still exist today, e.g., *Christian Flat Earth Ministry*, https://christianflatearthministry.org.

With the clarity of hindsight, all four of these methods of dealing with the challenge of heliocentrism can be seen as poorly designed constructions built upon a foundation that is intrinsically solid, but of little benefit to the builders. So where does this leave us when considering more contemporary issues like the age of the earth or evolution? Are those standing against the prevailing scientific wisdom fighting the good fight, or are they building the same faulty construction as our unfortunate eighteenth-century holdouts described above? This should not just be a matter of personal opinion. We should be able to discern the truth through a study of Scripture, and the Spirit's illumination.

The next three chapters will work toward an answer to a variant of Question 1: Does the infallibility of the Bible rest on a literal interpretation of the creation story? We'll start broadly in Chapter 3, considering how references to nature are employed throughout the Bible and how they relate to our understanding of inerrancy. Chapter 4 will draw attention to what can be learned from a comparison between the opening chapters of the New and Old Testaments before focusing full attention on the Genesis text in Chapter 5.

PART 2

THE MEANING OF SCRIPTURE

3

NATURE AND BIBLICAL INERRANCY

The doctrine of inerrancy is a belief that the Bible, by virtue of being inspired by the Holy Spirit, is free from error in all it intends to teach.[1] Nothing false is affirmed or defended. In short, it is *true*. This is a central doctrine of the Christian faith that is widely affirmed by believers. There is less unity, however, on what exactly this means. One common understanding says that if the Bible is truly inspired by God and without error, then it must be true for every subject upon which it touches. This view, which I will call *comprehensive inerrancy*, is characterized well by a quote from John McArthur,

> Scripture *always* speaks with absolute authority. It is as authoritative when it instructs us as it is when it commands us. It is as true when it tells the future as it is when it records the past. Although it is not a textbook on science, wherever it intersects with scientific data, it speaks with the same authority as when giving moral precepts.[2]

This understanding does not discount the use of figurative language in Scripture. But when observations of nature are made that are not clearly metaphorical, phenomenological, or common figures of speech, there is an expectation that the Author of Creation has inspired truthful and accurate descriptions of the physical realm.

Others have argued that this view goes beyond Scripture's own claim for itself, and imposes a modern Western definition of inerrancy that the orig-

---

1. *Chicago Statement of Biblical Inerrancy*, Article XI, reads, "We affirm that Scripture, having been given by divine inspiration, is infallible, so that, far from misleading us, it is true and reliable in all the matters it addresses."
2. McArthur, "Creation: Believe it or not," 14–15.

inal writers would not have recognized.[3] According to 2 Timothy 3:16–17, "All Scripture is inspired by God and profitable for teaching, for reproof, for correction, for training in righteousness; so that the man of God may be adequate, equipped for every good work." This verse makes no claim of instruction on subjects such as medicine, technology, or nature. If the intention of Scripture is to communicate truths about the kingdom of God, is God not free to use illustrations from nature that were common to the perspective of readers at the time, without charge of error? Descriptions of nature that anticipated modern scientific discoveries would have served only to confuse the original audience and distract from the intended message.

The theological term for the second view is *divine accommodation* (or just *accommodation*). It is not a new idea dreamed up to allow room for the science of the industrial and nuclear ages, but is found in the writings of respected church fathers as far back as Origen (third century) and Augustine (fifth century).[4] John Calvin, though critical of heliocentrism, nonetheless argued that our "slight capacity" for understanding *necessitates* that God condescend to our abilities and comprehension, comparing it to a mother speaking in "baby talk" to her infant child.[5]

Either view (comprehensive inerrancy or divine accommodation) *could* be true regarding the Bible's "intersection with science." So how do we know which is *actually* true? For an isolated passage in Scripture, the answer can be difficult to ascertain. As an example, consider the inspired prayer of Samuel's mother, Hannah, in 1 Samuel 2:8, which includes the statement, "For the pillars of the earth are the LORD's, and He set the world on them." Few reading this today believe the earth rests on physical pillars. Among those who hold to biblical inerrancy, agreement is virtually universal that this passage is *not* providing instruction on the physical structure of the earth. But the rationale for that conclusion differs dramatically for the two views.

For the comprehensive-inerrancy view, reference to pillars of the earth must represent a figure of speech or metaphor for stability that was

---

3. Walton and Sandy, *The Lost World of Scripture: Ancient Literary Culture and Biblical Authority*; Greenwood, *Scripture and Cosmology: Reading the Bible Between the Ancient World and Modern Science*; Miller and Soden, *In the Beginning...We Misunderstood: Interpreting Genesis 1 in its Original Context*; Hill, *A Worldview Approach to Science and Scripture: Making Genesis Real*.

4. Origen, *Homilies on Jeremiah and 1 Kings 28*, 198–99; van Bavel, "The Creator and the integrity of the Creation."

5. Calvin, *Institutes of the Christian Religion*, 1.13.1. Calvin's quote is quite similar to the words of Origen more than a thousand years earlier (cited above).

well known *at the time of writing*.[6] If, on the other hand, the Israelites of Hannah's day actually thought that the earth rested on some sort of solid foundation, then this passage represents an example of divine accommodation; God condescended to the limited and imperfect human understanding of nature to communicate the truth of his authorship and sustaining power over his creation.

The only way to ascertain which view is correct, short of a direct revelation from God, is to survey the entire Bible for references to nature and compare the descriptions with archaeological discoveries of what people understood at the time of writing. If biblical descriptions of nature are found to deviate from the normative thinking of the day, but begin to align better with discoveries of nature through time and scientific discovery, then it would appear that instruction on nature was indeed intended. If, on the other hand, descriptions consistently fit the common, imperfect understanding of the original audience, then one must conclude that accommodation was at work.

This task is less daunting than it might seem. If the idea of divine accommodation is correct, it should take only one definitive example to demonstrate its merit: a concept of nature that is repeated throughout Scripture that is not mechanically scientifically correct based on modern knowledge, but fits well with ancient understanding. We'll consider three subjects where God's Word "intersects with science," topics that span the spectrum of scale in nature from tiny seeds to the vastness of the cosmos.

SEEDS

Truly, truly, I say to you, unless a grain of wheat falls into the earth and dies, it remains alone; but if it dies, it bears much fruit. (John 12:24)

And [Jesus] said, "How shall we picture the kingdom of God, or by what parable shall we present it? It is like a mustard seed, which, when sown upon the soil, though it is smaller than all the seeds that are upon the soil, yet when it is sown, it grows up and becomes larger than all the garden plants and forms large branches; so that the birds of the air can nest under its shade." (Mark 4:30–32)

---

6. Short, "Phenomenological language and semantic naïveté"; Barrick, "Old Testament evidence for a literal, historical Adam and Eve."

It is well known today that seeds do not actually die when planted, and that mustard seeds are not the smallest of all seeds (Fig. 2). Of course, the literary style of the verses above is parable, so we expect that fictional names or events may be used to illustrate the point. But Jesus based these parables on things that were real and familiar to his audience, things we would not expect to be fictionalized. God knows the nature of germination and the size of all seeds, so it is entirely reasonable to assume Jesus spoke with "absolute authority" on the nature of seeds as well as on the nature of the kingdom of God. If God says the mustard seed is the smallest of all seeds, even if within a parable, how could it not be so?

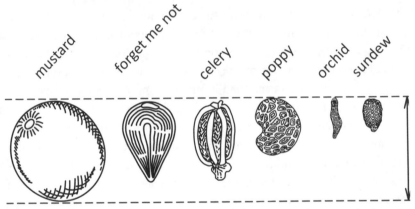

Figure 2—Examples of garden and flower seeds that are smaller than a mustard seed.[7]

And yet God was content to use the knowledge of the people at the time to convey his message without concern over how strictly accurate the description would be to those with greater scientific knowledge at a time far in the future. Could Jesus have told these parables using more technically accurate terminology and descriptions? Certainly. He could have provided a few caveats, saying, "The mustard seed is smaller than all the seeds *that you know of ...*" and "Though seeds don't *actually* die..." But with what result? The attention of his agriculturally savvy listeners would have undoubtedly focused on questions about seeds rather than the kingdom of God. The power of the message would have been diluted.[8]

7.　Orchid and sundew seeds are the European "common spotted orchid" and the South African "citrus-flowered sundew," respectively. The other seeds are common garden varieties.

8.　Miller and Soden, *In the Beginning... We Misunderstood*, 151.

It is additionally important to note that our understanding of these verses today is undiminished by greater knowledge of seed variety and physiology. We still recognize the message of something great arising from the smallest of beginnings, and the need to die to self to bear spiritual fruit. Instruction on nature was never the point.

FUNCTION OF THE HEART

If you confess with your mouth Jesus as Lord, and believe in your heart that God raised Him from the dead, you will be saved. (Rom. 10:9)

We consider it nearly self-evident today that all thoughts, emotions, and reasoning have their origin in the brain. We nonetheless routinely use phrases that associate feelings and emotion with our hearts. We follow our hearts, have longings in our hearts, pour our hearts into our passions, and even draw cartoon hearts as expressions of romantic love. We know that reference to the heart in each of these expressions is symbolic of functions that are really going on in our brains, so we naturally assume that the writers of Scripture had the same literary forms in mind; these expressions were all figures of speech.[9]

If a biblical expression was *intended* as a figure of speech, it means that native speakers *at the time of writing* knew the words were not literally true. But we forget that for most of human history, the function of the various bodily organs was not well understood, and the heart was commonly thought to have real powers of reasoning and emotion. During embalming, the ancient Egyptians (among whom the Hebrews lived) took great care to remove and preserve organs for the afterlife, returning the heart to the body, yet discarding the brain.[10]

Much later, with the rise of natural philosophy in Greek culture, there were active debates over which organs were primarily responsible for emotion, reasoning, and temperament. Aristotelian and Stoic philosophers believed human intellect derived from the heart. Followers of Plato and Hippocrates believed it resided in the brain.[11] Even Galen of Pergamum, who put some of these debates to rest with his meticulous medical examinations late in the *second century*, still placed the seat of the spiritual soul in the heart.[12]

---

9. Short, "Phenomenological language and semantic naïveté."
10. Wade and Nelson, "Evisceration and excerebration in the Egyptian mummification tradition."
11. Gross, "Aristotle on the brain."
12. Gill, "Galen and the Stoics: Mortal enemies or blood brothers?"

Given that God knows the inner workings of his creation, we might expect that he would inspire the writers of Scripture to set the record straight, assigning the will, intellect, and emotions to the brain. So what do we find? Throughout the Old Testament, functions of the brain are consistently attributed to the heart (*leb*[13]).[14] It is the heart that experiences joy and grief (Prov. 15:13), fear and courage (Ps. 27:14), arrogance, despondency, and lust (1 Sam. 17:32; Prov. 6:25; Hos. 13:6). The heart is the seat of intellectual reasoning (1 Sam. 25:37), and where trust and belief reside (Neh. 9:8; Prov. 3:5).

The New Testament, written in Greek at a time when debates were active over the functions of bodily organs, makes the same use of the heart as we find in the Old Testament.[15] The heart (*kardia*)[16] is repeatedly referred to as the source of motives (1 Cor. 4:5), understanding (Acts 28:27), belief (Rom. 10:9), and the center of our spiritual being (Eph. 3:17). If there was any doubt, Jesus himself weighed in, teaching that the mouth speaks what comes from the heart (Matt. 15:18–19), that men reason with their hearts (Luke 5:22), and calling upon listeners not to doubt in their hearts (Mark 11:23). The Greeks had a word for the brain (*enkephale*), but the New Testament writers did not make use of it.

If we were Christians of the first century wrestling with what to believe about the biological function of bodily organs, we might have reasonably assumed that God settled the matter in his infallible Word. The seat of human reason is in the heart. The words of Jesus confirm it. Still more, we may have felt frustration with Christian brothers and sisters who sided with the pagan philosophers, who attributed thought and emotion to the brain. Why did they allow science to trump the clear teaching of Scripture? Why trust unbelieving philosophers over the unchanging Word of God?

Yet it appears evident that God was content to use the common understanding of nature at the time of writing to communicate truth about the kingdom of God. And again, our understanding today is unharmed by the accommodation. Whether we think "believing with the heart" is a physical or symbolic reality, the intended message is the same. Belief is something to be contemplated, internalized, and owned at the center of our being.

---

13. Hebrew: לֵב (*leb*), "heart."
14. Branson, "Science, the Bible, and human anatomy"; Wolff, *Anthropology of the Old Testament*, 40–51.
15. Branson, "Science, the Bible, and human anatomy"; Baumgartel and Behm, "καρδια, καρδιογνωτζ, σκληροκαπδια," 605–14.
16. Greek: καρδία (*kardia*), "heart."

STRUCTURE OF THE COSMOS

Can you, with Him, spread out the skies, strong as a molten mirror? (Job 37:18)

Imagine for a moment that you are transported back to the first century, erasing all modern knowledge of the physical construction of the earth and the heavens. All you have are your senses and your Bible. Wishing to grow in understanding, you scour the Scriptures for references to the cosmos. You collect them and organize them by the specific subjects they address. Table 1 is a representative subset (limited to two pages) of what that listing might look like.[17] If you then start to read, adhering to the "plain sense" meaning of the verses, what understanding of the cosmos would result?

TABLE 1—REPRESENTATIVE VERSES RELATED TO COSMOLOGY
All the earth visible from a high point   • The tree grew large and became strong and its height reached to the sky, and it was visible to the end of the whole earth. (Dan. 4:11)   • Again, the devil took [Jesus] to a very high mountain and showed Him all the kingdoms of the world and their glory. (Matt. 4:8)
"Circle of the earth"[18]   • When He established the heavens, I was there, when He inscribed a circle on the face of the deep. (Prov. 8:27)   • He has inscribed a circle on the surface of the waters at the boundary of light and darkness. (Job 26:10)
"The ends of the earth" or "from sea to sea"   • O God of our salvation, You who are the trust of all the ends of the earth and of the farthest sea. (Ps. 65:5)   • And His dominion will be from sea to sea, and from the River to the ends of the earth. (Zech. 9:10)
Sky as solid surface   • The One who builds His upper chambers in the heavens and has founded His vaulted dome over the earth. (Amos 9:6)   • Can you, with Him, spread out the skies, strong as a molten mirror? (Job 37:18)

---

17. For a more complete tabulation, see www.solidrocklectures.com.
18. Note that circles are flat objects (two-dimensional).

TABLE 1—REPRESENTATIVE VERSES RELATED TO COSMOLOGY

Sky like a tent
- Their line has gone out through all the earth, and their utterances to the end of the world. In them He has placed a tent for the sun. (Ps. 19:4)
- It is He who sits above the circle of the earth, and its inhabitants are like grasshoppers, who stretches out the heavens like a curtain and spreads them out like a tent to dwell in. (Isa. 40:22)

Sky rolled up like a scroll
- And all the host of heaven will wear away, And the sky will be rolled up like a scroll. (Isa. 34:4)
- The sky was split apart like a scroll when it is rolled up, and every mountain and island were moved out of their places. (Rev. 6:14)

Sky with openings for rain
- On the same day all the fountains of the great deep burst open, and the floodgates of the sky were opened. (Gen. 7:11)
- For the windows above are opened, and the foundations of the earth shake. (Isa. 24:18)

Heavens supported by pillars
- The pillars of heaven tremble and are amazed at His rebuke. (Job 26:11)
- Then the earth shook and quaked, the foundations of heaven were trembling and were shaken, because He was angry. (2 Sam. 22:8)

Earth on foundations or pillars
- For the pillars of the earth are the LORD's, and He set the world on them. (1 Sam. 2:8)
- He established the earth upon its foundations, so that it will not totter forever and ever. (Ps. 104:5)

Earth immobile
- Indeed, the world is firmly established, it will not be moved. (Ps. 93:1)
- Say among the nations, "The LORD reigns; indeed, the world is firmly established, it will not be moved." (Ps. 96:10)

Sun travels about the earth, hastens back
- Also, the sun rises and the sun sets; and hastening to its place it rises there again. (Eccl. 1:5)
- [The sun's] rising is from one end of the heavens, and its circuit to the other end of them; and there is nothing hidden from its heat. (Ps. 19:6)

Following the order in Table 1, we find a dream where a tree was elevated to make it visible to all the nations of the earth, and a record of Jesus being taken to a high mountain where he could see all the kingdoms of the world. From these verses, you ascertain that the earth must be flat, or perhaps modestly domed, where one just needs to get higher than the tallest mountain to see the entire world. These descriptions would make no sense on a sphere. No elevation is high enough to see a nation on the opposite side of a globe.

The flatness of the earth appears to be reinforced with references to the "circle of the earth," and multiple passages that speak of "the ends of the earth." A sphere has no edges, no *ends*. A circle does. At those edges, a sea must surround the land, for you find frequent mention of the breadth of the earth running "from sea to sea."

The heavens above are described as a solid surface, even claiming it is as hard as a reflective metal plate (molten mirror). God stretched out this dome like a tent, which one day will be rolled up like a scroll. The sky has gates that allow the waters above to fall as rain. The heavens are supported by pillars that can be shaken at God's command. Still more verses testify that the earth is also seated firmly on pillars or on a solid foundation. The earth is immobile, fixed upon those pillars. It is the sun and stars that make their circuit across the dome, hastening each day back to their starting places.

If propelled into the twenty-first century, you are startled to discover that your biblical understanding of the earth and heavens looks *nothing* like what is commonly known today. To make matters worse, you find out that the information about the cosmos gleaned from Scripture fits quite well with the common understanding of all the nations surrounding Israel at the time of writing. Though the specific details varied with time and culture, the general understanding of the nations throughout the Ancient Near East (ANE), from Egypt to Babylon, depicted the cosmos in words and in art as a three-tiered system of solid sky, flat earth surrounded by seas, and a watery under-world supported by pillars. Figure 3 is a generalized depiction of the three-tiered system, with examples of roughly contemporaneous artwork from Egypt and Babylon in Figures 4 and 5.

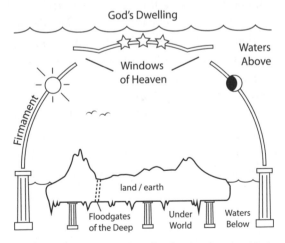

Figure 3—Depiction of the three-tiered universe, divided into the earth, the waters above the earth, and the waters below the earth.

Figure 4—The Egyptian god, Ra, travels daily over the arched goddess of the sky, Nut, who is held up and separated from Geb, the god of land, by Shu, the god of air.[19]

What do we make of all this? Those wishing to discount the Bible have focused on the *similarities* between the biblical and ANE cosmologies to claim that the small tribe of Hebrews simply borrowed their mythology from their neighbors, tweaking it to suit their purposes. Those wishing to "discount the discounters" have focused on the *differences* to insist that any similarities are incidental. A third, more likely explanation is that this view was simply the common understanding of people throughout the Ancient Near East.[20] The principal difference between Israel and its neighbors was not what the world *looked* like, but *who* was responsible for it.

It is of significance that we find no effort in all of Scripture to correct the misguided understanding of the physical nature of the cosmos of Israel's pagan neighbors. Where we see substantive (enormous) correction is in the understanding of the nature and character of the Creator.

---

19. Budge, *The Gods of the Egyptians*, plate 20.
20. For good descriptions of the various perspectives and more reasoned approaches, see: Greenwood, *Scripture and Cosmology*, chap. 2; Miller and Soden, *In the Beginning...We Misunderstood*, chap. 7.

OBJECTIONS TO ACCOMMODATION AND RESPONSES

Objection 1: Many of these expressions are simply phenomenological language.

Those embracing comprehensive inerrancy insist that much of this language is *phenomenological*, meaning descriptions are intended as observations from the perspective of a viewer, as opposed to statements of objective fact. Expressions such as the sun rising and the sun setting are simply descriptions from the perspective of human viewers on the earth's surface.

Use of phenomenological language is quite possible, but there are at least two problems if defending comprehensive inerrancy.

Phenomenological language should be used sparingly.

If the intention of Scripture was to include instruction on nature, we should not expect routine usage of phenomenological language, at least not without clear disclaimers. God, as the author and master of language, and knowing the discoveries that would one day be made, could have easily inspired writers to say the sun "*appears* to rise and set," or "*from your perspective*" the sun rises and sets, but he did not. The plain-sense reading of the text adheres to the commonly held belief that the sun orbited a stationary earth.

Figure 5—A Babylonian kudurru (boundary stone; 12th century B.C.), showing layers of the cosmos supported by pillars.[21]

Biblical descriptions go beyond the phenomenological.

Phenomenological designations are superficially plausible for simple statements like the sun rising or setting, but fail to account for more detailed

---

21. Drawn from a kudurru on display at the Louvre in Paris, Department of Near Eastern Antiquities: Mesopotamia.

descriptions found in places like Ecclesiastes 1:5 that refer to the sun hastening back to its starting point. The writer could not observe what happened to the sun during the night. Furthermore, there were competing views among Israel's neighbors regarding the daily fate of the sun. The Egyptians believed the sun went out or died and was reborn each morning. If intending to instruct on nature, the biblical description of the sun hastening back to its starting point should be considered a corrective statement, declaring that the sun does not die, but completes its orbit under the earth each night.

Objection 2: Many of these expressions really were figures of speech.

The argument here is that the ancient Israelites knew how the cosmos was constructed, with the same basic understanding we have today. Expressions such as *the ends of the earth, pillars of the earth, pillars of heaven,* and *floodgates of the sky*, were all known to people at the time as figures of speech.[22] We use some of these expressions today, after all, without thinking of them as factual statements about nature. There are at least three problems with this reasoning.

Illogical historical expectations

For the original audience to have considered these expressions to be figures of speech, it requires a rather odd history.

- God inspired the selection of words that would appear to conform with the pagan nations' literal concept of the cosmos.

- Israelites knew better, thus understanding these expressions correctly as figures of speech.

- Later Israelites and Christians *forgot* the proper understanding of the cosmos, reverting back to their neighbors' understanding and wrongly interpreting these verses literally for *thousands of years.*

- Modern science *rediscovered* the cosmology known previously only to ancient Israel, allowing us to rediscover these expressions to be figures of speech.

---

22. Short, "Phenomenological language and semantic naïveté"; Edward, "Literary forms and biblical interpretation."

Circular reasoning

The only reason we use some of these expressions in our language today is because we took them *from the Bible*. And the only reason we consider them figures of speech is because of our awareness of scientific studies demonstrating they are not realistic descriptions of nature. The original audience had no such knowledge, and the expressions fit quite well with societal beliefs at the time. To borrow an expression from an ancient culture, and then declare that they understood it figuratively because we commonly use such expressions figuratively today is circular logic.

Defending instruction of nature by claiming no instruction on nature

If claiming that hundreds of verses that touch upon nature *are not* teaching about nature (they are merely figures of speech or phenomenological), how does this provide a defense for an argument that the Bible *does* teach about nature?

Objection 3: Some verses actually predict modern discoveries.

The claim here is that the Bible contains truthful statements about the universe that were not discovered until hundreds or even thousands of years after they were written. Consider the verses below.

> He stretches out the north over empty space and hangs the earth on nothing. He wraps up the waters in His clouds, and the cloud does not burst under them. He obscures the face of the full moon and spreads His cloud over it. He has inscribed a circle on the surface of the waters at the boundary of light and darkness. The pillars of heaven tremble and are amazed at His rebuke. (Job 26:7–11)

> Covering Yourself with light as with a cloak, stretching out heaven like a tent curtain. He lays the beams of His upper chambers in the waters; He makes the clouds His chariot; He walks upon the wings of the wind. (Ps. 104:2–3)

> It is He who sits above the circle of the earth, and its inhabitants are like grasshoppers, who stretches out the heavens like a curtain and spreads them out like a tent to dwell in. (Isa. 40:22)

> I, the LORD, am the maker of all things, stretching out the heavens by Myself and spreading out the earth all alone. (Isa. 44:24)

Typical claims derived from these verses include:[23]

- "Stretching out heaven," is a description of the continuous expansion of the universe.

- "Circle" is better translated as "sphere"—predicting discovery that the earth is a globe (or indicating that the ancient Hebrews already knew the earth was a sphere).

- "Hangs the earth on nothing" refers to planet earth suspended in space.

There are at least two problems with this reasoning.

Haphazard hermeneutic

By the reasoning above, we are to interpret "stretching out heaven" and "hangs the earth on nothing" literally, yet within the *same verses*, we should not interpret literally the "pillars of heaven" or "beams of His upper chambers in the waters." From Job 37:18, we should interpret "spread out the skies" literally, but not the sky being "strong as a molten mirror." And though we are told that stretching of the heavens is to be understood as an expanding universe, "spreading out the earth," also in the same verse, is not to be understood as a continuously expanding *planet*. All this represents a haphazard hermeneutic.

Missed metaphor

Isaiah and Job did not just say that God stretched out the heavens, but did so *like a tent*. The Israelites were quite familiar with tents. They were erected and stretched taut with stakes to hold them fast against the desert winds. The tent formed a solid fabric around and above those inside. A tent that did not create a sturdy, *stationary* domicile was worthless. A tent is an apt metaphor for a solid, domed sky, not an ever-expanding cosmos.

Objection 4: "Accommodation" means that God affirmed falsehood.

A common objection equates accommodation with the "incidental affirmation of falsehoods."[24] If the intention of the Bible were to instruct on every-

---

23. Lisle, *Taking Back Astronomy*, chap. 2.
24. Grudem, *Systematic Theology*, 97–98.

thing with absolute authority, the charge would be reasonable. But the Bible nowhere makes this claim. It is a human expectation imposed on Scripture, not one derived from it. If there is no intention of teaching about nature and the common understanding of nature is tapped only to illustrate the intended message, there is no room for charging that falsehood is being affirmed, incidentally or otherwise.

Objection 5: "Accommodation" means no one could really understand the Bible until the discovery of Ancient Near Eastern tablets.

This is an understandable concern, but ultimately without basis. In fact, consider the sequence of discoveries. For most of human history, believers understood references to nature in the Bible to simply reflect common understanding. Whether God was *instructing* on nature or *accommodating* humans' limited understanding of nature did not matter, because there was no apparent conflict to worry about. Nature looked the way it was described.

Moving into the sixteenth century and forward, scientific studies began painting a picture of the natural world that was increasingly at odds with the descriptions in Scripture. Many, sadly or gleefully, concluded that the Bible is riddled with errors. By the nineteenth century, translations of newly discovered ANE texts began to accumulate, revealing that Israel's neighbors had very different views on the gods and their dealings with men, but that their understanding of the physical construction of the cosmos was remarkably similar to what is found in the Hebrew Scriptures.

This is significant, for if the ANE texts recorded a description of the cosmos that was distinctly different from what is found in the Bible, one could argue that the biblical writers were trying to correct the pagan nations' mistaken understanding of nature. It could also then be argued that modern science has demonstrated that this "corrected understanding" missed the mark—a confirmation of flaws in the Bible. But by virtue of our knowledge of the ANE texts, we know that there was no effort to correct the pervasive ANE understanding of the basic structure of the world. The Bible simply accommodated that common understanding to communicate its timeless message about the nature and kingdom of God.

Said another way, when there was no apparent conflict between science and the Bible, there was no need for ANE texts to assist understanding. The ANE tablets only became useful (not *essential*) for biblical understanding after scientific discoveries began to raise questions about how nature was addressed in Scripture. One might argue that the timing of discovery of the ANE libraries, following in the wake of growing apparent tensions between science and the Bible, was *providential.*

SUMMARY

The Bible is filled with references to nature that represent the common understanding of the Ancient Near East, whether seeds, or hearts, or the cosmos.[25] To suggest that the original audience knew their neighbors believed these things to be literally true, yet God inspired the words to be understood as figures of speech or merely phenomenological language, stretches credulity. Even the few verses that are pulled out as purported evidence of modern understanding all require departures from a "plain sense" reading to pry them loose from an ANE framework (e.g., tents don't eternally expand). The original audience would likely have been baffled at the logic applied to impose a twenty-first-century, Western cosmological worldview onto the text.

So is the Bible replete with errors? As the apostle Paul was fond of saying, *may it never be!*[26] If common knowledge of nature was being tapped as a tool of illustration, with no intention to instruct on the nature of nature, there is no error. Those who insist otherwise put God in a small box, where transient cultural norms and human sensibilities define the limits of God's sovereignty over his message. If accommodation does not live up to a person's expectation of God's perfection, it may well be that human expectation is at fault, not God.

So what does this mean for the creation story? Accommodation, found richly employed through the pages of Scripture, does not automatically disqualify Genesis 1 from being a literal account of the steps God employed to bring the world into existence. It should make us cautious, however, about uncritically assuming Genesis 1 *is* a literal account, based on a culturally biased adherence to *comprehensive* inerrancy. We still have ample hermeneutical work ahead of us to determine the intention and message of the creation story.

---

25. For additional examples of how nature is addressed in the Bible, see Lamoureux, *Evolution: Scripture and Nature Say Yes!*, chap. 5.
26. Ten times in Romans, three times in Galatians, and once in 1 Corinthians.

4

BEGINNINGS—MATTHEW AND GENESIS

In any study of Scripture, it is important to consider not only the particular verses of interest, but also how they fit in with the rest of the Bible. Detailed studies on the meaning of a word or the significance of the order in which words are strung together can be beneficial, but will fall short of full understanding if not placed in the larger context. This means more than just considering all the verses in Scripture that address the same subject. It means becoming familiar with the different literary forms employed by the writers, the historical context of the message, and even how different books are constructed. When considering how to best interpret the beginning of the Old Testament, it will prove to be a useful exercise to consider the opening of the New Testament. As we dive into Matthew Chapter 1, it may appear that we are taking an odd tangent from the subject of creation, but it represents another helpful step in our overall understanding of Scripture and our ability to answer our first question (page 24) concerning whether the infallibility of Scripture is dependent on a literal interpretation of the verses examined.

The book of Matthew opens with the genealogy of Jesus Christ. A list of forty-one names is provided starting with Abraham and ending with Jesus. The list ends with verse 17 stating, "So all the generations from Abraham to David are fourteen generations, from David to the deportation to Babylon, fourteen generations, and from the deportation to Babylon to the Messiah, fourteen generations." Upon careful examination, there are two apparent difficulties that arise. First, forty-one is not divisible by three. From Abraham to David, fourteen names are listed. From David to the exile (Jeconiah), fourteen more names are given if David is not double-counted. From Jeconiah to Jesus, *only thirteen* names are listed if we are consistent and do not double-count Jeconiah. The total adds up to forty-one.

The second problem is discovered by going back into the Old Testament to find the lineage described in Matthew. Table 2 shows the complete biblical lineage. Matthew's lineage from David to the exile is missing four of the generations listed in the Old Testament. Each name in the list from verses 2 to 16 is referred to as the father of the next name. Traditional explanations will note that *the father of* (*gennao*) can also mean *the ancestor of*, so generations may be skipped without error.[1] The word for *generations* (*genea*)[2] likewise is used elsewhere in Scripture to mean broadly grouped individuals, as well as for parent-child relationships. These explanations fall short, however, because Matthew is explicit about the total *number* of generations. He does not just identify lineage, he states a specific number of generations.

TABLE 2—A COMPARISON OF THE GENEALOGY OF MATTHEW 1:1–17 AND OLD TESTAMENT REFERENCES			
Groups of 14	Matthew Genealogy	OT Genealogy	OT Source
1	Abraham	Abraham	Gen. 25
2	Isaac	Isaac	
3	Jacob	Jacob	
4	Judah	Judah	1 Chron. 2
5	Perez	Perez	
6	Hezron	Hezron	
7	Ram	Ram	
8	Amminadab	Amminadab	
9	Nahshon	Nahshon	
10	Salmon	Salma	
11	Boaz	Boaz	
12	Obed	Obed	
13	Jesse	Jesse	
14	David	David	
1	Solomon	Solomon	
2	Rehoboam	Rehoboam	1 Chron. 3
3	Abijah	Abijah	

---

1. Russell, "Genealogy of Jesus Christ," 304–5.
2. Greek: γεννάω (*gennao*), "the father of"; γενεά (*genea*), "generations."

TABLE 2—A COMPARISON OF THE GENEALOGY OF MATTHEW 1:1–17 AND OLD TESTAMENT REFERENCES			
Groups of 14	Matthew Genealogy	OT Genealogy	OT Source
4	Asa	Asa	1 Chron. 3
5	Jehoshaphat	Jehoshaphat	
6	Joram	Joram	
		Ahaziah	
		Joash	
		Amaziah	
7	Uzziah	Uzziah[3]	
8	Jotham	Jotham	
9	Ahaz	Ahaz	
10	Hezekiah	Hezekiah	
11	Manasseh	Manasseh	
12	Amon	Amon	
13	Josiah	Josiah	
		Jehoiakim	
14 1	Jeconiah	Jeconiah	
2	Shealtiel	Shealtiel	
3	Zerubbabel	Zerubbabel	Ezra 3:2
4	Abihud	*end of OT record*	
5	Eliakim		
6	Azor		
7	Zadok		
8	Achim		
9	Eliud		
10	Eleazar		
11	Matthan		
12	Jacob		
13	Joseph		
14	Jesus		

---

3. Uzziah is actually called *Azariah* in 1 Chron. 3:12, but called *Uzziah* in 2 Chron. 26:1.

There are two possibilities here. Matthew was either sloppy or clever. The sloppy option is exceedingly unlikely for the simple reason that genealogies were quite important to Matthew's early readers (primarily Jews), and mistakes would have been quickly caught and corrected. The cleverness is seen in how Matthew has selected the names to build a *memory device* into the genealogy.[4] The genealogy is divided into three groups of equal size, with hinges between them representing pivotal names or events in Israel's history: King David and the great deportation. To maintain the equal numbers on either side of those hinges, names were left out of the middle set, and, perhaps because only thirteen names remained, Jeconiah was used both to end the second set and begin the final set to yield a consistent fourteen.

It is useful to identify the memory device in these verses, but it doesn't fully resolve our dilemma with a specified number of generations in each group. Genealogies are not exactly poetry, so we can't call on metaphor or symbolism to bail us out. Genealogies land squarely within an expectation of a straightforward telling of historical events.

The apparent dilemma is solved simply enough if we realize that Matthew's construction is not about the numbers, it is about the genuine lineage of Jesus, from Abraham and through David. Jesus is the king who fulfills God's promise to David to have a son on the throne forever (2 Sam. 7:8–17). The names are real. The history is real. The numbers are not wrong; they are not the point. They are a *literary device* to enhance memory of the intended message.

As clever as the construction may be, it still makes some readers uneasy to see anything identified within the biblical historical accounts that isn't strictly literal. We don't expect to find writers taking literary license here, especially not in a genealogy! As with the discussion of nature in the Bible (see chap. 3), the problem is not with the text, it is with the reader. We read with a twenty-first-century Western bias that tells us that records of history should stick rigidly to statements of fact. We unjustly project modern literary rules on ancient writers. That Matthew's early readers did not prompt a speedy correction is evidence that they apprehended the intended history of Jesus's lineage, and understood the license taken to form it into an easily remembered sequence. The point was never the numbers.

Matthew 1 is not the only Scripture passage that runs afoul of our modern sense of literary accuracy. Consider the parallel genealogy in the third chapter of Luke. Both Matthew and Luke identify the genealogy of Jesus through his father

---

4. Benson, *The New Testament of Our Lord and Saviour Jesus Christ, Vol. 1: Matthew to the Acts of the Apostles.*

Joseph. The genealogies identify the same lineage from Abraham to David,[5] but then diverge radically from David to Joseph (Table 3). The prevailing view among biblical scholars is that Matthew's genealogy is traced through Joseph and Luke's genealogy through Mary, even though Joseph is identified in both. Using our modern Western standard for literary accuracy, the account in Luke should have identified Joseph as the *son-in-law* of Eli rather than the *son*, but Luke did not write using a twenty-first-century English primer.[6]

TABLE 3—COMPARISON OF THE GENEALOGIES IN MATTHEW 1:1–17 AND LUKE 3:23–34 (THE DIFFERENT "FATHERS" OF JOSEPH ARE IN BOLD)

Matthew	Luke
Abraham	Abraham
Isaac	Isaac
Jacob	Jacob
Judah	Judah
Perez	Perez
Hezron	Hezron
Ram	Ram
	Admin
Amminadab	Amminadab
Nahshon	Nahshon
Salmon	Salmon
Boaz	Boaz
Obed	Obed
Jesse	Jesse
David	David
Solomon	Nathan
Rehoboam	Mattatha
	Menna
Abijah	Melea
	Eliakim
Asa	Jonam
Jehoshaphat	Joseph
	Judah
Joram	Simeon
Uzziah	Levi
	Matthat
Jotham	Jorim
	Eliezer
Ahaz	Joshua

---

5. Luke includes one additional ancestor between Abraham and David (Admin, v. 33) that is not found in Matthew.

6. A good argument against forcing ancient writers to abide by modern literary rules can be found in Packer, *God Has Spoken: Revelation and the Bible*, 104–5.

TABLE 3—COMPARISON OF THE GENEALOGIES IN MATTHEW 1:1–17 AND LUKE 3:23–34, THE DIFFERENT "FATHERS" OF JOSEPH ARE IN BOLD

Matthew Continued	Luke Continued
	Er
Hezekiah	Elmadam
Manasseh	Cosam
	Addi
Amon	Melchi
Josiah	Neri
	Shealtiel
Jeconiah	Zerubbabel
Shealtiel	Rhesa
	Joanan
Zerubbabel	Joda
Abihud	Josech
	Semein
Eliakim	Mattathias
	Maath
Azor	Naggai
Zadok	Hesli
	Nahum
Achim	Amos
Eliud	Mattathias
	Joseph
Eleazar	Jannai
	Melchi
Matthan	Levi
Jacob	Matthat
	Eli
Joseph	Joseph
Jesus	Jesus

SUMMARY

There are two conclusions to be drawn from this discussion. First, when addressing accuracy, we should not assume an ancient writer was obligated to follow modern rules of writing. Second, the *intent* of a passage plays a critical role in determining its appropriate interpretation. The central message of the genealogies in Matthew and Luke is that Jesus fulfilled the prophecies ascribed to the Messiah that he would be a descendent of Abraham through the line of David. The genealogies were created using actual historical ancestors, linked together in a culturally consistent context that always started with the father (even if tracking the maternal line), and using a memory tool that took culturally acceptable liberties with the full and exact lineage. To drive home the point, biblical inerrancy here requires that this historical text *not* be understood according to its literal or "plain sense" meaning. A literal reading unnecessarily forces internal inconsistencies that undermine the defense of inerrancy.

The opening of the New Testament begins with the intention of illustrating the very real lineage of Jesus with a memory tool that employs the use of words and numbers in ways that run counter to their literal meaning. Could the Old Testament begin in the same fashion, conveying a central message and utilizing a memory tool that differs from a strictly literal meaning of words employed? The central theme of Genesis 1 and 2 is God's authorship. Nothing exists that was not brought into being by his will. Perhaps taking literary license with the actual sequence of events, creation is neatly broken into seven days as a memory tool, emphasizing that God did not simply start the process and let it go, he created everything: planets and light, fish and birds, animals and humans. At this stage in our discussion, this would be a premature conclusion, but if true, it would be incredibly poetic, opening the Old and New Testaments in a parallel manner.[7] On to Genesis!

7. Theologians who believe in the inspiration of the Bible do not necessarily believe the current *ordering* of books in the Bible is also inspired.

5

GENESIS—INSIDE AND OUT

Few Christians will disagree that a central message of Genesis 1 is that the world did not come into existence on its own; it is the handiwork of an awesome and personal Creator. But what about the details of the creation process? Was the intent *also* instruction on the specific order and duration of creation events? Did God create the earth in a literal six-day sequence, or should we leave room for literary license in the description? Literary license would be remarkably consistent with what we see in the opening of the New Testament, but it does not automatically follow that the two bodies of Scripture must open in the same manner. In this chapter, we are ready to plunge directly into the Genesis text (still independent of scientific challenges) to see what it reveals.

The approach to Scripture in the preceding chapter utilized a method of hermeneutics that follows two steps. The first is to identify the literary style. Is the text poetry, vision, parable, historical narrative, or a letter? If the text is identified as poetry or vision, then we fully expect the writer to use nonliteral expressions when conveying the message. As an example, there is no serious debate on the physical impossibility of Solomon's lover having doves for eyes, or teeth that looked like actual sheep (Song 4). The entire book of Song of Solomon is recognized as poetry with rich usage of figurative language to convey a woman's beauty and expressions of love. On the other hand, if a text is recognized as historical narrative, it is assumed to be relating events and people just as described unless there are solid textual reasons to suggest otherwise. This brings us to the second step of deciding what is a "solid textual reason."

In the case of the genealogies in Matthew and Luke (both contained within historical narratives), we looked for internal consistency. If a strictly literal interpretation was intended, there should be no inconsistencies between

Matthew, Luke, and the Old Testament, nor should there be fundamental violations of logic. Since Joseph obviously did not have two fathers (comparing Matthew and Luke), and since the Old Testament identifies more than the forty-one ancestors listed in Matthew, we recognize the literary license taken in these passages. Note that literary license is not a veiled way of saying "less true." It is simply a recognition that writers of Scripture sometimes used words and descriptions in ways they never intended to be taken in an absolute literal sense. The chroniclers of Jesus's lineage did not intend for anyone to believe that Joseph had two biological fathers or that there was disagreement about which son of David the lineage of Jesus passed through.

We will take a similar approach with Genesis 1 and 2. For the purpose of this discussion, we'll start with the often made assertion that these chapters are historical narrative.[1] As historical narrative, we will assume that the words are to be taken in a straightforward, literal sense unless there are textual reasons to suggest otherwise. If a literal interpretation is intended here, we should not find inconsistencies within or between the two chapters. If you have not done so recently, it is worthwhile to take a moment to read through Genesis 1 and 2.

Looking internally within Scripture, there are several problems that quickly arise when forcing the creation story into a literalistic mold. These are summarized in Table 4, with several discussed in more detail below. Note that none of these are perceived conflicts with modern science. They are all either problems that arise with scriptural consistency, or logical problems with a common knowledge of how God's natural creation functions.

TABLE 4—SCRIPTURAL DIFFICULTIES WHEN IMPOSING A LITERALISTIC INTERPRETATION ON GENESIS 1 AND 2	
Reference	Problem with literalistic interpretation
Gen. 1 Heaven and earth made in six days.	Gen. 2:4 Heaven and earth made in one day. ("fixed" in NIV)
Gen. 1:3–5 Light created on Day 1.	Gen. 1:14–18 No sources of light were created prior to Day 4.

---

1. Kelly, *Creation and Change: Genesis 1.1–2.4 in the Light of Changing Scientific Paradigms*; Hoffmeier, "Genesis 1–11 as history and theology."

TABLE 4—SCRIPTURAL DIFFICULTIES WHEN IMPOSING A LITERALISTIC INTERPRETATION ON GENESIS 1 AND 2	
Reference	Problem with literalistic interpretation
1 John 1:5; Rev. 21:23 "God is light."	Gen. 1:3–5 If God is the source of light created on Day 1, this implies that God was dark prior to Day 1, and not omnipresent thereafter.
Gen. 1:3–5, 14–18 Light separated from dark.	Has no *physical* meaning. (Light separated from the absence of light?)
Gen. 1:14–18 Day 4: Sun, moon, and stars were created to separate day from night and light from dark.	Gen. 1:3–5 Light had already been separated from darkness on Day 1.
Gen. 1:5, 8, 13 "…and there was evening and there was morning…"	Gen. 1:3–16 Has physical meaning only from a fixed point on a rotating planet next to a stationary light source, yet occurs for three days with no people and no sun.
Gen. 1:6–8 Creation of the firmament or "expanse."	Literally means a solid dome holding back waters above (not an "atmosphere").
Gen. 1:24–28 Day 6: God created animals and birds first, then he created man.	Gen. 2:18–20 God created man first, then he created animals and birds. ("fixed" in NIV and ESV)
Gen. 2:2 God was done creating on Day 6.	Gen. 3:18 God created thorns and thistles after Day 6. (Or sin/Satan took over as master creator.)
Gen. 2:2 God rested from his labor of creation.	Taken literally, God is not the one now lifting the Himalayas, nor creating new land in Hawaii, nor bringing new babies into existence.
Exod. 31:16–17 Regarding creation, God rested and was refreshed.	Taken literally, God got tired and needed a break.

The subject headings below approximately follow the sequence in Table 4. In some cases, two or more issues identified in the table are grouped together under a topic.

"In the day"

Genesis 1 describes the creation in six consecutive days, while a literal interpretation of Genesis 2:4 requires creation in a single day: "This is the account of the heavens and the earth when they were created, in the day that the LORD God made earth and heaven." The Hebrew word for *day* (*yowm*) is the same word used to describe the completion of each day in Genesis 1.[2] The objection to calling this an inconsistency should be immediate, for the phrase *in the day* is clearly a figure of speech meaning a period of time of undefined length. By definition, however, a figure of speech is an expression whose actual meaning is different from the literal meaning of the words. Thus, at least one verse in Genesis should not be interpreted literally.

Light before Light Sources

Puzzlement over the creation of light on Day 1 before sources of light on Day 4 is not unique to the modern era. Christians and theologians have long pondered what was physically occurring during those formative days.[3] Simply claiming that God was the light (with reference to 1 John 1:5) is an insufficient answer, for it would require that God was dark prior to Day 1, and not omnipresent thereafter.[4] Morning and evening without a sun would only be possible if God first turned himself on and then fixed his position on one side of the earth.

The conundrum only increases with the realization of what light is. Light is not a static object like paint on a canvas. Light is generated by photons streaming outward from an energy source. Consider what this means for the creation of light with a three-day lag before creation of the sun. To get evenings and mornings, we need light to come from one direction toward the earth. This leaves two possibilities. For one, God could have continuously created photons for three days emanating from a point where the sun would eventually reside, though this departs from a plain-sense reading of a singular creation event of light on Day 1. Alternatively, to complete the creation of light in one day, God could have spread out photons along a path *behind* the

---

2. Hebrew: יוֹם (*yowm*), "day."
3. Origen, *De Principiis*, Book 4, Entry 16; Augustine, *The Literal Meaning of Genesis*; see also Young, "The contemporary relevance of Augustine's view of creation."
4. Morris, "Sunlight before the Sun."

point where the sun would eventually be placed (Fig. 6). This means a beam of photons distributed along a pathway away from earth, through the eventual position of the sun 93 million miles away, and out an additional *50 billion miles*. In this scenario, the sun would have been created just as the last of the trailing photons reached the location where the sun was to be placed.

Stars would have an even more complicated history, since all of them are much greater than 50 billion miles away from us. A focused beam from each star would need to be aligned *in front* of where the star would eventually be placed. All this is certainly within the power of an almighty creator, though it seems contrary to the nature of a nondeceptive God who brings *order* to his creation rather than *confusion*.

Day 1: three days' worth of directed photons

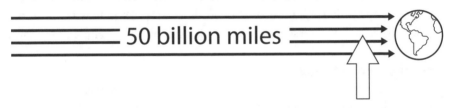

Day 4: insert sun

Figure 6—Unlikely creation of light on Day 1, fifty billion miles from the *eventual* location of where the sun would be created on Day 4.

Light Separated from Darkness

There is great spiritual significance to God's separation of light from darkness. Light illuminates. Darkness obscures. The English expression "to bring to light" captures the idea well, where thefts, lies, slanders, oppressions, murders, and other manifestations of evil cannot survive when all is fully revealed and brought to attention, when it is brought into the light.

But what about a literal understanding with a *physical* separation? This proves more problematic, because it actually has no physical meaning. Light has a physical existence made of photons that can be identified and measured.[5] Darkness is not a substance or entity or even a force that can be isolated. It is simply the *absence* of light.

---

5. Photons are simultaneously particles and energy waves.

By analogy, consider a jar of beans set before you. They are poured out onto the table and you are given a simple instruction: separate beans from the absence of beans. You object, "That has no meaning; the absence of something is not an independent 'something'!" Which is exactly the point. Something wonderful is expressed when God separates light from darkness, something much deeper than what a nonsensical "plain sense" reading would imply.

Light and Dark Separated Twice

In Genesis 1:14–18, the sun, moon, and stars are created in Day 4 for the express purpose "to govern the day and the night," and "to separate the light from the darkness," yet Genesis 1:3–5 says that light and dark were already separated back on Day 1. It may be argued that the separation occurred on Day 1 followed by the creation of celestial bodies on Day 4 to govern that separation, but this requires a departure from the literal reading. The most straightforward interpretation of the words of 1:14–18 is that the celestial bodies brought about the separation of light, making Days 1 and 4 redundant.

"Evening and Morning"

The description in Genesis 1 of each of the first six days of creation closes with the phrase "there was evening and there was morning...." Most discussions focus on the length of time referred to by these verses, but a critical observation is generally overlooked. Physical nightfall and subsequent dawn only have meaning from the perspective of someone (1) at a fixed geographic location, (2) on a rotating planet, and (3) adjacent to a stationary light source.[6]

There are a couple of problems here for a literal reading. First, with no humans or even animals on the planet for the first four days, fixing the point of reference to a particular spot on the newly formed planet makes little sense. From God's perspective, and for the creation as a whole, day and night are present on opposite sides of the globe *continuously*. A literal reading requires that the perspective be a backwards-in-time projection of humans who will be placed at a specific spot on the planet, but who won't actually exist until Day 6.

Some argue that references to evening and morning prior to creation of the sun are simply common expressions of the passage of a literal day.[7]

---

6. Or, from an ANE perspective, someone on a flat (or domed) earth with a light source making a daily circuit above and below.
7. Kulikovsky, "Evenings and mornings."

Ironically, this argument calls for a nonliteral, figurative understanding of the first three pairs of evening and morning. In other words, a *figurative* interpretation is called upon to defend a *literal* interpretation.

Firmament

On Day 2, God divided the waters above from the waters below, separating them by an object (*raqia*), translated variably as an *expanse* (NASB, ESV), *vault* (NIV), or *firmament* (KJV).[8] The sun, moon, and stars were later placed within the *raqia* (Gen. 1:15), and when birds were created, they flew above the earth and in or across the *raqia*.

The plain-sense reading is a description of a solid surface that holds back the waters of heaven, under which the birds of the air fly. This reading is consistent with the Ancient Near Eastern understanding of a three-tiered universe, and represents the traditional Hebraic tradition and interpretation of the church leading all the way up to Copernicus. The Septuagint, a translation of the Old Testament into Greek by Jewish scholars before the time of Christ, translated *raqia* as the Greek word *steréoma*,[9] meaning a solid surface, also consistent with the understanding of a solid dome above the earth.

Ironically, the only reason that one would interpret *raqia* as anything other than a solid dome (firmament) is if greater weight is given to modern science than to thousands of years of traditional biblical understanding. Those who insist that God intended all along for *raqia* to be understood as the *atmosphere* or *space* expect us to accept a very awkward history, where[10]

- the original Hebrew readers knew that the description *really* meant an atmosphere with water vapor, even though the wording is in apparent agreement with their neighbors' three-tiered universe;

- this true meaning was then lost for millennia; and

- the real meaning was then rediscovered by scientists only a few hundred years ago.[11]

---

8. Hebrew: רָקִיעַ (*raqia*), "expanse" / "vault" / "firmament."
9. Greek: στερέωμα (*steréoma*), "solid surface" / "firmament."
10. Vaterlaus, "Underneath a solid sky."
11. Alternately, some simply deny that ANE cultures or the early church believed in a flat earth or solid domed sky, e.g., Younker and Davidson, "The myth of the solid heavenly dome: Another look at the Hebrew רָקִיעַ (*raqia*)."

Order of Creation

Yet another problem arises with the order of creation of man and cattle. In Genesis 1:25–26, God created the beasts of the earth, including cattle, prior to the creation of humans. But in Genesis 2:18–19, we read,

> Then the LORD God said, "It is not good for the man to be alone; I will make him a helper suitable for him." Out of the ground the LORD God formed every beast of the field and every bird of the sky, and brought them to the man to see what he would call them....

A literal interpretation of these verses requires that terrestrial animals and birds were created *after* Adam. The apparent contradiction is "fixed" in the NIV and ESV by translating verse 19 to read "Now the LORD God *had formed*" all the beasts of the field. In fairness, there are cases in Hebrew where translation into a particular tense (pluperfect in this case) is justified by the immediate context of the wording. In this verse, however, the justification is not found within the immediate context, but has to be inferred (assumed) from the text of Genesis 1. This makes the choice of English wording more a matter of *interpretation* than *translation*. The NASB and NKJV remain more true to the Hebrew text.

God Rests

One may also question the wisdom of a literal interpretation of Genesis 2:2, which tells us God rested from his labors. We need rest because we tire. Does God grow tired that he should need rest? Of course, rest *can* simply mean to cease from activity (like a rest in a musical score) without being linked to fatigue, but other verses suggest this is not a sufficient explanation. Exodus 31:16–17 tells us, in the context of honoring the Sabbath, that God made the earth in six days, and on the seventh he rested and was *refreshed*.[12] There is no purpose to being refreshed unless one is first worn down. A literal interpretation here thus requires us to believe that God was wearied from his labors and needed a break. Yet Isaiah 40:28 assures us that God, the Creator of all the earth, does not grow weary.

Some have attempted to argue that *refreshed* can mean something akin to "stood back and enjoyed," though this is stepping *away* from a literal meaning

---

12. Hebrew: וַיִּנָּפַשׁ (*way-yin-na-pas*), "was refreshed."

in the *defense* of a literal interpretation.[13] The more defensible explanation for rest and refreshment is as an anthropomorphism, describing the actions of God in human terms by way of example.[14] Ending six days of work with a day of rest and refreshment is a figurative representation of completion of the lattice of creation. Chaos was fashioned into order, the formless was turned into functioning realms, and the empty realms were filled with luminaries and life (more on this in a few pages).

Cessation of Creation

Genesis 2:2 further tells us that "by the seventh day God completed His work which He had done." The plain-sense meaning is that God stopped creating by the end of Day 6. We can watch new land form as lava spills into the sea on the island of Hawaii and measure the growth rate of the Himalayan Mountains. We witness the creation of new life with each conception and birth. Astronomers even see new stars come to life daily in the vast cosmos. Adherence to a literal interpretation of Genesis 2:2 requires that God is not the author of these events since he has rested from his creative efforts. Indeed, even you and I are not to be considered his creative handiwork. One might suggest that the creation story is only concerned with God's miraculous creation, while what we see now are natural processes. Aside from the fact that the text does not support such a division, it would require that God is only the author of what is made miraculously. An understanding freed from a literalistic human bias acknowledges God as the continuing creator of new life, new lands, and new stars.

Thistles and Thorns

If God was done creating in the first six days, and no new species or "kinds" of organisms have appeared since Day 6, we have a problem when we get to Genesis 3:18. After Adam and Eve sinned, God's curse included the proclamation that the earth would now bring forth thorns and thistles. A literal interpretation here requires that thorns and thistles were absent on the earth until the curse. Yet thorns and thistles represent the arrival of completely new species.

---

13. Baldwin, *Creation, Catastrophe, and Calvary: Why a Global Flood Is Vital to the Doctrine of Atonement,* 61.
14. Blocher, *In the Beginning, The Opening Chapters of Genesis,* 57; Collins, *Science and Faith: Friends or Foes?,* 86; Miller and Soden, *In the Beginning...We Misunderstood: Interpreting Genesis 1 in its Original Context,* 53–54.

Literalist arguments, aware of the problem of thorns and thistles, have themselves evolved to the point where some now suggest that genetic defects introduced by the fall caused new species to develop such as plants with thorns and animals with fangs.[15] The appearance of carnivores like lions and killer whales, if not present prior to sin, represents new kinds of organisms not just at the *species, genus,* or even *family* taxonomic level, but new *orders* of creatures.[16] The implication is that the pre-fall creations were miraculous and part of the creation week, while subsequent variations of life-forms arose from cursed natural processes. But such interpretations are *imposed* on Scripture rather than *derived* from Scripture. In fact, it is difficult to argue from Scripture that there is any substantive difference in the creation of plants before the fall and thorns after. In Genesis 1:12, God said, "Let the earth sprout vegetation ..." and it did. In Genesis 3:18, God said of the land, "both thorns and thistles it shall grow for you," and it did. God spoke and it came to pass, both times.

It is also important to consider the organisms themselves. These plants and animals are exquisitely crafted for their environmental niches, often providing essential ecological functions. To suggest that these are the products of a cursed world and not the creative works of God is to suggest that Satan, or sin, is the creator of such magnificent, well-crafted organisms. Satan may be an author of suffering and pain, but the notion that he is a creator, on par with God, is not supported by any historical doctrine of the church. (We'll dive more deeply into this issue when we address death and sin in Chapter 6.)

It should be clear at this stage that a literal interpretation of Genesis 1 and 2 is not so straightforward. Even the most outspoken literalists stray substantially and frequently from the literal meanings in their interpretations of the story. If in fact there is a "plain sense" reading of this text, it is not a literal one, for a truly literal reading turns an orderly creation back into chaos.

So how should Genesis 1 be understood? I believe there is a much better way to understand this foundational story that is not only free of the inconsistencies and contradictions inherent to a literal reading, but that also gives us a grander view of both the Creator and his creation. A case will be made for

---

15. Sarfati, *Refuting Evolution 2*, 56; Gish, *Evolution: The Fossils Still Say No!*, 29.
16. Each level of biological taxonomy includes a wider and wider grouping of organisms: species, genus, family, order, class, phylum, kingdom.

what we might call a *commonsense* reading. We will apply some basic God-given common sense to the structure of the story to gain a deeper, *more* biblical understanding. The basic ideas shared in the remainder of this chapter are not new. Theologians both modern and ancient have already accomplished the heavy hermeneutical lifting. My intention here is to collect and represent the insights of others in a concise and comprehensible presentation.

A MARRIAGE OF HISTORY AND POETRY

The creation story opens with the grand statement that God made everything (the heavens and the earth), followed by the observation that the earth was *tohu wa-bohu*, translated as variations of "formless" (*tohu*) and "empty" (*bohu*).[17] In English, we miss the literary use of rhyme in this introductory phrase. After bringing matter and energy into existence, God began to solve the twofold problems of being formless and empty. Creation unfolds in a striking parallel structure, with the first three days aligning with the last three days (Table 5). This parallel structure has been noted at least as far back as Thomas Aquinas (thirteenth century),[18] and developed more fully by a number of modern theologians.[19]

TABLE 5—PARALLEL STRUCTURE OF GENESIS 1	
creation of heavens and the earth	
Tohu (formless)	*Bohu* (empty)
realm of light and dark	filling with sun, moon, stars
realm of sea and sky	filling with fish and birds
realm of land with plants	filling with animals and man
rest	

The days are not only aligned, they fit neatly under the headings of *tohu* and *bohu*, formless and empty. The first three days solve the problem of being formless (*tohu*). On Day 1 God begins giving his creation form and order, creating the realm of light and dark. On Day 2, he gives form to the realm of sea and sky. And on Day 3 he gives form to the terrestrial realm, complete with plants necessary for sustaining life.

---

17. Hebrew: וָבֹהוּ תֹהוּ (*tohu wa-bohu*), "empty and void."
18. Aquinas, *Summa Theologica*, Part 1. Quest. 70, Art. 1.
19. Blocher, *In the Beginning*, chap. 2; Kline, "Space and time in the Genesis cosmogony."

These days are coupled with the next three days that solve the problem of being empty (*bohu*). Day 4 fills the realm of light and dark with the sun, moon, and stars. Day 5 fills the realm of sea and sky with fish and birds. And Day 6 fills the terrestrial realm with animals and humans.

All this is set in the context of a human workweek, complete with a day of rest. The idea of rest is found not only in the climax, but within each day. C. John Collins has noted that the unique wording for the close of each day is *also* linked to the need for human rest. Rather than bracketing each day with "morning and evening," the normal order is reversed to say "there was evening and morning, a day." The norm for humans is to work during the day and rest at night, so each day of creation ends with a time of rest; rest that God does not need.[20]

The alignment of the two sets of three days is often referred to as the *framework view*. The creation story is cast in the literary framework of parallel days aligned under *tohu* and *bohu*, all within the structure of a human workweek. The truth of God's authorship is communicated with rich poetic and allegorical form. Note that "poetic" and "allegorical" are not code words for nonhistorical. In fact, one might argue that it helps to communicate the historical truth far more powerfully than a simple record of events might imply.

This story is telling us so much more than a sequence or timing. It tells us that God did not just create things (filling empty space), but created the very realms in which things can exist (giving form and order). He is not the deist God who got things started and sat back wondering what would happen next, but is the Author of every step along the way. The celestial bodies were not gods to be worshiped, as Israel's neighbors believed, but were grand creations of God to mark time and seasons. The natural world is not an accident of warring gods, also a belief of Israel's neighbors, but is the intentional creation of a singular, benevolent God who declared his work to be good.

And what of all those apparent inconsistencies or contradictions from Table 4? All but one immediately fall away. Light and dark separated on Day 1 and on Day 4 are describing the same event from the interconnected perspectives of forming and filling. The separation is not a physical description (which would have no meaning), but a word picture to communicate that it is God who gives and withholds light. There is no need to figure out the sequence of light from nonexistent sources because the story was never about *sequence* in

---

20. Collins, *Science and Faith*, 84–86. Collins holds more to "analogical days" for Genesis 1, though the argument for the nights for rest is valid for both the framework and analogical-day views.

the first place. Likewise, the pattern of daily human rest, with each day ending with evening and morning and finishing with a Sabbath rest allegorically fits the structure of a *human* workweek. Lastly, the different order of the appearance of animals and man given in Genesis 1 and 2 requires no translational fix, as the order of events was never the point of Genesis 1.

The only remaining apparent inconsistency is the arrival of thorns and thistles after creation was completed. This also has a straightforward explanation if Scripture is not arbitrarily forced into a literalistic mold. The garden was a place of protection from an arguably less desirable existence outside. This is evident from the fact that the garden had boundaries (why boundaries if all the earth was perfect for human habitation?), and an angel was placed at the entrance after the curse to ensure that no one could reenter (Gen. 3:24). If thorns and thistles already existed outside the garden, man was blessed with their absence until cast out. The curse was not the *creation* of thorns, but the *exposure* to thorns.

But what of the fact that God cursed *the ground* in Genesis 3:17? Doesn't this support the idea that thorns did not exist until the ground was cursed? Visiting a related Scripture passage helps to answer this (again drawing on insights from C. John Collins).[21] In Deuteronomy 28:17–18, God warned his people of the consequences of disobedience, saying,

> Cursed shall be your basket and your kneading bowl. Cursed shall be the offspring of your body and the produce of your ground, the increase of your herd and the young of your flock.

We know Israel did disobey and did experience these curses, but few would suggest that their baskets, bowls, crops, or cattle physically twisted into new diabolical forms. Rather, people's *experience* with each of these was transformed from something positive to something negative. Lions eating deer posed no problems for Israel, but lions eating sheep did. Weeds were not a problem if growing outside fields, but resulted in empty bowls when proliferating in the midst of the wheat. The wording of Deuteronomy 28, as in Genesis 3, appears at first to say that the objects themselves are cursed, but knowing how these curses were fulfilled in Israel's history informs us that it is not the physical objects that became twisted, but the way in which Israel began

---

21. Collins, *Science and Faith,* 150–51.

to experience them. Thorns could have existed on earth from the beginning, but outside of Adam and Eve's experience until after their own disobedience.[22]

OBJECTIONS TO FRAMEWORK VIEW AND RESPONSES

Objection 1: Genesis 1 is not Hebrew poetry.

The objection raised most often is that Genesis 1 is not poetry. Parallelism is a hallmark of Hebrew poetry, so why would anyone declare Genesis 1 to be free of poetical form? There are two principal reasons. The first is that the detailed structure of Genesis 1 does not exactly match the structure in Hebrew poems found elsewhere in the Old Testament. But it doesn't exactly match the form of historical narrative found elsewhere either. Genesis 1 is unique. This has led some scholars to describe the passage as "semi-poetry" or "exalted prose."[23] Given the clear use of parallel structure introduced with a rhyming wordplay, both elements of Hebrew poetry, it may well be a marriage of history and poetry, a poem of perhaps greater antiquity than others, giving rise to its unique form.

The second reason for rejecting a poetic designation is a presuppositional commitment to the text being straightforward narrative. This seems evident from the degree of confidence placed on thinly supported arguments. In *Coming to Grips with Genesis*, contributing author Robert V. McCabe builds a lengthy case for a literal interpretation, based largely on the use of the Hebrew "*waw* consecutive," a word often translated as "then." The crux of the argument is that a listing of events described as this, *then* this, *then* this—as is found in Genesis 1—must be prose because it indicates a specific sequence.[24] Why a specific sequence cannot be poetic is left unanswered.

Objection 2: Parallel structure fails on closer examination.

Several have challenged the parallel structure directly by claiming the days do not really align, arguing that the luminaries of Day 4 were placed in the heavens of Day 2 (not Day 1), and fish were placed in the seas of Day 3 or the water made prior to Day 1 (not in the "waters below" of Day 2).[25] Whether

---

22. If this makes sense to you, but you find yourself concerned that it is all motivated by modern scientific challenges, you can find some of the same ideas expressed by Augustine over a thousand years ago: Augustine, *The Literal Meaning of Genesis*, 94; Young, "The contemporary relevance of Augustine's view of creation."
23. Young, *Studies in Genesis One*, 82; Collins, *Genesis 1–4: A Linguistic, Literary, and Theological Commentary*, 44.
24. McCabe, "A critique of the framework interpretation of the creation week."
25. Ham, *The Lie: Evolution*, 211; Mortenson, "When was Adam created?," 142–43.

these represent genuine misalignment depends on which parts or themes of each verse are deemed central.

To unpack this, let's examine Table 6, which is similar to Table 5, but with excerpts from each day and key Hebrew words included. If attention is only given to *placement* of the luminaries on Day 4, then an argument can be made against a parallel with Day 1 because the expanse (*raqia*) was made on Day 2. If we are considering *purpose*, however, the parallel is strong, for Days 1 and 4 both serve to separate light from dark and day from night.

The objection of aligning the water of Day 2 with the fish of Day 5 is that the seas (*yam*) are named on Day 3. But if we give attention to *purpose*, again, the purpose of the expanse (*raqia*) on Day 2 was to separate the waters on the earth from the waters above the dome of the sky, giving rise to the realms of ocean and sky. This is consistent with the choice of words for the water in which the fish swim. Day 5 does not use the word for seas (*yam*) from Day 3, but the waters (*mayim*) of Day 2.

The parallels survive the objections.

TABLE 6—EXCERPTS FROM EACH DAY IN GENESIS 1 WITH KEY HEBREW WORDS[26]	
Gen 1:1–2 creation of heavens (*shamayim*) and earth (*erets*) and waters (*mayim*) of the deep	
Day 1, Gen. 1:3–5 "Let there be light…. God **separated the light from the darkness**. God called the light day, and the darkness He called night."	**Day 4, Gen. 1:14–19** "Let there be lights in the expanse [*raqia*] of the heavens [*shamayim*] to **separate the day from the night**."
Day 2, Gen. 1:6–8 "God made the expanse, and separated the **waters** [***mayim***] which were below the expanse from the waters which were above the expanse [*raqia*]…. God called the expanse heaven [*shamayim*]."	**Day 5, Gen. 1:20–23** "Let the **waters** [***mayim***] teem with swarms of living creatures, and let birds fly above the earth in the open expanse [*raqia*] of the heavens [*shamayim*]."
Day 3, Gen. 1:9–13 "God called the dry land earth [*erets*], and the gathering of the waters He called seas [*yam*]."	**Day 6, Gen. 1:24–25** "Let the earth [*erets*] bring forth living creatures after their kind: cattle and creeping things and beasts of the earth after their kind."

---

26. Hebrew: הַשָּׁמַיִם (*shamayim*), "heavens"; אֶרֶץ (*erets*), "earth"; הַמַּיִם (*mayim*), "waters."

Objection 3: Jesus believed Genesis 1 was literal.

Some insist that Jesus believed in a literal six-day creation, for his words are recorded in Mark 10:6 saying, "But from the beginning of creation, God made them male and female."[27] But according to Genesis, humans were not made at the beginning of creation, they were made at the end. Jesus did not trip over his words here; he wasn't making a statement about the days of creation at all. His statement reflects the fact that from the beginning *of their creation*, humans were specifically designed to function in paired unions of the two forms, male and female. His statement is about marriage and human sexuality, not the timing or mode of creation.

SUMMARY

Literalists will often say the issue is not a matter of *interpretation* of Genesis 1 and 2, but simply whether one *believes* what it says.[28] The implication is that one only needs to interpret the text if one chooses not to believe what the words say. We have seen, however, that a great deal of interpretation underlies a superficial, literalist reading of the creation story. In fact, few (if any at all) truly believe the supposed "plain sense" meaning of the words, for a host of nonliteral explanations are required to buttress the purported literal view.

On the other side, there are many who argue that Genesis *can* be interpreted in a more figurative or poetic form, without giving up the doctrine of inerrancy and without relegating the story to myth. I will be bolder and suggest that the most Bible-honoring, internally consistent, and *commonsense* understanding of Genesis 1 is a marriage of poetry and history. The zealously promoted literalistic view sells well in many churches, but it is no more defensible than the geocentric interpretations argued with equal zeal in the days of Galileo.

If the focus of the creation story is about the *who* more than the *how*, then we are free to allow God's natural creation to inform us on the details of what that creative process looked like. The study of earth's history does not have to be limited to hunting only for evidence of a story already fully understood. We can follow Job's admonition to his critics, saying, "speak to the earth, and let it teach you" (Job 12:8).

---

27. Sarfati, *Refuting Evolution 2*, 41; Wieland, "Jesus on the age of the earth."
28. Mortenson, "Adam, morality, the Gospel, and the authority of Scripture," 490.

This does not mean that scientific explanations are automatically correct. It is still possible that scientific conclusions may genuinely conflict with Scripture, or that some theories are simply incorrect (even if not in conflict with the Bible). In the next chapter, we will begin addressing Question 2 (page 23), which asks if specific scientific theories or claims conflict with the intended message of the Bible.

PART 3

CONFLICT?

6

DOES MODERN SCIENCE CONFLICT WITH SCRIPTURE?

If the first question has been satisfactorily addressed, we are ready to ask Question 2: Does the science conflict with the intended message of Scripture? Note that we are not yet addressing the *credibility* of scientific claims. We are only looking to see if current scientific understanding fits or clashes with Scripture's intended meaning. This is not as simple as just addressing the general subjects of the earth's age or of evolution, for it is possible that a subset of scientific claims under these broad headings may be found to be free of conflict with Scripture, while another subset could remain at odds with the biblical message. With this in mind, this chapter has been divided into six sections, each addressing a particular scriptural concern that relates to age or origins.

For each subject, we'll first review the fundamental biblical message, followed by a description of the current scientific understanding, and then see what sort of synthesis or conflict may arise. Each section includes a table directly comparing the relevant biblical and scientific claims. At this stage, we won't dive deeply into the history or defense of scientific theories. That will be saved for Question 3 (discussed in Part 4).

THE ORIGIN OF THE UNIVERSE: *EX NIHILO*

"In the beginning God created the heavens and the earth." (Gen. 1:1)

Bible

Various opinions on the interpretation of the creation story agree on one point if they share a belief in the authority of God's Word: God created all that is here. Though Genesis does not say explicitly that the world was made from nothing, Hebrews 11:3 adds that bit of clarity, saying, "By faith we understand that the worlds were prepared by the word of God, so that what is seen was not made out of things which are visible."

God did not merely reshape that which already existed. He brought all that exists into being by the power of his divine will. Following the initial inception of the universe, God may have molded and shaped what is now present, but the first creation event was *ex nihilo,* out of nothing.

Science

The study of the universe and its origins is known as *cosmology.* It is generally thought among cosmologists that the universe started as a dimensionless point, or *singularity,* roughly 14 billion years ago. Rapid expansion of energy at an unimaginable temperature (the so-called "big bang") initiated the beginning of time and space in a baby universe devoid of the physical matter we are now familiar with. During the first microsecond of the expansion, some of the energy converted into matter (nuclear bombs do the same thing in reverse), followed by a clustering of matter into what would eventually become galaxies, stars, and planets.

The expansion continues today. Left to itself, the universe will experience one of three fates. If there is sufficient mass in the universe, gravitational forces could eventually halt expansion and collapse all matter back to the center in what is called the "big crunch." If there is insufficient mass, expansion will continue indefinitely. Stars will eventually burn out, light will fade, and temperatures will approach absolute zero. A third possibility is that repulsive forces acting over great distances may accelerate expansion to the point where galaxies, stars, and planets get torn apart in what is called the "big rip."[1] In all three scenarios, life in the universe—if left to natural processes—ultimately ends.

Several theories were postulated in the twentieth century that considered recurring cataclysmic collapses and reverberating big bangs that continue in infinite oscillations. In principle, such oscillations should be limited in number before running out of steam, much as a dropped rubber ball bounces a little lower each cycle until coming to rest.[2] While some have argued that the basic laws of physics may be very different at those transition points, allowing

---

1. Cowen, "Wrenching findings: Homing in on dark energy."
2. Ross, *The Fingerprint of God: Recent Scientific Discoveries Reveal the Unmistakable Identity of the Creator,* chap. 10.

unending oscillations,[3] the subject has largely been made moot by current astronomical observations. All evidence indicates that the expansion rate of the universe is either accelerating (growing faster and faster with time)[4] or is at least expanding at a constant rate.[5] There is no indication of slowing in preparation for a rebound.

In all these scientific versions, the universe in which we live had a beginning. According to the "standard model" of cosmology, the pre-universe condition is referred to as a *void*. This is not another term for a vacuum or empty space; it literally means *nothing*. Driven largely by discomfort with the idea of something from nothing, a new field of study emerged known as *M-theory*. Researchers in this field are convinced that our universe is actually one of an infinite number of universes constantly being formed like froth on a beer or bubbles in Swiss cheese. All the universes taken collectively are referred to as the *multiverse*.[6]

Though mathematically based, M-theory is fundamentally different from theories of standard cosmology. Evidence for the big bang and the history of the universe exists in the form of physical observations and measurements of energy emanating from distant stars that conform to theoretical calculations. M-theory is speculative and has yet to be uniquely supported by any physical observations. Further, the existence of other universes would be inherently unobservable from within our own universe, limiting our knowledge of them to mathematical calculations that allow only for the *possibility* that they are real.

Synthesis

Scientific inquiry will yield proof for only that which is observable within the confines of time and space. The existence of other universes or descriptions of conditions prior to the creation of our universe may be mathematically plausible, but fall outside our ability to scientifically test. As such, belief in a self-existent universe initiated by a quantum fluctuation in a pre-universe void derives more from a philosophical commitment to materialism than from science. Having said this, the existence of more than one universe is not inherently in opposition with biblical Christianity; the Bible simply does not address the existence of anything outside our own experience.

---

3. A layman's explanation can be found in Bojowald, "Follow the bouncing universe."
4. Palmer, "Nobel physics prize honours accelerating universe find."
5. Nielsen, Guffanti, and Sarkar, "Marginal evidence for cosmic acceleration from Type 1a supernovae."
6. Kaku, "What happened before the big bang?"; Nadis, "Making multiverses."

TABLE 7—ORIGIN OF THE UNIVERSE	
The Bible	Science
The universe had a beginning.	The universe had a beginning.
The universe was created from nothing. (Heb. 11:3)	According to the standard model, the beginning of the universe is described as coming from nothing (*void*).
Time and space began when the universe began.	Time and space as we know it were initiated at the big bang.
The possible existence of multiple universes is not addressed in Scripture.	Though there is no unique physical evidence, our universe *may* be one of many.

Though I am not a fan of the multiverse, I find some irony in the strength of Christian reactions against the idea of any universe other than our own, considering the immense popularity of C. S. Lewis's *Chronicles of Narnia*. The whole series is based on the hypothetical notion of multiple universes in which God acts in different, yet wholly consistent ways within each. The only issue that is truly in conflict with Scripture is the supposition that matter and energy, whether in one universe or many, is eternal. Standard cosmology, summarized in the first three rows of Table 7, is remarkably biblical.

THE ORIGIN OF LIFE: "BROUGHT FORTH FROM THE EARTH"

> Then God said, "Let the earth sprout vegetation, plants yielding seed, and fruit trees on the earth bearing fruit after their kind with seed in them"; and it was so. (Gen. 1:11)

> Then God said, "Let the earth bring forth living creatures after their kind: cattle and creeping things and beasts of the earth after their kind"; and it was so. (Gen. 1:24)

Bible

The Genesis account tells us that God started his creation off by bringing the heavens and the earth into being. The initial universe was created *ex nihilo*: from nothing. Once created, the rest of creation appears to be a reshaping of what God previously made. Genesis 1:11 and 24 point out that God commanded the earth to bring forth plants and animals, and it obeyed.

The added phrase of "after their kind" was likely a statement about the orderliness of God's creation. His creation was not an accident of warring gods, with natural phenomena varying with their capricious moods. The creation reflects its Author. As we interact with nature, we can be confident that it follows the natural laws that God set in motion. In the short span of human history, sheep can be counted on to produce sheep and cows to produce cows.

Science

Evidence suggests that life began on earth roughly 3.5 billion years ago under an oxygen-deficient atmosphere. The mechanisms for the formation of life from nonliving materials are poorly understood, but it is thought that life was probably first formed under one or some combination of the following scenarios: (1) in the ocean where essential elements were readily available and circulated, (2) protected from harmful ultraviolet rays under rocks or in deep water, (3) in contact with a thermal-energy source such as sun-warmed tidal pools or at deep ocean thermal vents, or possibly (4) by interaction with catalysts such as clay surfaces that increase the rate of molecular combination.

The appearance of life-forms based on the fossil record is summarized in Table 8. Evidence of the earliest life is equivocal, but the first single-celled organisms may date to within the first billion years of earth's 4.6-billion-year history.[7] Subsequent developmental advances included the appearance of photosynthetic varieties (cyanobacteria) believed to be responsible for eventual increases in atmospheric oxygen levels, but life remained as individual or colonies of single-celled organisms for at least another billion years. Increases in complexity within the last 1.8 billion years started with the first appearance of cells containing a nucleus (eukaryotes), then multicellular organisms, and eventually a great diversification of life beginning about 0.6 billion years ago.

---

7. Rosen, "Tiny fossils could be oldest signs of life."

TABLE 8—APPEARANCE OF LIFE-FORMS		
Time		Life-forms
First billion years		none (?)
Second billion years		single-celled bacteria with no cell nucleus
		photosynthetic bacteria (produce oxygen)
Third billion years		Single-celled bacteria with a cell nucleus
Fourth billion years		multicellular organisms (proto-plants/animals)
Last 0.6 billion years (600 million years)	600–450 million years ago	shelled organisms, fish
	450–300 million years ago	land plants, amphibians
	300–200 million years ago	reptiles, insects
	200–100 million years ago	dinosaurs, mammals, birds, flowering plants
	100–0 million years ago	primates, humans

Changes in the design and function of organisms in successive generations are thought possible due to changes in the genetic code that occur by several different processes, including copying errors during cell division, transfer of genetic information between different organisms, and even programmed change carried out by specialized sections of DNA. All forms of change are collectively referred to as *mutations*. Changes in form and function resulting from mutations may have deleterious, advantageous, or neutral effects on an organism's ability to survive and reproduce. Those with new features better adapted for a particular environment will tend to populate that environment, with offspring possessing the same features. Those ill-suited for their environment either migrate or die out. The cumulative effect of small changes from one generation to the next add up to large changes when looking across thousands of generations.

In a population, changes in form or function may occur due to simple genetic drift, with changes causing neither harm nor gain, or by natural selection, where change is driven by greater reproductive success. If a population of organisms remains well mixed, the whole population changes over time. If portions of the population are separated by geographical barriers, or as a result of developing different preferences for food sources or mate characteristics, the subpopulations begin to change independently and can eventually give rise to separate species.

TABLE 9—ORIGIN OF LIFE	
The Bible	Science
The earth "brought forth" life at God's command. (Gen. 1:12, 24)	Life originated from nonliving earth materials.
In man's experience, plants and animals produce offspring of the same type.	Over the span of many human generations, organisms change relatively little. Over longer time periods, larger changes follow orderly natural laws.

Synthesis

"Let the earth bring forth"

According to Genesis, God commanded the earth to give rise to life. Interestingly, these verses hold true whether God formed plants and animals from the earth all at once or if they appeared through a long series of generations beginning with nonliving earth materials. So what does science currently claim? According to modern scientific understanding, the earth gave rise to life.

The parallel here between the Bible and science is remarkable, but not sufficient to assuage the concerns of many Christians because of their perception that natural selection is replacing God as the driving force for creation. Indeed, many secular scientists do insist that natural selection is the ultimate driving force, eliminating all need of a personal creator. This conclusion naively assumes that a *supernatural* driving force could not give rise to a *natural* driving force. Unfortunately, many Christians often follow the bad example set by these secularists and insist that a natural force cannot be real based on the same faulty assumption.

In this light, consider a hypothetical God-versus-gravity debate. A ball released at the top of an incline rolls down the slope. Scientists studying the phenomenon discover that the behavior of the rolling ball is predictable, and develop a theory that the behavior is controlled by something they call *gravity.* Some of these scientists go so far as to say that God is not necessary to account for the behavior of the ball because they have a good naturalistic explanation for the observed phenomenon. In reaction, some Christians insist that God is the driving force behind all of creation, therefore gravity cannot be true.

Though the idea of a God-versus-gravity debate may seem far-fetched, it is not terribly different from the very real God-versus-natural-selection debate. Christians and non-Christians alike are too quick to assume that supernatural and natural driving forces are mutually exclusive. If natural selection is a real driving force, there is no reason to believe that it is not one of many natural phenomena designed by an awesome supernatural Creator.

"After their kind"

As each group of organisms is created in Genesis 1, a repeated phrase is used that organisms were made and then reproduced, each "after their kind." The same phrase is found in Genesis 6 when God told Noah to bring creatures aboard the ark, each "after their kind." For most of human history, creation of groups of organisms according to their kind was understood to be a statement of the orderliness and stability of God's creation, with plants and animals producing offspring of the same type, roughly equivalent to what we think of as a species today.[8]

With a little knowledge of Ancient Near East mythology, it makes a lot of sense for this affirmation to be included. Israel's neighbors believed nature to be the chaotic, unpredictable outgrowth of the actions of capricious gods. There was no telling what monstrosity could arise from the union of two creatures if the gods got careless or mischievous. But the God of Genesis is not capricious. There is order to the creation. In human experience, sparrows will give rise to sparrows and sheep will give rise to sheep.

This is not a statement against evolution. Quite to the contrary, evolutionary theory *affirms* that nature is not controlled by mercurial gods, but acts in an orderly and logical fashion. That orderliness is what allows us to selectively breed to enhance desirable traits in crops or livestock, and even to manipulate the genetic code with reasonable foreknowledge of what it will produce.

Ironically, young-earth creationists have turned the traditional interpretation of this text upside down. Realizing that representative species from

---

8. Augustine, *The Literal Meaning of Genesis*, Book 3, Articles 18–20, 227–28; Calvin, *Commentary on Genesis*, Vol. 1, Article 24.

the entire earth could not fit on the ark,[9] leading young-earth advocates now claim that creatures that we would not recognize today entered the ark, with offspring evolving at hyperspeed after exiting to a dramatically changed environment.[10] As an example, a single cat-kind pair leaving the ark gave rise, in a matter of a few generations, to all of today's lions, tigers, cougars, jaguars, leopards, cheetahs, bobcats, panthers, lynx, ocelots, and house cats, as well as the many extinct varieties of saber-tooth cats. With a biblical *kind* defined closer to a biological *family*, not even sheep, goats, and cows would have been on the ark in forms recognized today, for they are all part of the *bovid* family. (Sheep and goats are even part of the same *caprinid sub*family.) Noah presumably brought on pairs of a *bovid kind*, which soon gave rise to goats, sheep, and cows. Stated another way, in the young-earth view, creation "after their kind" could allow a goat to give birth to a sheep or gazelle to a giraffe.[11]

All this departs radically from a literal/traditional understanding of Genesis.

- The fact that God differentiated clean from unclean animals in Genesis 7:2, long before such divisions appeared in the dietary laws passed on by Moses, implies that the animals Noah brought on his boat were the same as those known to Moses, which are still recognizable today.

- Of the roughly 100 animals identified by name in the Bible, every single one is from the modern land of Israel or its surrounding trading partners, and all but a few with uncertain translations are familiar to us today.[12]

- Genesis 4 contains references to men who gave rise to diverse skills and technology: Jabal who gave rise to those who live in tents, Jubal who fathered those who play the lyre and pipe, and Tubal-cain who forged implements of bronze and iron. If ancestral animals unfamiliar to us on the ark gave rise to diverse classes of creatures, one might expect a similar mention in Genesis. No such references appear in Scripture.

---

9. Woodmorappe, *Noah's Ark: A Feasibility Study*; Sarfati, "How did all the animals fit on Noah's ark?"
10. Morris, "The microwave of evolution"; Catchpoole and Wieland, "Speedy species surprise."
11. Lightner, "Mammalian ark kinds," 191–92.
12. *Leviathan* and *behemoth* are the most uncertain. Theologians differ on whether these are descriptions of real or allegorical creatures.

- The Bible makes no mention that there was anything out of the ordinary in nature in the immediate post-flood world.

- The traditional, and straightforward reading of "after their kinds" has always been something akin to species producing the same species.

Current scientific understanding, with minor changes in the forms of organisms over human experience, is closer to the plain-sense meaning of Genesis than is the modern, young-earth view.

THE ORIGIN OF MAN: "DUST FROM THE GROUND"

> Then the LORD God formed man of dust from the ground, and breathed into his nostrils the breath of life; and man became a living being. (Gen. 2:7)

> Cain said to the LORD, "My punishment is too great to bear! Behold, You have driven me this day from the face of the ground; and from Your face I will be hidden, and I will be a vagrant and a wanderer on the earth, and whoever finds me will kill me." (Gen. 4:13–14)

> The Nephilim were on the earth in those days, and also afterward, when the sons of God came in to the daughters of men, and they bore children to them. Those were the mighty men who were of old, men of renown. (Gen. 6:4)

Bible

The creation of man differs from the creation of other life-forms only in detail. Adam, like all the creatures before him, was brought forth from what God had previously created: "of dust from the ground." Eve was likewise brought into being from materials already present, though in this case, Adam's side is described as the source of the material used for her creation. If the rivers named in Genesis 2 are the same as today (Tigris and Euphrates), Eden was in the Middle East within the Fertile Crescent.

Adam and Eve are described as the first humans, with Eve's name meaning the "mother of all living." Eve gave birth to two sons, Abel who tended herds and Cain who raised crops. When Cain's sacrifice was rejected by God and Abel's was accepted, Cain became jealous of Abel and killed him. Cain's punishment was exile from the land of his parents. Cain feared that he would be killed by others he encountered. God assured Cain of his protection and placed a mark on Cain that would shield him from attack.

The moral decay of the human race following the first sin was both immediate and universal. Several generations later, God saw the wickedness of men and decided to wipe out all but Noah and his family. One behavior in particular merited calling out—"the sons of God saw that the daughters of men were beautiful; and they took wives for themselves, whomever they chose." Unions that produced the enigmatic Nephilim. Whoever these people were, their genetic influence carried on even after the flood, for they "were on the earth in those days, and also afterward" (Gen. 6:1–4). During the conquest of Canaan, Israel again encountered their descendants: "There also we saw the Nephilim (the sons of Anak are part of the Nephilim); and we became like grasshoppers in our own sight, and so we were in their sight" (Num. 13:33).

Science

Shared ancestry

Fossil remains of over 6,000 individuals have been found with features that fall intermediately between ancient apes and modern humans, with older specimens more apelike and younger specimens more humanlike.[13] It is not argued that we evolved from modern apes, but that humans and modern apes share a common ancestor population within the last 15 million years. Diverging populations over time produced myriad species, with common ancestry more recent between some species and more distant in time between others. Fossils combined with genetic evidence for modern species indicate humans share the most recent common ancestor with chimps, humans+chimps share an older common ancestry with gorillas, and humans+chimps+gorillas share a still older common ancestry with orangutans. Note that an ancestral human+chimp population does not mean a mix of interbreeding humans and chimps. It means a single apish population, with subgroups eventually separating and giving rise in one case to chimps, and in the other to a variety of more upright and larger-brained species eventually leading to modern humans. The popular literature usually refers to these species collectively as *hominids*, though technically they

---

13. Richard Potts, director of the Human Origins program at the Smithsonian Institution, has compiled a personal database of hominin fossil discoveries. At present, the database includes entries for over 6,000 separate individuals ranging from 20,000 to 7 million years in age. Note this is not 6,000 fossil fragments, but fossil remains originating from over 6,000 different individuals.

are classified as part of a smaller group known as *hominins*.[14] We will stick with *hominids* here, only because it is more familiar to most readers.

Over the course of hominid existence, several species lived at the same time. Most of these species eventually died out, with only one line giving rise to modern humans. Determining the exact lineage is difficult, for more than one species at any given time possessed intermediate features between more ancient hominids and us.[15] What is clear, however, is that younger species take on increasingly more humanlike features, with anatomically modern human skeletons appearing only within the last 200,000 years in Africa.[16]

Cultural development

Though modern-looking skeletons date to hundreds of thousands of years, *culturally* modern man is a much more recent phenomenon. *Culturally modern* is a subjective (and sometimes contentious) term, but can be thought of as having a self and societal awareness that goes beyond cooperative living, tool-making, and burial of the dead, to include abstract thought leading to complex language skills, technological innovation, creation of visual and auditory art, and contemplation of the supernatural.[17] These traits are not preserved in skeletons, but evidence is preserved in the form of tools, burial arrangements, artwork, musical instruments, village layouts, and remnants of what was eaten or raised.

Mapping the appearance of such traits in time and place depends on spotty discoveries of the buried remnants of ancient activities. Our understanding continuously adjusts with new findings.[18] At present, the earliest evidence of culturally modern traits has been found in Africa, dating to 60,000 to 70,000 years ago, with subsequent migrations into the Middle East and Europe within the last 40,000 to 60,000 years, and into the Americas by 20,000 years ago. The creation of urban centers, cultivation of plants for food, and herding were still later advances that first appeared in the Middle East in what is known as the Fertile Crescent within the last 11,000 years.

---

14. *Hominids* technically include the African great apes and their ancestors: Wood and Constantino, "Human Origins: Life at the top of the tree."
15. McDougall, Brown, and Fleagle, "Stratigraphic placement and age of modern humans from Kibish, Ethiopia"; summary article: Bower, "Human fossils are oldest yet."
16. A recent study argues for a date of 300,000 years, though the "anatomically modern" designation is contested: Richter et al., "The age of the hominin fossils from Jebel Irhoud, Morocco, and the origins of the Middle Stone Age."
17. The term *Cro-Magnon* was once used to identify the appearance of modern man in the Middle East and Europe, but has fallen out of use among anthropologists today.
18. Wilcox, "Updating human origins."

Relation to other hominids

Prior to human DNA studies, there were two competing schools of thought on human evolution. The multiregional hypothesis was that an earlier hominid species, such as *Homo erectus*, had spread widely across the globe, with separated populations independently adapting to yield the different races we see today. In contrast, the Out of Africa hypothesis argued that a more isolated population of hominids in Africa gave rise to modern humans, who then migrated into the Middle East and around the world. Isolation of subpopulations then gave rise to the genetic diversity observed today. Genetic studies comparing the DNA of humans of diverse ethnicity now strongly support a variant of the Out of Africa hypothesis, with an initial northward migration out of Africa within the last 250,000 years, followed by subsequent waves that merged or genetically subsumed earlier migrations.

During the early waves of migration, humans leaving Africa encountered Neanderthals and their lesser known cousins, the Denisovans.[19] DNA extracted from Neanderthal and Denisovan fossils indicate that some interbreeding took place. All non-African human populations today contain 1 to 4 percent Neanderthal DNA, and Melanesian and South Asian populations possess similar amounts of Denisovan DNA.[20] Neanderthal skulls and skeletal structures have distinct features that easily differentiate them from those of contemporary humans, but the general appearance of Neanderthals was still very humanlike. Some cultural similarities between the two groups also existed, such as toolmaking, communal living, and burial of their dead. Artifacts and cranial development, however, suggest that humans had a substantial cognitive advantage over their Neanderthal neighbors. Contemporary humans crafted tools out of a much wider variety of raw materials, applied heat treatments in tool fabrication, developed projectile weapons such as the bow and arrow, created sophisticated works of art and jewelry, made figurines likely used in worship, and conducted more obviously ritualistic burials. Soon after the spread of modern man, the Neanderthals disappeared. The reason for their demise is not well understood, but one leading hypothesis is that our

---

19. Humans may have also encountered more distant cousins such as *Homo floresiensis* and *Homo luzonensis* on Southeast Asian islands: Brown et al., "A new small-bodied hominin from the Late Pleistocene of Flores, Indonesia"; Détroit et al., "A new species of Homo from the Late Pleistocene of the Philippines."

20. Neanderthal DNA: Pääbo, *Neanderthal Man: In Search of Lost Genomes*; Green et al., "A draft sequence of the Neandertal genome"; Denisovan DNA: Jacobs et al., "Multiple deeply divergent Denisovan ancestries in Papuans"; according to my 23andMe results, I have more Neanderthal DNA than 52% of their clients.

ancestors drove them to extinction, either through competition for the same food sources or through direct conflict.[21]

Common mother, common population

Statistical analyses that consider large numbers of DNA segments collected from people around the world arrive at two conclusions that can seem contradictory. The first, based on the diversity within the human genome, is that the human population from which all living humans derive was never smaller than about 10,000 individuals. The second, based on studies looking specifically at mitochondrial DNA (mtDNA), which is passed on to offspring by the mother, is that all humanity can trace their ancestry back to a single female, termed *Mitochondrial Eve*.[22]

The two conclusions are not in conflict. As an example on a smaller scale, suppose a couple has five daughters who all marry and each have their own children. All of the third-generation cousins will trace their mtDNA back to the same maternal grandmother—a common ancestral mother. At the same time, the cousins will have nuclear DNA from their fathers that represents contributions from a larger population alive at the same time as the grandmother. The cousins all come from both a common ancestral mother *and* a larger contemporaneous population. Put in different terms, the cousins do not have a *sole* progenitor, but they do share one *common* or *universal* progenitor.

Based on the degree of genetic diversity in humans and estimated mutation rates, the age of the most recent common ancestor of *all* humans alive today is on the order of 200,000 years. Over multiple generations, however, genetic contributions from ancient ancestors gets diluted and can be entirely lost in subsequent generations (i.e., I may retain no recognizable DNA from a particular ancestor ten generations earlier). These are referred to as *ghost ancestors*.[23] The result is that it is not only possible but statistically likely that a more recent universal ancestor existed that is not directly discernible from population genetics. The age of the most recent universal common ancestor could be as low as a few thousand years.[24]

---

21. Fagan, *The Journey from Eden, The Peopling of Our World*, chap. 11.
22. The same thing can be done with Y-chromosomes to trace back to a common genetic father, who may or may not have been at the same time as Mitochondrial Eve.
23. Gravel and Steel, "The existence and abundance of ghost ancestors in biparental populations."
24. Chang, "Recent common ancestors of all present-day individuals"; Rohde, Olson, and Chang, "Modelling the recent common ancestry of all living humans."

TABLE 10—ORIGIN OF HUMANS	
The Bible	Science
Man was created from "dust from the ground." (Gen. 2:7)	Man was created through the successive evolution of various life-forms ultimately derived from nonliving earth materials: "dust from the ground."
The first humans lived in the Middle East near the Tigris and Euphrates Rivers (part of the Fertile Crescent). (Gen. 2:14)	The oldest current evidence of "culturally modern man" comes from Africa, and later from the Middle East and Europe.
All humanity today derives from the same initial couple.	All humanity today can trace their origin to a common parent.
Cain raised crops and Abel tended herds. (Gen. 4:2)	Earliest evidence of agriculture is found in the Fertile Crescent.
At the time of his exile, Cain was one of only three humans on earth, but he was fearful of others he would encounter. (Gen. 4:13–15)	Humans derived from a population of at least 10,000, and human ancestors coexisted with other hominids including Neanderthals.
The "daughters of men" and the "sons of God" engaged in forbidden unions producing offspring known as the Nephilim. (Gen. 6:1–4)	Interbreeding took place within the population from which humans derived, and to a lesser extent with Neanderthals and Denisovans.
The genetic contribution of the Nephilim persisted through the flood and up to at least the conquest of Canaan. (Num. 13:33)	The genetic markers of interbreeding persist to this day.
Animal husbandry and agriculture by Abel and Cain (Gen. 4:2) *suggests* a relatively recent age for Adam and Eve.	Though population genetics points to an ancient common human ancestor, universal genealogical ancestry could have been more recent.

Synthesis

Materially, the biblical account of man's creation is no different from the creation of other life on earth. Of plants and terrestrial animals, God commanded "the earth to sprout" or "the earth to bring forth" life. To create Adam, God "formed man of dust from the ground." According to scientific accounts, man was formed from the same earth-dust as all other creatures.

The details of the scientific account leave us with some possibly uncomfortable questions, however, regarding nonhuman to human transitions, the appearance of a soul, and whether this mode of creation is consistent with God's character.

Specialness of humans

Our first reaction to human evolution may be that we are not like the animals. Humans are unique and must have been specially created even if nothing else was. The concept that humans might share a common origin with other life-forms is an affront to our dignity and sense of value. One must ask, however, if the indignation comes from an understanding of biblical truth or simply from an inflated sense of material worth. During the days of Galileo, it was strongly felt that humans, and thus the earth, were both the figurative and literal centerpieces of God's creation. To suggest that the earth was not the center of the universe was to degrade the God-ordained position of humankind. It was a useful exercise in humility to realize that humans travel on a speck of relative insignificance in the vast cosmos. Humanity's value is derived from something other than its relative location. If the physical origin of humans is no different than the origin of worms, it would be another fitting lesson in humility. We are not special because we were created in a different manner than all other life; we are special because of God's singular love and endowment.

The ultimate artist

But would God really create in such a prolonged manner, making small changes from one generation to the next and spinning off myriads of life-forms, many destined for extinction? Is this consistent with God's character? An answer might be found by noting that humans are made in God's image and then looking at our own creative instincts. Genesis 1:27 tells us, "God created man in His own image, in the image of God He created him; male and female." The fact that both men and women are in the image of God clearly tells us that this expression means something of greater significance than physical appearance. It means, at least in part, that aspects of God's nature are uniquely manifest in mankind. Elements of God's character are found in the human desire for relationships, in the ability to converse, employ logic, administer justice and mercy, and in the desire to create works of beauty.

We now have the ability to push a button and get an instantaneous work of computer-generated art. While entertaining, this process is a cheap substitute for the work of a real artist. A true artist will take a lump of clay and begin to mold it and shape it. It is rarely done in an hour or a day. Over time, the lump takes on a form that progressively changes until the final moment when the artist declares that it is finished. If our creative nature is truly a reflection of God's nature, then it is entirely consistent that God would start with a lump of clay (earth materials) and begin to form and shape life through myriad generations until he arrived at what he was ultimately after. This in no way suggests that all forms prior to man were mistakes or castoffs. Inasmuch as God is infinitely more creative than humans, each work along the way is an amazing creation in its own right.

God who chooses

At some stage, when God had a hominid population with the requisite biological structures in place, such as neural wiring capable of supporting complex language and abstract thought, he may have selected one to endow with something beyond biology. The gift of an eternal soul, with moral accountability and the capacity to commune with God, would have set this individual apart from all other creatures, including the hominid population from which he was selected.[25] The result would have been a creature biologically equivalent to his neighbors, but with a unique spiritual nature that set him apart—a new species akin to what John Stott first referred to as *Homo divinus*.[26] The subsequent description of Eve's creation from the side of Adam may represent a miraculous event, or a figurative reference to the creation of Adam and Eve from the same stock or in the same manner. In either case, God is solely responsible for the appearance of humankind on earth.

The idea of God choosing one individual or group out of many is also consistent with what Scripture tells us of God's character. For reasons we do not understand, God chose Abraham alone from among the people of the earth. He chose Isaac over Ishmael, Jacob over Esau, and Israel over all other nations. The selection is not a random process where any righteous or handsome specimen will do, for God indicates that his selection was made before those he has chosen were even born. Of Jacob and Esau, God says, "for though the twins

---

25. A number of Christian writers now argue that Adam may represent a *population* of first humans rather than an individual. Old Testament professor C. John Collins describes four different biblically defensible views, ranging from a genuine first individual man to representative chief of a first tribe: Collins, *Did Adam and Eve Really Exist? Who They Were and Why You Should Care.*
26. Stott, *Understanding the Bible*, 63.

were not yet born and had not done anything good or bad ... Jacob I loved but Esau I hated" (Rom. 9:11, 13). Likewise, Jeremiah was chosen for his role as a prophet before birth: "Before I formed you in the womb I knew you, and before you were born I consecrated you; I have appointed you a prophet to the nations" (Jer. 1:5). It is consistent with God's revealed character to choose one hominid from among many to endow with a soul and initiate the human race.[27]

The timing of such a selection is not easily deciphered. Arguments could be made for the first anatomically modern human, the first culturally modern human, or some more recent descendent prior to the appearance of agriculture in the Fertile Crescent. For later dates, one has to reconcile the existence of culturally modern humans spread across the globe. (We'll return to this question at the end of this section.)

The Bible and current scientific understanding are in agreement that all humanity shares a common ancestor. If there is conflict, it is with an interpretation of Genesis that insists that Adam and Eve are the *sole* progenitors of the human race. A return to Genesis will help us explore this further, first considering Cain's punishment (Gen. 4) and then the strange case of the Nephilim (Gen. 6).

Cain's fear

Cain's fear of others he would encounter has long been a puzzle. At the time of Cain's banishment, he was the second child of the first humans in existence. Who else was there to fear? The most common explanation is that Adam and Eve had other children that populated the area into which Cain was exiled. Genesis 5:4 does say Adam and Eve had other sons and daughters, and a population can rise rather quickly from a single fertile pair, but it turns out to be an inadequate explanation. There are problematic timing and location issues.

- *A timing problem*: The first three sons of Adam and Eve are explicitly named. Abel, the firstborn, died childless (no genealogy). Cain, the second born, did not have his first son, Enoch, until after Cain was already exiled (Gen. 4:16–17). Seth, the third son, was not born yet when Cain killed Abel. In Genesis 4:25, Eve states that God gave her

---

27. Some argue that spiritual awareness may have evolved along with the physical form of a hominid population. In my estimation, this creates a logical conundrum of how a hominid might have been in possession of a *partially* eternal soul. One either has or does not have a relationship with God leading to eternal life or death. This is developed in more depth in Davidson, "Genetics, the Nephilim, and the historicity of Adam."

a son, Seth, to *replace* Abel. There is no indication of a delay between Cain's crime and his punishment, so Cain's banishment most likely occurred before Seth was even born. If Cain's fear was of his relatives, it would have to be an unlikely fear of their future birth and settlement in the land of his wanderings.

- *A location problem*: Recall that Cain was *banished* for his crime. He was sent off to a new location away from his parents. If those whom Cain feared in the land of his banishment were his own relatives, it means that there must have been a series of earlier crimes and banishments that sent them all packing to the new location. Yet Scripture is silent on any such events. It is unlikely that any such earlier exiles occurred at all. It is also insufficient to suggest that these other offspring wandered off on their own, for the point of the Cain and Abel story is to relate the alienation that derives from sin. The separation was not just a move from one set of relatives to another.

Consider, however, the possibility that Adam and Eve had been taken from a population of hominids and set apart, endowed by God with an eternal spirit. The population from which they were drawn would have been biologically equivalent, though lacking the divine spark that made Adam and Eve what we think of as truly or fully human.[28] It would make perfect sense for Cain to personify those he encountered and to fear their hostility.

The Nephilim

If we fast-forward several generations in Genesis, we find by Chapter 6 that humankind, with only one exception, had universally degenerated into wickedness. At the top of the list of infractions was sexual unions between the "sons of God" and the "daughters of men," which gave rise to the Nephilim. The Nephilim were exceptional in their physical prowess, referred to as "mighty men of old, men of renown." Men of great physical stature encountered later in the land of Canaan were described as descendants of the Nephilim (Num. 13:33).

Traditional interpretations of these verses vary widely.[29] One interpretation is that the sons of God were noblemen who took wives from among

---

28. Analogous models have been proposed by Kemp, "Science, theology, and monogenesis"; Wilcox, "A proposed model for the evolutionary creation of human beings: from the image of God to the origin of sin"; Alexander, "Human origins and genetics."
29. Sailhamer, "Genesis," 18.

the common people. Another is that the sons of God refer to the righteous line of Seth who intermarried with the unrighteous line of Cain. Still another is that they are fallen angelic beings that took human wives who gave birth to children of great physical size and prowess. Each of these interpretations represents a reasonable attempt to understand the passage, but none are free of logical difficulties.

The idea that the sons of God were nobles is not likely, given the use of the Hebrew word *'elohim*, translated in this instance as "God."[30] Though *'elohim* can be used as an honorary title, similar to addressing a magistrate as "lord," the word is never used elsewhere in Scripture to distinguish between people of different classes. Unions between noblemen and commoners also fail to account for offspring of unique stature.

The interpretation that the sons of God are the righteous line of Seth is often accepted not on its own merit, but because the other options are deemed worse. This interpretation is also weak, for there is no indication that God forbade marriage between the offspring of Seth and Cain, nor is there reason to believe that unions between them would give rise to anything other than normal human beings. Further, the idea of a "righteous line of Seth" is a misnomer. If the line of Seth were truly righteous, they would not have so readily taken wives from among the unrighteous, nor would there have been need for the flood. The wickedness of mankind fully encompassed both lineages, with the sole exception of Noah.

Identification of the sons of God as fallen angels comes from passages such as Job 1:6, where Satan is identified as among "the sons of God" presenting themselves before Yahweh.[31] Jude 6 makes a reference to angels who "abandoned their proper domain," and 2 Peter 2 speaks of the sin of angels followed by mention of human sins in the days of Noah, possibly linking the events in time. I find several problems with this understanding.

- Biblical identification of the "son(s) of God" is imprecise, with application to unfallen angels (Job 38:7), righteous earthly humans (Gal. 3:26), resurrected humans (Luke 20:34–36), and Jesus (Matt. 8:29).

---

30. Hebrew: הָאֱלֹהִים (*'elohim*), "God."
31. Several theologians whom I highly respect take this position, e.g., Collins, *Reading Genesis Well*, 186–188; Copan and Jacoby, *Origins: The Ancient Impact and Modern Implications of Genesis 1–11*, 146–55; Hieser, *The Unseen Realm: Recovering the Supernatural Worldview of the Bible*.

- Jesus made statements that would seem to preclude the possibility. Matthew 22:30 and Luke 20:34–36 record Jesus saying that angels in heaven do not marry. Proponents argue that the statement does not apply to *fallen* angels because these are not among the "angels in heaven," yet the description of Satan and the sons of God in Job 1:6 is described as occurring in the context of a heavenly council.

- While angels and demons may take on a physical form, siring offspring requires that they have DNA to pass on. (This is not the same issue for the virgin birth of Christ, as no sexual reproduction was involved.)

- Fallen angels would certainly wish to corrupt healthy sexual expression, but there is no other biblical passage that suggests they have desires for sexual intimacy with humans, that they would go to the trouble of establishing formal unions of marriage, or that they would limit their interest to *women* (especially given explicit biblical condemnation of homosexuality).

- There is no indication that the desires or behaviors of fallen angels were altered after the flood, and no reason to expect that illicit behaviors prior to the flood were truncated afterward. Yet there is no mention again of such unions from the time of Noah to the present.

In this context, we will consider again the possibility that the descendants of Adam and Eve lived near their ancestral hominid population, and, depending on the timing, perhaps even crossed paths with Neanderthals. Though of human likeness, these creatures would have been considered "strange flesh." As biological equivalents, sexual attraction and unions could have been physically possible, but intolerable in God's sight in much the same way as the acts of Sodom and Gomorrah:

> Sodom and Gomorrah and the cities around them, since they in the same way as these indulged in gross immorality and went after strange flesh, are exhibited as an example in undergoing the punishment of eternal fire. (Jude 7)

It is possible that "daughters of men" and "sons of God" refer to humans and their neighboring hominids, where "sons of" can mean the offspring or creation of God. If intermixing was widespread, as Genesis 6 implies, this could readily account for the genetic diversity that leads geneticists to claim a minimum population size of 10,000, while also tracing our ancestry back to a common mother.[32] It could also account for why such unions are described as occurring in the early days of human existence, and then never again. The only thing missing is why these unions might have produced unusual offspring. As biological equivalents, there is no obvious reason why children of a human and neighboring hominid would have been unique. This could be as simple as the presence of a subgroup of contemporary hominids with a more robust body plan. Given the ubiquitous human tendency of assigning names to things we think are odd or different, it would have made perfect sense to apply a unique term to the offspring of such unions.[33]

One might speculate further, given the genetic evidence we have today, if the Genesis story dates back to a period of overlap between humans and Neanderthals. This could have occurred if the date was several tens of thousands of years ago, or if a population of Neanderthals persisted beyond what we find in the fossil record, or even if a highly hybridized subpopulation existed at the same time as the first true humans. Neanderthals were not the brutish ape-men depicted in cartoons. Though of diminished cognitive potential relative to humans, Neanderthals were nonetheless similar to humans in appearance and many behaviors. They lived in groups, fabricated tools, placed items related to daily life in the graves of their dead, and may have engaged in rudimentary art.

Neanderthals were not taller than humans, but their bone structure was designed for a greater musculature and greater strength. Reproduction between humans and Neanderthals, now documented within the human genome, could have plausibly produced individuals of admirable strength and prowess in hunting or battle. It is also possible for hybrids to combine genes in a way that produces traits not found in either parent, a phenomenon known as *heterosis*. It is thus possible that some of these offspring could have had unusual stature as well as strength, giving people another reason to identify them by a special name.

---

32. It would be natural here to question whether the union of a human with a soul to a hominid without a soul would produce a child with a soul. There is no way of answering this question, other than to speculate that perhaps the child possessed a soul by analogous reference to Paul's claim that the child of a believing and unbelieving parent is sanctified, or considered clean, through the believing parent (1 Cor. 7:14).
33. Davidson, "Genetics, the Nephilim, and the historicity of Adam."

Bestiality?

A common reaction to the model above is what may be termed "the *eww*-factor." Doesn't this suggest bestiality? Sex between humans and non-humans? *Eww!* Technically, the answer is *yes*, though if used as a critical argument, it is a red herring. First, the illicit unions would have occurred between creatures that were biologically equivalent, with physical distinctions *less* than what Hollywood frequently depicts in romantic encounters between humans and human-looking aliens or mutants.[34] Second, such unions would fall within the same biblical category as any other forbidden sexual practice, some of which can illicit the same visceral reaction. Third, *ickyness* has never proven to be an obstacle in preventing sinful human behavior. As a species, we've made a virtual profession of it. And lastly, if this was a real objection, the fallen-angels model would fail under the same logic.

Remaining questions

A natural question that flows from all this, assuming the scientific observations are accurate, is what does this mean for the age of Adam and Eve? How far back does this push a possible first human couple? At the end of the scientific description, I noted recent advances in the understanding of common ancestry, with scientists publishing work demonstrating that universal common ancestors for all living humans are likely to be a much more recent phenomena than indicated by genetic studies alone. Christian writers David Opderbeck and Jon Garvey independently noted the potential impact on discussions about Adam and Eve, followed by more recent work by S. Joshua Swamidass, including an entire book devoted to the subject.[35]

A scientifically plausible recent date for a common ancestor would seem to resolve a host of apparent science-Bible tensions, though some theologically sticky questions remain. The primary issue gets back to the presence of other hominids/humans at the same time as Adam and Eve. For all proposed evolutionary models, there was a time in which multiple

---

34. E.g., *Star Trek* (James Kirk and various green girlfriends); *Guardians of the Galaxy* (Peter Quill and Gomora).
35. Opderbeck, "A 'historical' Adam?"; Garvey, "Adam and MRCA studies"; Swamidass, "The overlooked science of genealogical ancestry"; Swamidass, *The Genealogical Adam and Eve: The Surprising Science of Universal Ancestry*. Swamidass has proposed that Adam and Eve could have been *de novo* creations whose offspring then interbred with an evolved population. This would require that they were specially created with a genetic makeup that mimicked that of their evolved neighbors, making it functionally equivalent to selecting an existing hominid.

generations passed with hominids or culturally modern humans in existence who did not trace their genealogy back through Adam and Eve. Time was required for tribes disconnected from Adam and Eve to die out, or for adventurous members of the Adamic clan to venture into distant lands to spread their seed—with the eventual result of all living humans tracing at least one family lineage back to the same couple. This could have occurred sometime between Adam and Abraham, or some have argued as late as the arrival of Christ, in time for Paul to make a truthful statement in Romans 5 that all humans share in the sin of their common father, Adam.[36]

If the timing of Adam and Eve is pushed back to the early appearance of culturally modern behaviors, it is not difficult to imagine Adam's offspring migrating outward and displacing or genetically absorbing other hominid groups over a period of a few millennia. If only a few thousand years ago, one has to account for the global presence of modern cultures that did not yet have a direct genealogical connection with Adam and Eve. What was the spiritual status of these individuals? Was the *imago dei*—the image of God—conferred on only those with at least one parent deriving from the Adamic tribe, or was it conferred more broadly upon a larger group that included those not yet sharing the same recent ancestry? What was the impact of Adam's sin on these individuals?

Such questions lie beyond the scope of scientific investigation, and can only be partially answered by biblical study.[37] So where does such uncertainty leave us? I will suggest that it leaves us in the same place as dozens of other theological questions for which we are provided *sufficient* but not *exhaustive* answers. We have sufficient information to recognize that the study of God's natural creation is not a threat to his written Word. Science and Scripture both affirm all life derived from earth materials, selection of one or a group to set apart from among others is consistent with the character of God, a spiritual endowment of the image of God could well have set the stage for a real first act of rebellion, and all humans alive today derive from the same familial root, both spiritually and physically. The details of when, where, and how it all played out are intriguing, but not essential to Christian faith and unity.

---

36. S. Joshua Swamidass, *The Genealogical Adam and Eve.*
37. C. John Collins provides a good assessment of the biblical constraints: Collins, *Did Adam and Eve Really Exist?*

DEATH AND THE FALL

> The LORD God commanded the man, saying, "From any tree of the garden you may eat freely; but from the tree of the knowledge of good and evil you shall not eat, for in the day that you eat from it you will surely die." (Gen. 2:16–17)

> Therefore, just as through one man sin entered into the world, and death through sin, and so death spread to all men, because all sinned. (Rom. 5:12)

> For the creation was subjected to futility, not willingly, but because of Him who subjected it, in hope that the creation itself also will be set free from its slavery to corruption into the freedom of the glory of the children of God. For we know that the whole creation groans and suffers the pains of childbirth together until now. (Rom. 8:20–22)

Bible

Christians agree on at least one point regarding the verses above: sin brought about separation of man from his Creator—spiritual death. This condition set into motion circumstances that would eventually lead to man's physical death as well. Disagreement has long existed, however, among Bible-believing theologians over the extent to which sin influenced the rest of creation, and whether plant and animal death already existed prior to the fall.

Arguments used to support the absence of death of any kind prior to the fall include:

- No death before sin is the simplest reading of the Scriptures quoted above.

- Genesis 3 tells us that it was not simply man but the very ground that was cursed following sin.

- If heaven is a return to the creation as it was before sin, then prophesies found in Isaiah 11 and 65 tell us that animals did not eat one another nor die prior to sin. (The wolf and the lamb will graze together, and the lion will eat straw like the ox.)

- In Genesis 1:29–30, God told Adam and Eve that plants were given for food "to every thing that moves on the earth which has life." This suggests that there was at least no carnivory—no animal death.

- How could God create a world with death in it and call it good?

Biblical arguments supporting plant and animal death from the very beginning of creation

Simple vs. right

The simplest reading does not always yield the right understanding. Just think of the consequences of insisting on the simplest reading of Jesus's command in Mark 9:45: "If your foot causes you to stumble, cut it off; it is better for you to enter life lame, than, having your two feet, to be cast into hell."[38]

Physical vs. spiritual death

The death spoken of in Romans 5 and Genesis 2 is *spiritual* death for humans, not *physical* death in general. Justification for this interpretation comes from an analysis of related verses in Genesis and Proverbs. In Genesis 2:17, God warned that "*in the day* that you eat from [the fruit] you will surely die." This cannot refer principally to physical death, for neither Adam nor Eve physically died on the day they ate the fruit. The immediate death they experienced was spiritual: separation from God. Physical death was a secondary consequence of the spiritual chasm opened between them and God and perhaps also of being cut off from the life-sustaining produce of the garden.[39]

Proverbs 12:28 says, "In the way of righteousness is life, and in its pathway there is no death." The death from which the righteous are spared is clearly not physical death, for we know that, materially, the righteous die just as the unrighteous. The death the righteous are spared is of the eternal variety—spiritual death. In the same way, Romans 5:17–21 speaks of life given through the righteous act of Christ. The recipients of this grace still experience material death, but are spared the death of true consequence. The death to which we became subject by sin, and the one from which we may be spared, is spiritual.

---

38. This section benefited significantly from Collins, *Science and Faith: Friends or Foes?*, chap. 10.
39. One understanding of the "Tree of Life" was that Adam and Eve maintained immortality for as long as they continued to eat from the Tree. Once losing access to the Tree, they aged and eventually died. Miller and Soden, *In the Beginning...We Misunderstood: Interpreting Genesis 1 in its Original Context*, 169–70.

Death came explicitly to humans

If the intention of Romans 5:12 was to communicate that sin brought death to all creatures, it should have ended by saying "death spread to all" or "death spread to all creation." But it does not. It very specifically says that "death spread to all *men*." There is no reason to add the last three words unless this death was meant to be limited to humankind.

Righteousness and animals

Romans 5:17 relates a divinely inspired analogy between Adam and Christ: just as the sin of one brought death, the righteousness of One brought life. If we are to be consistent with the application of this analogy, Christ did not come to bring life to animals, so it is not likely that Adam brought them death.

Heaven is not a return to Eden

The idea that heaven is a return to creation as it was prior to sin is a human concept, not an undisputed biblical concept.[40] If Isaiah says the wolf and lion will eat grass and straw in heaven, it does not necessarily follow that they did so at the start of creation. Scripture describes several aspects of heaven that will clearly be different from the initial creation:

- Night was an integral part of the creation, marking the passage of time. In heaven, there will be no night (Rev. 21:25; 22:5).

- The sun and moon were created in the beginning for light. In heaven, there will be no sun or moon, for God's glory will illuminate it (Isa. 60:19; Rev. 21:23).

- The sea was part of the creation. In heaven, there will be no sea (Rev. 21:1).

- Satan was allowed into the garden and humans were susceptible to temptation. Neither Satan nor temptation will be found in heaven.

- Isaiah 65:25 speaks of a day when the lion will eat straw like an ox and Isaiah 11:6 says the lion will lie peacefully with a calf, yet the same prophet says elsewhere that lions will not be present at all (Isa. 35:9).

---

40. Miller and Soden, *In the Beginning... We Misunderstood*, 171.

The juxtaposition of these verses suggests they are metaphorical statements of the peace to come and should not be used to assess biological conditions at the time of creation.[41]

The curse did not twist nature

When God cursed the ground in Genesis 3:17, it changed the way Adam and Eve would experience nature without requiring any fundamental change in how the natural world operated. Recall the curses of Deuteronomy 28:17–18. God warned Israel that their baskets and bowls, crops and herds, and even their children would be cursed if they were disobedient. Israel did not regard these words and did experience these curses, but without any supernatural conversion of baskets and bowls into twisted versions of their original forms, nor did crops and herds suddenly change their biological functions. Rather, the curse reflected how Israel would experience these things—empty baskets and bowls as crops and herds were weakened, stolen, or destroyed.

In this context, consider the biological design in carnivores. Animals such as lions, wolves, and alligators have claws and teeth specifically designed for catching prey and tearing flesh. Eagles have talons and beaks optimized for the same use. Sharks and killer whales are likewise outfitted for catching and eating other animals. None of these features prohibit a vegetarian snack, but plant consumption is not what these claws, talons, beaks, and teeth were *designed* for. The traditional interpretation of sin and the fall requires one of two possibilities. One is that the claws, talons, beaks, and teeth of lions, wolves, eagles, sharks, and killer whales all suddenly morphed from plant-eating implements into flesh-eating tools when Adam sinned. The second is that God created these creatures *poorly designed* for their pre-sin environment, but optimized for a diet that would not begin until after sin.

Our analysis of Deuteronomy 28 argues strongly against morphing body parts at the moment of the fall. The second choice is no more appealing, for it requires that God formed a world in which his creations would not be ideally suited to their environment until after sin corrupted it. It makes more sense that material death existed from the start, but initially outside of human experience. As mentioned in Chapter 5, the description of Adam and Eve's stay and eviction from the garden of Eden suggests that life outside the garden

---

41. Further, when Isaiah 65 addresses the end of infant mortality, v. 20 includes the statement, "*For the youth will die at the age of one hundred.*" If Isaiah 65 is a literal description of heaven, death is still present.

had always been less human-friendly than life inside. The garden had boundaries. After the curse, God placed an angel to guard not just the Tree of Life, but access to the whole garden. Thorns, thistles, and material death may have always existed beyond the garden's borders.

Subjection to futility

Romans 8 does not say that the creation was subjected to futility *by sin*, but *by God*, perhaps from the very start of creation. The implication is not that God created the world flawed, but that it was created, from the very start, with a yearning to see the Messiah. Alternatively, C. John Collins argues that the corruption and futility was implemented at the time of the fall—creation had to bear the brunt of man's sinful behavior. It was not a twisting of nature, as noted above, but creation's experience with a corrupt inhabitant.[42]

Decay: seeds and digestion

Death and decay within at least the plant kingdom before the fall is implicit in the creation account itself. Genesis 1:12 and 29 state that plants produced seeds, and that plants were given as food to eat. The production of seeds has meaning only in the context of death. If nothing dies, seeds have no lasting purpose. It could be argued that God created plants with seeds to propagate plant growth in unvegetated areas, but this would have led to rapid overpopulation and the need for either death, or cessation of seed production. At the very least, plants were created with the *expectation* of death and decay prior to sin, meaning the creation was prepared for, and likely subjected to, material decay from the very start.

Consumption of plants for food further indicates decay. If plant material passes into and out of an organism without decay, no energy is released to maintain the metabolism of the consumer. Eating has no purpose without decay.

Vegetarian diet

In Genesis 1:29 and 30, God gives "every plant yielding seed ... and every tree which has fruit yielding seed" as food for Adam and Eve, and "every green plant" as food for all the beasts and birds and crawling creatures. It is not until the fall that we read of animal death in order to make skin garments for Adam and Eve (Gen. 3:21). We'll draw attention to three points here.

---

42. Collins, *Reading Genesis Well*, 237.

First, these verses may be describing conditions and constraints present within the boundaries of Eden that were not the same beyond the garden. If conditions were not different outside of Eden, there would have been no reason to cast Adam and Eve out of the garden after sin, for Eden would have been cursed the same as everywhere else. The human experience with nature *inside* the garden was free of carnivory, or at least free of fear of personal loss to such behavior.

The second point comes from Genesis 9:3 where the subject of diet is revisited. As Noah exits the ark, God tells him that "every moving thing that is alive shall be food for you; I give all to you, as I gave the green plant." The implication from a "simple reading of the text" is that all from Adam to Noah had been vegetarian, yet we know that animal sacrifices dated all the way back to Cain and Abel. Throughout the Old Testament, animal sacrifice involved eating a portion of the offering (e.g., Lev. 7:15–21). In fact, Genesis 4:4 tells us that "Abel, on his part also brought of the firstlings of his flock and of their fat portions." Specific mention of the fat is important, for the fat was to be reserved for the Lord, to be entirely consumed in the sacrificial fire and not eaten (Lev. 3:16–17). Explicit mention of the fat portions of Abel's sacrifice would have been understood by Hebrew readers to mean that other portions were eaten.[43]

The statement to Noah also appears to be a reaffirmation of permission to eat animals, rather than a new command. Though the local animal population was dramatically thinned, and great care was taken to preserve the life of these animals, Noah was assured it was still permissible to harvest a portion for food. The story of Noah comes many generations after the fall, so one may wonder why it is pertinent to whether there was animal death before the fall. It is pertinent because it illustrates that a "simple reading of the text" is not always adequate to understand its meaning. In this case, the same wording of every green plant is used before and after sin, yet it cannot be easily interpreted to universally exclude carnivory.

A third point some will make is that *provision* of plants is not the same as *prohibition* against eating animals.[44] Though this argument is not one I am particularly fond of, it has been argued that every green plant provided for food simply established plants as the base of the food chain. Carnivores depend on plants for their survival as much as herbivores, and are effectively eating plants every time they eat another animal. If plants die out, carnivores will quickly follow.

---

43. Collins, *Reading Genesis Well*, 191.
44. Snoke, *A Biblical Case for an Old Earth*, 66.

God's definition of "good"

In Isaiah 55:8, God tells us that "My thoughts are not your thoughts, nor are your ways My ways." The apostle Paul affirms the gap between God's thinking and ours in Romans 11:33, saying, "Oh, the depth of the riches both of the wisdom and knowledge of God! How unsearchable are His judgments and unfathomable His ways!" These verses are frequently read from Christian pulpits and congregations heartily voice their "amen!" But what do we do next? Far too often, we use our next breath to describe God's character and actions in ways that fit quite neatly within our own sense of what is right and proper.

In the context of our current discussion, if *we* feel that animal death is bad, then *God* must also believe it to be bad. We see a young gazelle chased down by a cheetah and feel bad for the prey when it fails to escape the predator's deadly jaws. God must feel the same way. Surely God would not have created a world where baby gazelles are torn asunder and call it *good*. But does this sense derive from Scripture or from our tendency to put God in a box fashioned in the image of ourselves? [45]

Consider Psalm 104. The song opens with the wonder of God's works during creation, and continues with how he sustains it. In verses 21–31 we read:

> The young lions roar after their prey and seek their food from God. When the sun rises they withdraw and lie down in their dens. Man goes forth to his work and to his labor until evening. O LORD, how many are Your works! In wisdom You have made them all; the earth is full of Your possessions. There is the sea, great and broad, in which are swarms without number, animals both small and great. There the ships move along, and Leviathan, which You have formed to sport in it. They all wait for You to give them their food in due season. You give to them, they gather it up; You open Your hand, they are satisfied with good. You hide Your face, they are dismayed; You take away their spirit, they expire and return to their dust. You send forth Your Spirit, they are created; and You renew the face of the ground. Let the glory of the LORD endure forever; let the LORD be glad in His works.

These verses praise God for the great things he has done, which includes providing food for lions and creatures of the sea. They receive it and are satisfied with *good*, and God is *glad*. In case you are wondering, the Hebrew word for "good" here is the same word used when God referred to his original

---

45. Martin and Vaughn, *Beyond Creation Science*, 215–17.

creation as good in Genesis 1.[46] If God feeds animals to other animals and calls it good, who am I to tell him he cannot?

Science

Both creation and decay existed from the birth of the universe as stars formed and immediately began a long process of burning out. Death and decay existed from the beginning of life. Organisms such as sharks, dinosaurs, raptors (birds), and mammals with clearly carnivorous teeth, claws, and beaks existed long before the appearance of humans.

TABLE 11—DEATH AND SIN	
The Bible	Science
Spiritual and subsequent physical death for man was introduced by sin (Rom 5).	The role sin played in the physical death of the first man cannot be addressed by science.
Death within the plant and animal kingdoms prior to the fall is not explicitly addressed.	Death and decay within the plant and animal kingdoms existed long before the appearance of mankind.

Synthesis

Scientific study cannot reveal information about the role sin played in the eventual death of the first humans, so the potential conflict is limited to the question of whether there was death at all prior to the fall. We already saw that there are differences of opinions among Bible-believing scholars regarding death before the fall. But what about suffering?

Where there are predators, there must be some measure of suffering on the part of the prey. There is also evidence of disease in pre-human fossils. How could a loving God create a world that included suffering and call it good? We might ponder the observation that there are differences in the pain experienced by a spiritual, self-aware human and the rest of creation, but it doesn't resolve the tension. Animals still feel pain.

To address this, consider related questions that we wrestle with. How can a loving God send anyone to eternal torment? How can a mother be truly happy in heaven if her child is in hell? Or, if suffering arose from sin, how can a loving God allow innocent animals to suffer now because of human sin thousands of years ago?

---

46. Hebrew: טוֹב (towb), "good."

The last question is particularly important, because death and suffering are often described as something God did not plan—it was *sin* that brought corruption into the world. But this undermines the sovereignty of God. Nothing happens that God does not at least superintend. To suggest that God had no control over the consequences of sin is to make sin an equal to God in dominion. *God* dictated the consequences of sin and demonstrates his power over it throughout time in declaring that *all* things—even human sins—work together for good for those who love him and are called according to his purposes (Rom. 8:28). Even now, when natural disasters strike, do we think that God merely sheds a tear at the unintended storm or tremor? We can think this way only if we keep our Bibles closed, for Amos 3:6 tells us, "If a calamity occurs in a city has not the LORD done it?" If animal suffering was a result of man's sin, God declared it to be so.

Do I fully understand how God could create a world where animals experience suffering and call it good? Not really. But placing the blame on sin doesn't help, because it just bumps the same question to a later moment in time. Do I understand better how God may have justified the suffering of innocent animals as a consequence of man's sin? Not at all.

Ultimately, the explanation for any creation scenario is that God's ways are not my ways. God does not need my permission to be truly loving while pouring out eternal judgment on the wicked. He does not need my understanding to give genuine joy to the mother whose child is not with her in heaven. Nor does he need my approval to feed a baby gazelle to a cheetah and call it good. God's ways are not my ways!

NOAH'S FLOOD

> Behold, I, even I am bringing the flood of water upon the earth, to destroy all flesh in which is the breath of life, from under heaven; everything that is on the earth shall perish. (Gen. 6:17)

> In the six hundredth year of Noah's life, in the second month, on the seventeenth day of the month, on the same day all the fountains of the great deep burst open, and the floodgates of the sky were opened. (Gen. 7:11)

Bible

God gave instructions for Noah to build a boat that would preserve Noah, his family, and representatives of all living creatures from the floodwaters God would bring upon the land. The ark was built, and God directed animals to come to the ark. Unclean animals came in pairs, while clean animals and birds were loaded in groups of seven (or seven pairs). God closed the door to the ark behind Noah and brought torrential rains upon the land for forty days and forty nights until all the land was immersed. The floodwaters persisted for 150 days until the ark came to rest on the mountains of Ararat. The people and animals left the ark and repopulated the land. Noah planted a vineyard and enjoyed its fruits within the remaining years of his life.

Science

Evidence of catastrophic floods covering immense areas have been found in places such as the Mediterranean Sea, the Black Sea, and the northwestern states of the US, though at different times in earth's history. The area surrounding the Black Sea is of particular interest, for it borders modern Turkey and the mountains of Ararat directly to the south (Fig. 7). Evaporite deposits and thick layers of coarse sediments north of the Bosporus Strait indicate that the water level in the Black Sea was once much lower than it is today. Some have postulated that, prior to about 7,500 years ago, the Mediterranean Sea was once isolated from the Black Sea by a narrow strip of land. A global rise in sea level at the end of the last ice age eventually resulted in the Mediterranean overflowing this strip of ground, spilling into the Black Sea several hundred feet below. Rapidly flowing water quickly cut a channel through unconsolidated sediments, increasing flow to such a torrent that the underlying bedrock was ripped up and hurled into the Black Sea. Water from the Mediterranean may have poured into the Black Sea at a rate of as much as ten cubic miles per day, raising the water level by six inches a day.

This hypothesis is described in detail in the book *Noah's Flood*, by William Ryan and Walter Pitman. These authors, neither of whom claim any religious convictions, chose the title based on the idea that the flood "myths" present in many cultures arose from an actual event along the shores of the Black Sea.

Similar evidence exists for floods of immense proportions in different places around the globe at different times, but no credible evidence has been found that the entire world was immersed at one particular time. Knowledge of the diversity of life today also makes it apparent that a ship of the size described in Genesis could not have held representatives of every land-dwelling species over the entire world even if all were juveniles.[47] Adding all the extinct species magnifies the impossibility.

---

47. A ship the size of the one featured in the Answers in Genesis *Ark Encounter* theme park in Kentucky is equally insufficient.

TABLE 12—NOAH'S FLOOD	
The Bible	**Science**
All the land was covered by water when the fountains of the great deep burst open, and the floodgates of the sky were opened (Gen. 7).	Evidence exists for massive localized floods at various times in earth history, including one fitting the time and location of the biblical narrative. Evidence of a single, globe-covering flood is not found in nature.
Representatives of all known land-dwelling animals were taken on the ark, clean and unclean (Gen. 7:1–12).	A ship as described in Genesis could have held representatives of animal species known to the region at the time, but not those of the entire world or through all of earth history.

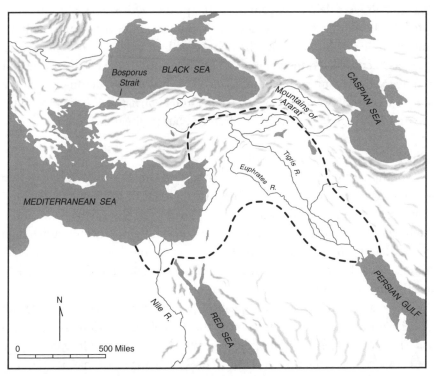

Figure 7—Map of the Black Sea, the mountains of Ararat, and the Fertile Crescent (inside dashed line) where modern civilization developed.

Synthesis

Extent of flood

There is no inherent conflict between science and Scripture over the occurrence of a massive flood early in human history. If there is a conflict, it is only in the magnitude of such an event. The issue is not even whether the flood story is literal history, but in the *degree* to which the wording must be taken literally. Recall our analysis of the genealogies of Matthew and Luke. The genealogies are literal in the sense that they identify real individuals in the lineage of Jesus, but they are not strictly literal in their identification of the total number of ancestors, nor in the way the lineage through Mary is described.

The wording of the extent of Noah's flood in Genesis is all encompassing, with descriptions that include God's intention to "destroy all flesh in which is the breath of life, from under heaven" (Gen. 6:17), and waters that eventually cover "all the high mountains everywhere under the heavens" (Gen. 7:19). There are three ways in which these words can be understood. One is that animals were delivered from the entire planet before the world was inundated. We'll call this the *global flood*. A second is that the flood covered all the land inhabited by humans, who had not spread yet to all the continents. This idea has been referred to as the *universal flood* (not in the cosmic sense, but in universally encompassing humankind).[48] A third understanding is that the flood covered the world known to Noah—the *known-world flood*. The latter two options are both versions of widespread but regional floods.

Global vs. regional

For this section, I will lump the *universal* and *known-world* views together to contrast with a *global* flood. The two regional-flood views understand scriptural references to the "entire world" or to "all the earth" to mean all the inhabited lands known to the people at the time of writing, rather than to *planet* earth. If the Genesis flood story was the only place where this was argued, it would be a hermeneutical stretch, but we actually find evidence of this throughout all of Scripture.

There are many verses that speak of "all the earth" that are clearly not global. Consider the famine in Egypt in the days of Joseph. Genesis 41:57 tells us, "The people of *all the earth* came to Egypt to buy grain from Joseph, because the famine was severe in *all the earth*." Few Christians insist that people from

---

48. Ross, *The Genesis Question: Scientific Advances and the Accuracy of Genesis*, 140.

Australia and the Americas were arriving in Egypt in boats to transport food back home, yet the reference to the earth here is clearly universal.

In Daniel 4:1, the prophet-magistrate addresses the king of Babylon saying, "Nebuchadnezzar the king to all the peoples, nations, and men of every language that live in *all the earth*." The Babylonian empire was vast, but certainly not global. There were many cultures and languages unknown to Daniel on continents beyond the great oceans.

Universal language used for the known world continues in the New Testament. In Romans 1:8, Paul commends the Christians in Rome telling them that "your faith is being proclaimed throughout *the whole world*." In Acts 11:28, a brief reference is made to the prophesy of Agabus, fulfilled in the reign of Claudius, of a famine that occurred "*all over the world*." Though communication and the later famine were widespread, there were many distant nations that knew nothing of the church in Rome, nor of the Middle Eastern famine.

We see the same language in the prophesies that pronounce a coming judgment on the world. In Isaiah 13:11, God says, "I will punish the world for its evil." Systematic judgments are then proclaimed in chapters 13–24 on representative nations from the world: Babylon, Assyria, Philistia, Moab, Damascus, Ethiopia, Egypt, Arabia, and Tyre. Nothing beyond the Middle East—the *known* world at the time of Isaiah—is mentioned.

In fact, in all of Scripture, with its many references to *all the earth*, *all the nations of the earth*, or *all the world*, not one place outside of the Middle East or the Roman Empire is ever mentioned. None of this is an argument for biblical mistakes due to ignorance. The argument is that God inspired language, repeatedly and consistently, about the physical world that was consistent with the common understanding of people at the time of writing. If there were lands beyond the experience or knowledge of the people when various Scriptures were recorded, God did not feel the need to correct their ignorance with qualifiers of "all the earth *that you know of*."

Consider a possible sequence of events during the days of Noah. For this rendering, we'll use the ancient catastrophic flooding of the Black Sea, but the description could fit a different location and time equally well. After following the command of God to build an ark, animals of every kind known to Noah appear and enter the ark. Torrential rains begin to fall at the same time that water begins to pour into the Black Sea from the Mediterranean. The ark, built on the shores of the sea, soon begins to rise. The ark drifts far into the sea during the rain. For months after the rain, land is too far beyond the horizon to be visible. No evidence of animal life can be found, and even fish have died from the rapid introduction of salt water from the Mediterranean. All flesh as far as the eye can see dies. As Noah relates the story to his children and grandchildren in the years following the flood, he describes what he observed: the whole of the land was covered with water.

One may object to this on the grounds that Noah did not have to rely only on his own observations, for God is the ultimate Author of Scripture. According to the Genesis account, God told Noah that all the land under heaven would be covered. While this is true, Paul also did not have to rely on his own experience and knowledge when he said the church in Rome was spoken of throughout the world. For reasons God has not revealed to us, he allowed his Word to be written, in part, through the eyes of its writers. God did not inspire Solomon to write that the earth rotates daily beneath the sun, but that the sun rises and the sun sets. This was what Solomon observed, and what he was inspired to record, without regard to the future literary expectations of Western civilization.

Universal vs. known-world

In the *universal flood* view, the flood waters did not cover the planet, but did encompass all of humanity. This understanding requires that the flood occurred before human populations migrated beyond the lands of the Fertile Crescent, with all humans perishing except Noah and his immediate family. This view is consistent with a more literal reading of Genesis, but is hard to reconcile with archaeological evidence of human migrations into East Asia tens of thousands of years ago,[49] or with genetic evidence indicating a minimum human population of several thousand (never as little as eight).

A *known-world flood* would allow for humans on distant continents to have lived beyond the scope of Noah's flood. In this view, the flood is a representative story, paralleling the representative judgments Isaiah pronounced on the lands surrounding Israel. Just as all the lands known to Noah were destroyed, there will come a day when judgment is poured out on all the lands known today—which is now the entire planet. Floods today are not a violation of God's promise (Gen. 8:21), for the promise was not about the cessation of natural disasters, but about the scale of his judgment. Destruction and renewal of *all* the known lands will never again happen until the final day of judgment.

---

49. https://en.wikipedia.org/wiki/Early_human_migrations; Martin and Vaughn, *Beyond Creation Science*, 129–49.

GENEALOGIES AND THE TIME SINCE CREATION

> When Adam had lived one hundred and thirty years, he became the father of a son in his own likeness, according to his image, and named him Seth.... Seth lived one hundred and five years, and became the father of Enosh. (Gen. 5:3, 6)

Bible

Genesis 5 and 11 contain the genealogies of Adam to Noah, and Noah to Abraham, respectively. The list includes not only names, but also the age of each man at the time when he "became the father of" his offspring. Summing these ages between Adam and Abraham yields approximately 2,000 years. Reasonable estimates of the date of Abraham, based on the number of generations between Abraham and Christ, would place his time on earth somewhere near 2000 B.C. If the genealogies of Genesis 5 and 11 represent a complete list of generations, this places the creation of Adam at about 4000 B.C., with a total age of roughly 6,000 years. However, as mentioned in Chapter 4 "the father of" can also mean "the ancestor of," meaning that generations may be skipped without error. In this case, the age of a father is given when an unnamed son was born who would give rise to the son named in the text.

The example given earlier of skipped generations in a genealogy came from Matthew 1 in the New Testament (Table 2), but similar examples may be found in the Old Testament. Exodus 6:14–27 records a genealogy from Levi to Moses with a total of four generations.[50] These verses identify the "sons of Levi" which includes Kohath, then the "sons of Kohath" which includes Amram, and then Amram's wife who bore Aaron and Moses. Nothing seems unusual about this until discovering these names elsewhere in Scripture. Genesis 46 lists the names of Jacob's sons and grandsons that he took with him to Egypt. Genesis 46:11 mentions Kohath as one of Levi's sons. When the Israelites left Egypt 430 years later (Exod. 12:40–41), the clan of Kohath numbered 8,600 males (Num. 3:27–28), or approximately 17,000 people if we assume an equal number of females.

If Kohath and all his offspring had the same number of children, it would require that Kohath and every child and grandchild have at least 25 children to get to 17,000 in three generations. If marriages took place between

---

50. Collins, *Science and Faith*, 108–9.

tribal members (husband and wife both descendants of Kohath), the average number of children per couple would have to be even greater. There were clearly names left out of the lineage. The actual number in Moses's lineage from Levi was probably closer to the twelve listed in Joshua's line from the tribe of Ephraim (1 Chron. 7:20–27).

Skipped names in the lineage from Adam to Moses means that the chronology can only be used to set a *minimum* age on Adam and Eve's appearance. On the ages of the earth or the universe, the Bible is silent.

Science

Radioisotopic dates on hominid fossils place the first appearance of anatomically modern humans approximately 200,000 years ago. The oldest evidence of behavior considered culturally modern is currently found in Africa at sites dated to over 60,000 years ago, with later occurrences in the Middle East and Europe. The first evidence of domestic agriculture is found in the Middle East within the last 11,000 years. The oldest rocks and meteorites found on earth indicate an age of our planet and solar system of 4.6 billion years. The age of the universe is 13.8 billion years.

TABLE 13—GENEALOGIES AND AGE	
The Bible	Science
The first humans appeared a *minimum* of 6,000 years ago.	Humans practicing domestic agriculture date back at least 11,000 years.
The age of the earth and universe is not addressed.	The earth is 4.6 billion years old, residing in a universe that is 13.8 billion years old.

Synthesis

The genealogies in the Bible affirm that all humans share a common origin, emphasized with the use of genealogies tracing back to Adam and Eve. God is the author of that lineage, and entered into that same human lineage to share the experience of his beloved creatures and bear the penalty of sin on their behalf. That is the message of the genealogies. As we saw in Matthew 1, the numbers, whether total ancestor count or ages, are not the point.

SUMMARY

Whenever Scripture touches on nature, it does so using the understanding of people at the time to communicate truth about the kingdom of God. We find nothing in Scripture that instructs us on the nature of nature, with one notable exception. We do find words that tell us to expect that nature reflects the character of its Creator (e.g., Rom. 1:20). Nature does not declare the corruption of sin; it declares the glory of God. This means we should expect that when nature is examined, it will communicate a truthful story. The ability to explore nature to discover not only how things work, but what life and the planet looked like in days before any human walked the earth, is a wondrous gift. A gift that should not be squandered by putting God into a human box, declaring in advance what story we are allowed to see in rocks, in life, and in the stars. In the next part of the book, we will explore more deeply what scientists see in nature that speaks to a rich and ancient history.

PART 4
THE CREDIBILITY OF MODERN SCIENCE

7

CONFUSING SCIENCE AND PHILOSOPHY

Before diving directly into Question 3, regarding the credibility of the science of origins, we need to spend a few pages clarifying the difference between science and philosophy. This may seem an odd tangent at first, but confusion on this issue has proven to be an obstacle that has prevented many from seriously considering scientific evidence because of a misperception that Christian faith and evolutionary science are *inherently* in conflict. If a scientific theory is based on the assumption that God does not exist, why should a person with religious convictions even consider it? We need to address this misperception before unpacking the physical evidence.

NATURALISM, MATERIALISM, DARWINISM, AND EVOLUTION

The confusion has arisen partly over the term *naturalism*. There are two definitions of naturalism that overlap but are profoundly different. The first applies to the philosophical position that the natural world is all there is. This is synonymous with *materialism*. This represents an a priori belief that the material or natural world is all that truly exists. Concepts of God and the supernatural are all constructs of the human imagination. What we can physically sense and measure is *it*—there is nothing else. The second definition of *naturalism* is not a philosophical position but merely an approach to experimentation. This naturalism simply says that in any experiment, we assume there is a natural explanation for the observed phenomenon. The possibility that the observed phenomenon was set in motion or designed by God is neither affirmed nor denied.[1]

---

1. Some have sought to solve the confusion created by the different definitions of *naturalism* by attaching descriptive qualifiers such as *philosophical naturalism* (the philosophy)

The pursuit of natural explanations is often misunderstood as an effort to explain away God, as though *natural* and *God* are antonyms. If God created nature, however, natural explanations are merely discoveries of the mechanisms God instituted to govern that creation. In most of science, secular and religious people alike *insist* that this approach be employed. Consider a chemist mulling over an intractable, multifaceted chemical reaction. After years of study, she submits her findings to a journal stating that a miracle must take place between steps 14 and 15 in the reaction. What Christian would fault the editor for rejecting this manuscript? We fully expect there to be a natural explanation for the reaction, while also fully believing that it is authored by God.

So what happens when we turn our scientific questions to the subject of origins? Many argue that God has already answered wonderings of "how" and "in what order," equating all attempts at finding natural explanations with a tacit commitment to materialism. If the only plausible interpretation of the six days of creation in Genesis is a literal one, this might be a fair claim. If the message of the creation days is *authorship* rather than *process*, however, then the search for natural explanations is nothing worse than an effort to see the details of God's handiwork. It is akin to seeing the painting of a master and not just wishing to know if the sky was painted before the mountains, but desiring to know what the first brush stroke looked like, whether the colors were blended on the canvas or on the palette, or how the texture of the paint may have changed after the long passage of time. These questions do not deny the existence and brilliance of the painter; they reflect a desire to understand the painter's work.

It should be clear that a philosophical position of naturalism, better identified as *materialism*, is antithetical to Scripture (by virtue of denying all forms of the supernatural) while the day-to-day assumption of naturalism in experimental work is not. Failure to recognize this distinction runs deep in our society, however, promoting the misconception among both the religious and the nonreligious that the pursuit of natural explanations (i.e., *science*) leads inevitably to materialism. Many will note that science does not *have* to lead to materialism, but in actuality, science *cannot* logically lead to materialism.

Science, defined here as the systematic study of the natural realm (rather than the more broad definition of any acquisition of knowledge), can be

---

and *methodological naturalism* (the approach to experimentation), e.g., Keith Miller, *Perspectives on an Evolving Creation*, 7.

summarized as any effort to understand natural processes and phenomena. As such, it is limited in its scope to that which is confined within the boundaries of time and space. Since it cannot address that which may lie outside its boundaries, it cannot make any conclusion about the existence or nonexistence of such a realm. To get to materialism, a large, blind leap of faith is required to believe that only that which is testable by science truly exists.[2]

Stephen Jay Gould was an atheist and spent his life promoting and defending evolution, but nonetheless chastised fellow scientists for overextending the application of scientific methods.

> Science simply cannot (by its legitimate methods) adjudicate the issue of God's possible superintendence of nature. We neither affirm nor deny it; we simply can't comment on it as scientists.[3]

At its heart, materialism is based on circular reasoning where it is assumed that everything that is real is testable by science, and that therefore scientific tests can be used to determine if something is real. Ironically, science does not provide a mechanism for testing the hypothesis that only what is testable by science is real.

The misconception that science equals materialism might be more understandable if it were only perpetuated by Hollywood (those with an agenda but little understanding), but such is not the case. The misconception has been widely promoted by the very people who should know better: scientists and professors. Prominent scientists like Richard Dawkins and Jerry Coyne[4] have been outspoken about their belief that scientific evidence demonstrates materialism. In the popular book *The Blind Watchmaker: Why the Evidence of Evolution Reveals a Universe Without Design*, Dawkins makes the claim that scientific investigation can prove that God does not exist, or at least that God had no dealings with this universe. The underlying assumption is the deeply flawed premise that if we can understand how a natural process works, God didn't design it, create it, or guide it. In Dawkins's own words:

---

2. Francis Collins, former director of the Human Genome Project, states this well in his assessment of Richard Dawkins's atheistic arguments: "The major and inescapable flaw of Dawkins's claim that science demands atheism is that it goes beyond the evidence. If God is outside of nature, then science can neither prove nor disprove His existence. Atheism itself must therefore be considered a form of blind faith." Collins, *The Language of God: A Scientist Presents Evidence for Belief*, 165.
3. Gould, "Impeaching a self-appointed judge (review of Phillip Johnson's *Darwin on Trial*)."
4. Coyne, *Faith vs. Fact: Why Science and Religion Are Incompatible*.

The basic idea of *The Blind Watchmaker* is that we don't need to postulate a designer in order to understand life, or anything else in the universe.[5]

To say that a miracle need not be invoked to explain the development or continued existence of some process or organism is far from proving the process or organism had no designer. One might as well be clear and say that God is only allowed to exist if he violates the natural laws he set into place. In the end, the only thing that is proven in *The Blind Watchmaker* is Dawkins's religious commitment to materialism.

When highly regarded scientists fail to recognize the limits of science and smear the distinction between science and philosophy, it is no wonder that religious people react with the same faulty assumptions. Phillip Johnson, a lawyer and author of *Darwin on Trial*, has written extensively attacking the entire field of evolutionary science on the presupposition that it is all based on an a priori belief in materialism. Johnson's attacks on naturalism/materialism hit dead center. His attacks on evolutionary science miss the target, in large part because he is still aiming at materialism.

Johnson equates evolution with *Darwinism*, which is materialism applied to the origin and diversity of life. When addressing Darwinism, Johnson does well to note that it is "inherently naturalistic and therefore antagonistic to the idea that God had anything to do with the history of life."[6] There are many scientists who will boldly and naively support this assertion with statements that evolution is "unguided" and "without purpose." But the *science* of evolution makes no such claims. As a science, evolution is merely the name given to a study seeking to fit pieces of the life-history puzzle together in the most sensible way.

One may object and point out that words like "random" can be found frequently in every textbook about evolution. While this is true, it does not follow that it is undirected. Consider our understanding of dice. We freely speak of the roll of the dice as being random. Do we think it is unguided as well? Perhaps, unless we remember Proverbs 16:33, which tells us, "The lot is cast into the lap, but its every decision is from the LORD."

Casting the lot was the biblical equivalent of rolling dice and was the principal means for determining which portion of the land of Canaan was given to each Israelite tribe (Josh. 18, 19), and the method of identifying Achan, the man who violated the ban against taking spoils from Jericho (Josh. 7).

---

5. Dawkins, *The Blind Watchmaker*, 147.
6. Johnson, "What is Darwinism? Why science clings to a fractured paradigm," 20–26.

Random is a scientific word meaning we cannot predict the outcome using scientific tools. It does not rule out supernatural guidance any more than the random nature of dice rules out God's ability to predetermine the result.

If evolution is true, it should be understood not as *Darwinism* but as the name people have given to the study of what God's creativity looks like. God does not select, guide, prod, or adjust evolution as if it is an independent force that he must rein in. God creates. Humans apply names to the subsequent artistry.

BUT DOES LIFE *LOOK* INTENTIONAL?

For those who are familiar with the works of authors like Dawkins or Coyne, an additional philosophical objection to evolution may yet remain, because many writers insist that the nature of life's development and diversification demonstrates there was no intelligent designer at work. At this stage, we will not dive into the nuances of the Intelligent Design movement (that gets its own chapter later). For now, we are only concerned with the question of whether observations from an evolutionary perspective effectively rule out divine governance.

For those arguing against God's active guidance, the premise is that a supernatural engineer would have made the diversification much more efficient than what is observed, and would not have permitted so many dead-end lineages. Richard Dawkins uses an example of the bony flatfish that starts life with an eye on each side like normal fish. As it grows, one eye moves to the other side and the fish transitions to life on the bottom.

> The whole skull of a bony flatfish retains the twisted and distorted evidence of its origins.... No sensible designer would have conceived such a monstrosity if given a free hand to create a flatfish on a clean drawing board.[7]

Not all scientists who share these views are atheists. Kenneth Miller is a cell biologist who claims belief in a benevolent God, though one with a very hands-off approach to the creation of life-forms. In his book *Finding Darwin's God*, Miller writes,

> The advocates of design are faced with a logical contradiction. They would like to claim that the perfection of design seen in living organisms cannot

---

7. Dawkins, *The Blind Watchmaker*, 92.

possibly have been achieved by a random, undirected process like evolution, and that an intelligent agent is required to account for such perfection. But when one looks at the record, the products of this intelligent design consistently fail to survive.... Whatever one's views of such a designer's motivation, there is one conclusion that drops cleanly out of the data. He was incompetent.[8]

The evidence cited for these assertions can be broken into three categories:

Presence of DNA, organs, or developmental features that serve no purpose for the organism

Genetic code can be found in all living organisms that had a function in ancestral life-forms but that does not serve any recognized purpose in the current organism. A variant of the same observation is that organisms often have organs or fetal developmental features that had a necessary function in ancestral forms, but not in the current organism. Examples include an unused yolk sac in embryonic humans and functionless pelvic or lower leg bones in some whale species.

Existence of "poorly designed" organs

A commonly used example is the human eye. The light receptors are said to be "wired backwards" with the photon sensor pointed inward instead of outward. The wires to each sensor pass over the top of the retina to the optic nerve bundle which results in a blind spot.[9]

The vast majority of life-forms that existed on earth are extinct. Most species failed to survive to the present.

There are people who will take issue with each of these categories, claiming that vestigial DNA or organs do not exist, nor are there poorly designed organs, but for the sake of this argument, we will assume the observations are valid. The first two categories are cited as evidence of inefficiencies that make perfect sense if life developed through the accumulation of random copying errors acted upon by natural selection, but not if guided by an intelligent designer. The third is used to suggest that if

---

8. Miller, *Finding Darwin's God*, 102.
9. Many more examples can be found in Lents, *Human Errors: A Panorama of Our Glitches, From Pointless Bones to Broken Genes.*

God was responsible for the diversity of life on earth, he was a bumbling engineer who had great difficulty making something capable of long-term survival.

These observations may indeed be evidence for the evolutionary development of life-forms, but they fall far short of becoming evidence against authorship by a Creator. Underlying each assertion is the unspoken statement, "If I were God I would not have created this way; therefore God did not do it!" The offered evidence says more about the people making the assertions than about the existence or actions of God.

If God chose to create through successive generations, then it makes perfect sense that vestiges of previous generations would be present in later generations. This is not a sign of inefficiency, but a simple reflection of lineage, much as we recognize grandpa's eyes on baby's face. Vestiges without function need not be cast off immediately for a designer to exist. In fact, residual DNA that may not have a function now is thought to become one of the very means by which a new function develops in a later offspring as a result of a mutation on the "temporarily out of service" genetic sequence. Pretty neat design.

The idea of poorly designed organs, as with beauty, is in the eye of the beholder. To Dawkins, backwards-pointing light receptors in human eyes would never have occurred if created with foresight by an intelligent designer. There are many things that we could cite, however, that we might prefer in a new and improved body plan. Take the eye again. My optician tells me that the lens in each of my eyes is typical of human eyes which tend to stiffen with age. The focal lengths of my lenses were never quite right, and as they stiffen over time, I have more difficulty focusing and require stronger eyeglass prescriptions. Is this inefficiency evidence that God does not exist or that he had no hand in my creation? Hardly, yet the example is no different than the positioning of light receptors behind the retina. God chose to create beings with inherent limitations. Wonderfully made, but with designed limitations. Why he chose to do so may be a legitimate question, but unrelated to the question of his existence.

The last category of "evidence for life without design" is the perceived failure to create life capable of long-term success. Imagine here an artist who does not create out of need for someone else's approval, but simply for the joy of creating. Our artist molds clay into three-dimensional shapes of exquisite beauty. After enjoying sculptures for some period of time, the artist takes some of them and re-forms them into new shapes. Others he breaks down to make space for new sculptures, not because he was displeased with the old ones, but because he is ready for the next and does not need to cling to the old. If God chooses to retain some creatures as they were in the past, remold some lineages into new forms, and allow other lineages to end, how is that evidence against his intelligence or competence?

In the end, all the arguments against divine creativity reflect nothing more than their proponents' belief that nature would look very different if *they* were God.

CHOICE OF TERMINOLOGY

As we move on to the credibility of modern science, it will be necessary to keep track of some opposing views. This requires a set of labels—terminology—that can prove more challenging than one might think. Historically those advocating a biblical view referred to themselves as *creationists* and labeled those who held to long ages of earth history, or specifically to evolution, as *evolutionists*. The problem with these terms is that they have come to embody meanings that create an artificial dichotomy between faith and science. Creationists believe in the Bible. Evolutionists believe in nature. Yet there are many who believe that God initially created supernaturally, followed by continued, personally directed creation via divinely ordained natural means. Those who adhere to such a position are simultaneously creationists and evolutionists!

To make things more confusing, modern young-earth creationists increasingly argue for evolutionary adaptations of organisms at a rate far faster than proposed by conventional evolutionists. So if there are evolutionists who believe in an initial special creation and creationists who believe in a form of evolution, we clearly need better terms to identify the different positions being argued. This is not a segue into naming and defining all the various positions on the subject of origins.[10] My intention here is to simply provide insight into *my* choice of terms.

In the chapters to follow, I will identify those claiming a literal interpretation of Genesis 1 and 2 as either *young-earth proponents/advocates* or as *evolution opponents*, depending on the context of the discussion. It might seem that we could use the first term exclusively, but there are some young-earth

---

10. A good source for defining the various positions is Haarsma and Haarsma, *Origins: Christian Perspectives on Creation, Evolution, and Intelligent Design*, 299–302.

advocates who accept aspects of evolution and some who do not. We could refer to those completely disavowing all forms of evolution as *antievolutionists*, but I have chosen to use this term sparingly because too many associate the "anti" prefix on any position as pejorative (such as referring to "pro-life" as "anti-choice").

Those who believe in God and evolution are often lumped into a position known as *theistic evolution*, though I dislike the term for its vague definition and for the sense that it is somehow different from "normal" evolution.[11] If God created life-forms without violating any of the natural laws he set into motion, the study of life through earth history will look the same to theists and atheists alike (though inspiring less admiration in the atheist).[12] A relatively new term, *evolutionary creationism*, is a subset of theistic evolution, more narrowly defined as a view that acknowledges the truth of the Bible while also embracing the findings of astronomy, geology, genetics, and evolution.[13] These labels are important when discussing the *ultimate* driving force behind the origin and adaptation of life, but are not as critical for understanding how evolution works. The basic principles of genetics, adaptation, and inheritance look the same to the materialist, the theist, and the Christian evolutionist, in the same way that a chemical reaction looks the same for the materialist, the theist, and the Christian chemist. For this reason, I have chosen to simply use the term *evolutionist* to identify anyone in agreement with the science of evolution.

---

11. *Theistic evolution* can be used to include belief in a personal God intimately involved at all levels of creation, a more distant God who occasionally nudges the evolutionary process in particular directions, or even a deist god who merely got things started and now watches with some amusement to see what evolution will produce.
12. An atheist friend reacted strongly to this statement, but consider the logic. The theist is awed by the natural workings of creation *and* by the self-existent God capable of authoring and sustaining that creation. The atheist is awed by only the natural workings of creation. You do the math.
13. Lamoureux, "Evolutionary creation: Moving beyond the evolution versus creation debate"; Haarsma, "Evolutionary Creation."

8

QUESTIONS OF AGE—UNIVERSE AND EARTH

To this point, only the first two questions from Chapter 2 have been addressed:

1. Does the infallibility of Scripture rest on a literal interpretation of the verses in question?
2. Does the science conflict with the intended message of Scripture?

If the answer is *no* to both questions for a specific subject where science and Scripture intersect, we are ready to move to the final question which asks, "Is the science credible?"

The objective here is not an exhaustive review of all scientific subjects relevant to creation and the Bible. Such an endeavor would require not only many chapters, but many books. Indeed, many works already exist on the credibility of science from both Christian and secular viewpoints. There will also be no effort to *prove* any scientific theory, for this would also require multiple volumes, much of which would be laborious reading.

The objective is to provide simple, concise overviews of the development and current evidence for the scientific claims most relevant to creation, in language that nonscientists can grasp. Many of the descriptions provide summaries of the historical context of theories to better understand how we got to where we are. These are particularly useful where there are misperceptions that (1) modern theories were built on atheistic presuppositions, or (2) science had to shake off the fetters of religion to get where we are today.

THE BIRTH OF THE UNIVERSE

Within the secular population, there is a general belief that science now provides us with the information that religion once gave. Questions of how we came to be and how things work required mystical answers until such a time came when science could replace mythology with logical explanations of the world around us. This perception has led to a belief within both the secular and religious communities that advances in scientific discovery since the days of the Renaissance have only served to widen the gap between science and faith. Such a view, however, can only be maintained by ignoring *actual* history. Change in our scientific understanding of the origin of the universe provides a great opening example of a scientific view that has become *more* consistent with the Bible over the last century.

In the early eighteenth century, the development of Newtonian physics led to a commonly held belief that the universe was static and of infinite extent.[1] It was recognized that planets and stars revolved around common centers of mass, but no relative movement had been observed between our galaxy and more distant stars; thus the universe as a whole was thought fixed in space. This posed a problem, however, because it was also recognized that a finite universe filled with fixed stellar masses would have a gravitational center that would ultimately draw all matter in upon itself. It was assumed that the universe must be infinite in extent, thus having no center.

This theory posed no direct threat to biblical interpretations, for it could be argued that God had created the universe as an infinite system of fixed bodies. Secular scientists, on the other hand, could argue with equal conviction that the universe was infinite in time as well as space. The universe had no beginning, and no creator was necessary.

It was within this scientific and philosophical framework that Albert Einstein and his contemporaries began developing more advanced mathematical models of the behavior of natural phenomena at both local and cosmic levels. The first few years of the 1900s spawned significant advances in the understanding of electrodynamics, the dual particle-wave nature of light, and the counterintuitive interrelationships between matter, energy, time, and motion. Such advances eventually provided Einstein with the tools to develop a remarkably elegant mathematical model of the universe that could account

---

1. This section benefited greatly from Ross, *The Fingerprint of God: Recent Scientific Discoveries Reveal the Unmistakable Identity of the Creator.*

for nuances in the observed motion of planets and stars, the relationship between matter and energy, and the relative nature of time. It even allowed the accurate prediction that space itself was bent by gravitational fields.

The model that explained observed phenomena so well, however, posed a significant problem. In its unaltered form, the model required the universe to be expanding. This outcome was bothersome to Einstein because an expanding universe implied a beginning, and a beginning implied a nonnaturalistic inception of the universe. On mostly philosophical grounds, Einstein inserted an additional term, known as the *cosmological constant*, into his model to achieve a static system.[2]

The correction term was embraced by many of Einstein's peers. In part, the acceptance was legitimate because there was little direct evidence that the universe was expanding. The acceptance was not without bias, however, for many shared Einstein's personal distaste for the idea of a beginning. Arthur Eddington, a leading theoretician at the time, famously referred to a possible birth of the universe as being "philosophically repugnant."[3]

Not all were satisfied with this mathematical "fix," and physical evidence began to mount that eventually shattered the static universe theory. Though unknown to Einstein at the time, evidence against a stationary universe had begun to emerge even before the 1917 publication of his seminal work. In 1914, Vesto Slipher reported measurements indicating that distant nebulae were moving away from us at incredible velocities.[4] The first to formally link Slipher's observations with Einstein's equations to suggest the universe was expanding was a Belgian priest, Georges Lemaître, in 1927.[5] At the same time, Edwin Hubble and others were making additional measurements of both the distance and velocity of many more star systems. In 1929, Hubble published a landmark work stating that the more distant the galaxy, the higher its velocity away from our own.[6] The universe was clearly expanding. Having fought

---

2. The cosmological constant was eventually revived, but its modern employment is quite different than originally proposed. All modern adaptations of Einstein's work still yield an expanding universe of finite age, though there is some debate concerning the nature of the expansion. A sufficiently large value assigned to the cosmological constant yields an accelerating model, meaning that distant galaxies are moving away from us at ever-increasing speeds.
3. Eddington, "On the instability of Einstein's spherical world"; Eddington, "The end of the world: From the standpoint of mathematical physics," 450.
4. Slipher, "Spectrographic observations of nebulae."
5. Lemaître was also the first to propose the universe started from a "single quantum." Farrell, *The Day Without Yesterday: Lemaître, Einstein, and the Birth of Modern Cosmology.*
6. Hubble, "A relation between distance and radial velocity among extra-galactic nebulae."

for over a decade to defend a static universe, Einstein eventually conceded that the insertion of the cosmological constant was the biggest mistake of his professional life.[7]

Expansion of the universe was soon acknowledged by virtually all astronomers and cosmologists, though many remained ill at ease with the idea of a beginning. It is ironic that the term we now associate with the inception of the universe, the *big bang*, was coined by an astronomer who *opposed* the theory. Fred Hoyle accepted expansion, but insisted there was no need for a beginning, or "big bang," by postulating the eternal creation of matter in the space between galaxies.[8] Though Hoyle maintained his position to his death in 2001, no evidence or mechanism for the eternal creation of new matter was ever found. Today there is nearly universal acceptance, even by the most ardent atheists, that the universe had a real beginning.

With respect to the question of the eternal or temporal nature of this world, the scientific understanding today is more consistent with the Bible than it was a century earlier.

BEFORE THE BIG BANG?

For those wedded to a materialistic worldview, a true beginning is not permitted. A beginning of *our* universe is acceptable only if a naturalistic mechanism can be postulated for bringing it into existence. Many ideas have been floated, ranging from cosmic cycles of collapse and rebound, to the existence of an infinite number of coexisting universes (the so-called *multiverse*) that spawn new universes from quantum discontinuities.

There is a critical difference between the scientific models for the world in which we live and models of what may have come before. Mathematical constructs and explanations for the birth and structure of *this* universe can be tested by innumerable methods. As a famous example, recall that Einstein's mathematical model predicted that gravity bends space. In 1919, astronomical measurements were sophisticated enough to put the prediction to the test during a solar eclipse. It was known ahead of time that the eclipse would occur just as the sun was crossing the bright Hyades star cluster. As the sun approached, the position of the star cluster appeared to shift—by just the magnitude predicted by Einstein's equations.

---

7. Douglas, "Forty minutes with Einstein."
8. Mitton, *Fred Hoyle: A Life in Science.*

In contrast, the models for what is purported to have existed before the big bang have no comparable tests. Though mathematically based, there are no hypotheses which can be subjected to experimentation or physical discovery, leading a number of prominent physicists, astronomers, and cosmologists to argue that these hypotheses do not even qualify as science.[9] They are more mathematical philosophy than mathematical science.

THE AGE OF THE UNIVERSE

This section presents a significant challenge for a book designed with nonscientist readers in mind, because the methods used to calculate the age of the universe require a considerable education in math and physics to fully comprehend. Adequate explanation of any of the different methods requires many pages of technical terminology and advanced math that leaves the normal reader little more informed when finished. On the other hand, to glibly say that really smart people know what they are doing and come up with very old ages leaves the average reader still less informed, and justifiably suspicious that these smart people are probably not as smart as they think. Perhaps there are erroneous assumptions built into their calculations that will yield far younger ages once better understood?

There is a natural tendency to disbelieve that which we have trouble comprehending when we know that many advocating a particular position are antagonistic to our worldview. In the current context, it is true that many astronomers and physicists reject God, so it is tempting to write off their findings as biased. Recall, however, examples such as Albert Einstein and Edwin Hubble. Einstein's math and Hubble's measurements led to estimates of extreme age for the universe, but also to the eventual confirmation that the universe had a beginning. Though not fitting into a young-earth model, the scientific paradigm nonetheless shifted to one that was more consistent with the biblical account.

Is there a way to give the common reader (i.e., nonphysicist) more confidence in the accuracy of the methods used to estimate the age of the universe? My attempt at a reasonable solution is to provide a simplified, conceptual explanation of the most easily understood method, without discussion of the underlying mathematics, and to offer a few summary notes on the other methods.

---

9. Lennox, *God and Stephen Hawking*, chap. 3, includes quotes from prominent scientists in pertinent fields of study who do not consider *M-theory* to be a genuine scientific theory (e.g., Roger Penrose, Paul Davies, John Polkinghorne, Don Page, Jim Al-Khalili, Frank Close, Jon Butterworth).

Age from Expansion Rate: Velocity and Distance of Galaxies

The most readily understood method used to estimate the age of the universe became possible as soon as it was discovered that we could measure the velocity of distant galaxies and their distance from us. If we can map the position of galaxies in the universe and we know how fast they are moving away from us, we can calculate the time required to move from a common starting point to the current positions.

Imagine a set of points drawn on a balloon that is inflated at a constant rate. As the balloon is blown up, the points begin to move farther apart. If we sit at one spot, points on the far side of the balloon will seem to move away from us faster than closer points (Fig. 8). If we can determine the distance between points and the rate they are moving away from us, it is possible to calculate how long ago the balloon started inflating.

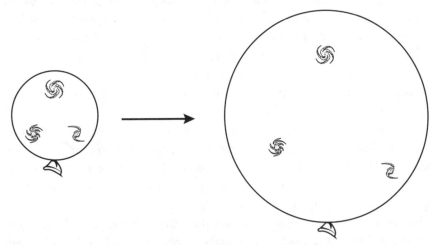

Figure 8—Expanding balloon as an analogy for the expanding universe. All points on balloon surface become farther apart as the balloon expands.

So how are distances and velocities of stars and galaxies determined? Velocities are determined by measuring the shortening or stretching of light waves that emanate from far-off galaxies. A similar phenomenon is familiar to us involving sound waves. A car speeding toward us compresses the sound waves, resulting in a higher frequency sound (higher pitch) reaching our ears. As the car passes, the sound waves are now stretched out, so a lower frequency sound (lower pitch) reaches our ears. With light, a star moving toward us shortens the wavelengths (higher frequency), resulting in bluer light, a phenomenon known as *blue shift*. Stars moving away from us stretch the wavelengths (lower frequency), producing redder light known as *red shift*. The galaxies closest to us include some that are moving toward us and some that are moving away, but distant galaxies are all moving away at tremendous speed—they all exhibit red shift. The magnitude of the red shift allows the velocity to be quantified. Consistent with the idea of an expanding balloon, galaxies farthest away are moving away at the highest velocities.

Distance can be determined by a number of different methods. The easiest method to understand takes advantage of something known as *parallax*, and is employed for calculating distances to nearby stars. Parallax refers to the apparent displacement of an object when viewed from two different vantage points. As an example, hold your finger up in front of your face. With your right eye closed, position your finger over the top of some distant object. Now close your right eye and open your left. You are now viewing from a slightly different position. The distant object pops into view as your finger appears to shift out of the way to the left. The closer you hold your finger to your eyes, the larger the apparent shift will be. If you know the distance between your eyes, and the angle formed between your eyes and the apparent positions of your finger, you can use simple trigonometry to calculate the distance.

The same method works with stars, but obviously not just by alternating closed eyes. The different viewing angles become possible as the earth revolves around the sun. The relative positions of stars are different when viewed six months apart (Fig. 9), allowing the distance to be calculated. For stars and galaxies great distances from earth, the parallax angles become too small to precisely measure and other more complex methods are employed.[10]

Once velocities and distances are known for multiple galaxies, their relative positions can be mapped, which yields the size of the region of the universe under study and the rate of expansion. Knowing the size and expansion rate then allows an estimate of the time required to go from an initial starting point to the current configuration.

But there is a complicating factor we have not yet mentioned. The expansion rate may not have been constant. The universe may have expanded more slowly or quickly in the past. But we don't have to make untestable assumptions to estimate possible deceleration or acceleration in the past. One method makes use of exploding stars, called supernovae, at variable distances from us. The light from

---

10. A summary of methods can be found under the heading of *Cosmic Distance Ladder* on Wikipedia, https://simple.wikipedia.org/wiki/Cosmic_distance_ladder.

more distant stars took longer to reach us, so we are seeing events that happened longer ago in the past. These snapshots of explosions from the past provide information about the rate of cosmic expansion at specific times in the past. Current measurements indicate the rate of expansion is increasing over time. Quantifying the expansion rate has been further refined by measurements of the cosmic microwave background radiation measured by the Hubble Telescope.[11] Taken together, this data allows calculation of the time required to move from a common starting point to where we are today: 13.8 billion years.[12]

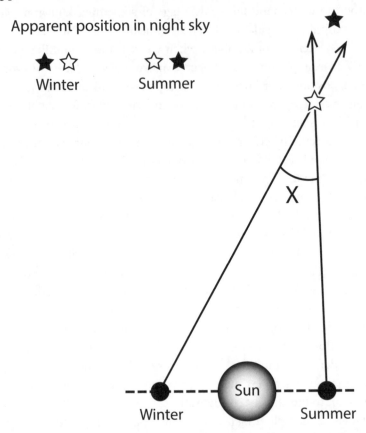

Figure 9—Diagram of earth, sun, and two stars during different seasons (not to scale). The farther away an object is from earth, the smaller the angle will be. Note also the apparent shift in positions, from the perspective of a viewer on earth, of a near and far star during different seasons.

11. How the cosmic microwave background radiation is employed to estimate expansion rate requires some of that advanced math that this book is not delving into.

12. Grant, "Planck refines cosmic history."

Age of Stars and Star Clusters

Several methods exist for estimating the age of individual stars and of clusters of stars. Age estimates of individual stars are considered less reliable, requiring assumptions that are difficult to reliably test. Astronomers have greater confidence in methods employing globular star clusters (regions of a galaxy with a high density of stars).[13] Measurements of the globular cluster of our own Milky Way galaxy indicate formation of the oldest stars 12.5 to 13 billion years ago, consistent with a slightly earlier inception of the universe as a whole closer to 14 billion years ago.[14]

GEOLOGIC HISTORY AND THE AGE OF THE EARTH

The systematic study of earth's rocks, features, and processes is a relatively young science.[15] Though elements of geologic science can be traced back to the ancient Greeks, formalization of geologic principles did not begin to appear in print until late in the seventeenth century. Nicholas Steno, a Danish physician living in Italy, noted that fossil-bearing rock layers appeared to have been laid down horizontally in laterally continuous layers that could be subject to tilting and deformation at a later time. These observations became the foundation for his principles of original horizontality, lateral continuity, and superposition that provided a basis for determining the relative order in which sedimentary rock units were formed.[16]

Geology blossomed into a full-fledged science during the eighteenth century, which witnessed lively debates between those who believed that crystalline rocks, such as granite, were formed from a chemically rich primordial sea during the earth's early history, and those who believed that these rocks were formed by a continuous cycle of subterranean volcanic activity. Advocates of a marine origin of crystalline rocks, championed by Abraham Werner, were known as *neptunists*, after the Roman god of the sea. Advocates of the opposing view, championed

---

13. Soderblom, "The ages of stars."
14. NASA has useful web resources for the lay-scientist: http://hubblesite.org/reference_desk/faq/all.php.cat=cosmology; https://map.gsfc.nasa.gov/universe/uni_age.html.
15. Much of the history of geology in this chapter comes from two sources: Levin, *The Earth Through Time*, and Peters, *No Stone Unturned: Reasoning About Rocks and Fossils*.
16. *Original horizontality*: sediments in steeply tilted strata were originally deposited in nearly horizontal beds and were tilted at a later time. *Lateral continuity*: matching strata on either side of a valley were once continuous. *Superposition*: in undisturbed strata, younger sediments sit on top of older sediments. These terms apply only to sediments and sedimentary rock (layers referred to as *strata*), not to igneous rocks, which can intrude between existing layers.

by James Hutton, became known as *plutonists*, after the god of the underworld. Research in geochemistry and rock formation eventually proved the plutonists to be correct in the origin of crystalline rock.

James Hutton, a renowned geologist and author of the first exhaustive geology book, is perhaps most famous for his statement that "the past history of our globe must be explained by what can be seen to be happening now." This statement was later abbreviated to the more familiar phrase "the present is the key to the past" by Archibald Geikie, and given the name *uniformitarianism* by William Whewell.

The term—and the expression "the present is the key to the past"—is often misunderstood to mean that *rates* observed today were uniform throughout the past. It is better understood to represent a belief that the basic laws of chemistry and physics observed today have been uniform through time. Applied to the study of rocks, if we repeatedly see that ripple marks are formed in loose sand by a steady flow of wind or water, we can have reasonable confidence that ripple marks preserved in an old sandstone are evidence that the sandstone was once loose sand exposed to the flow of wind or water.

In the years following Hutton, there were active debates between *gradualists*, those who believed that the earth was shaped mostly by slow processes of deposition and erosion, and *catastrophists*, who believed most of the earth's layers could be explained by a series of global cataclysms. Today, applying uniformitarian principles, it is recognized that the earth has been shaped by both slow *and* catastrophic events, with rates of formation or erosion varying dramatically in activity and scale. While it may take centuries in a cave to add an inch to the top of a limestone stalagmite, a hundred feet of volcanic ash may fill a dozen mountain valleys in a matter of minutes. What we see left behind from limestone formation and volcanic ash deposits today helps us recognize similar processes in the past.

There is a temptation to view all scientists such as Hutton as secularists who looked only for ways to explain away God, but our views are often colored by the authors we read. Introductory chapters in geology textbooks will often attribute Hutton with using the principle of uniformitarianism to see in the earth's layers a record of a "succession of former worlds" with "no vestige of a beginning, no prospect of an end." What is rarely shared is that the driving force behind Hutton's scientific views was a deistic belief that the earth had been created by a benevolent God who endowed his creation with regenerative forces to continuously reshape its surface.[17]

---

17. Peters, *No Stone Unturned*, 54.

Relative Dating

During the eighteenth century, the ability to determine the geologic history at a location was limited to *relative-dating* techniques developed by Nicholas Steno and later expanded by Charles Lyell. Relative dating simply establishes a sequence of events, without knowing when each event took place. We can use a book, fashioned and then damaged, as an analogy. If we find a book torn in half, with fewer pages in one half relative to the other, we can reasonably deduce a sequence where (1) the pages were stacked and bound, (2) the book was torn, and then (3) some pages were lost from one side. The pages had to be there in order to be torn, and the tear had to predate the loss of pages from only one half. The same basic principles can be applied to stacked rocks with cracks, faults, and eroded surfaces.[18]

While this approach worked well for determining the relative ages of rock layers at one location, there was no way of knowing how those ages related to layers at some distant location. This began to change as a result of observations published by William Smith, an English surveyor in the early nineteenth century.

William Smith was responsible for the placement of canals used for navigation and drainage throughout England and Wales. Through a detailed study of outcrops and rocks exposed during the construction of these canals, Smith observed that different layers contained unique assemblages of fossils that could be traced laterally over wide distances. In his studies, the sequence of fossils observed in one place was never reversed in another location, even though the rock type might change. This meant the vertical change from one set of fossils to another was not just due to a change in the local environmental conditions at the time, but represented a wholesale replacement of one set of organisms with another set at a later time. From this information, he deduced that the earth's history must have been divided into time intervals with unique sets of life-forms. The transition in life-forms over time was termed *biotic succession*.

Initially there was no sense of increasing complexity of life over time, but simply changes from one suite of organisms to another. Smith's discoveries predated Darwin's published work on evolution by several decades. At nearly the same time, Georges Cuvier and Alexander Brongniart made similar observations across the English Channel in France. They further noted that abrupt changes in life-forms preserved in successive rock formations were often separated by erosional surfaces. From this, they argued that the earth's history included periodic catastrophic events, the most recent being Noah's flood, that

---

18.   As a humorous aside, I remind my students that *relative dating* does not mean taking your cousin to a movie.

wiped out existing life-forms and allowed new ones to be introduced. Cuvier and Brongniart were thus catastrophists, though not necessarily creationists.

Once it was recognized that unique fossil assemblages represented periods of similar time that could be traced between countries, studies began to identify time-equivalent links between rock formations throughout Europe. Names assigned to each successive time interval were drawn from local history or culture in the area where the most detailed studies were done. As an example, the time represented by rock formations studied by Adam Sedgwick in north-western Wales was termed *Cambrian*, where *cambria* is the Latin word for Wales (and also the origin of the names of the city and university of Cambridge where Sedgwick worked) (Fig. 10). Rock with Cambrian fossils could be identified in many parts of Europe.

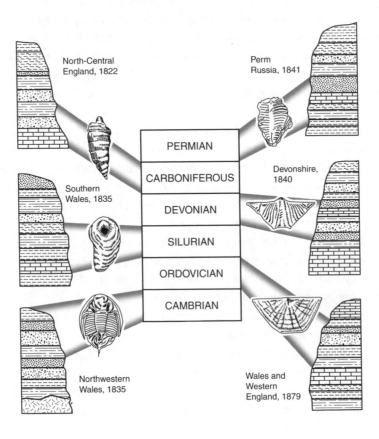

Figure 10—Illustration of how the geologic column and different intervals of geologic time were constructed from different rock outcrops in Europe and Asia.

In some locations, another sequence of layers sat directly above Cambrian layers, each with distinctly different assemblages of fossil organisms. These were given their own names such as *Devonian*, *Silurian* and *Ordovician*. Piecing all this information together eventually gave rise to the idealized geologic column (Fig. 11).

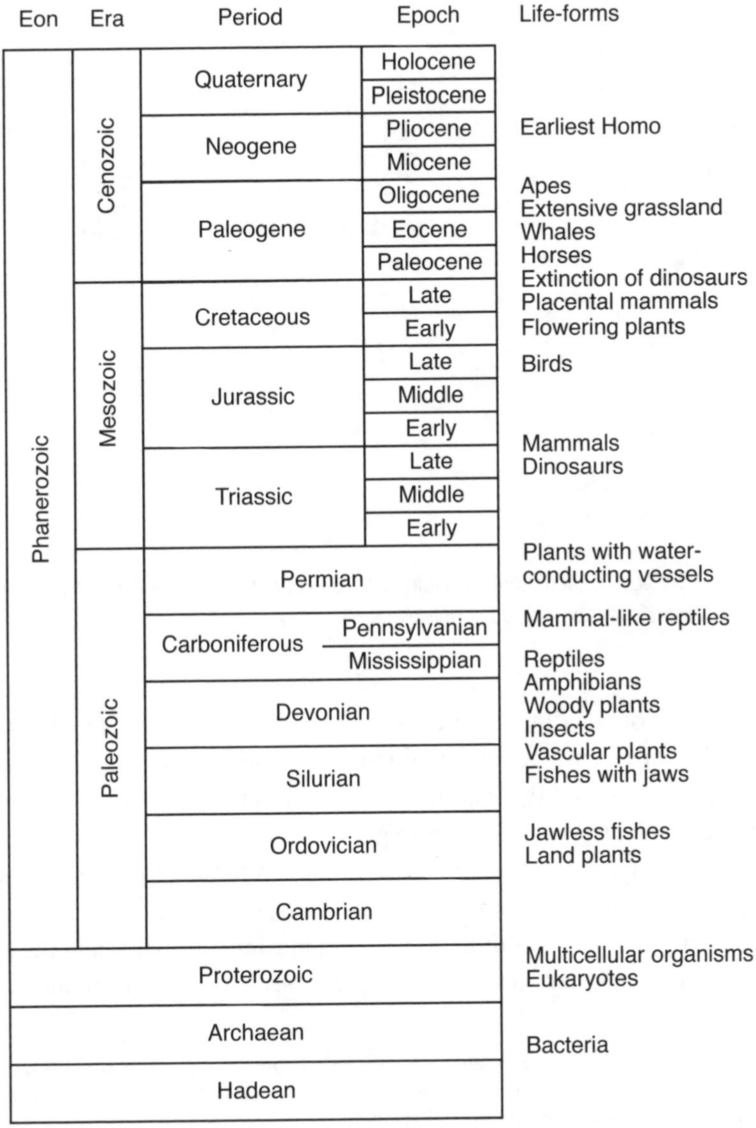

Eon	Era	Period	Epoch	Life-forms
Phanerozoic	Cenozoic	Quaternary	Holocene	
			Pleistocene	
		Neogene	Pliocene	Earliest Homo
			Miocene	
		Paleogene	Oligocene	Apes Extensive grassland
			Eocene	Whales
			Paleocene	Horses Extinction of dinosaurs
	Mesozoic	Cretaceous	Late	Placental mammals
			Early	Flowering plants
		Jurassic	Late	Birds
			Middle	
			Early	Mammals
		Triassic	Late	Dinosaurs
			Middle	
			Early	
	Paleozoic	Permian		Plants with water-conducting vessels
		Carboniferous	Pennsylvanian	Mammal-like reptiles
			Mississippian	Reptiles Amphibians
		Devonian		Woody plants Insects
		Silurian		Vascular plants Fishes with jaws
		Ordovician		Jawless fishes Land plants
		Cambrian		
Proterozoic				Multicellular organisms Eukaryotes
Archaean				Bacteria
Hadean				

Figure 11—Composite Geologic Column

Until fairly recently, it was never suggested that the entire geologic column could be found in one place. Rather, it represented a completed puzzle made from overlapping sequences found in many places around Europe. Today, however, with advances in drilling technology and the global hunt for oil, there are now at least two dozen places around the world where every period of the geologic column is represented in a single stack, *all in the expected order* (Fig. 12).[19]

Figure 12—Locations of sedimentary basins where every period of the Geologic Column, shown in Figure 11, is represented in one place.[20]

Absolute Dating

Identification of different periods of earth history continued through most of the nineteenth century without any knowledge of the actual age of the rock formations or the length of time represented by each period. Only relative relationships were known (e.g., Cambrian rock must be older than Ordovician, which is older than Silurian). Early attempts to determine absolute ages focused primarily on the total age of the earth. Efforts to calculate an age based on observed accumulation rates of marine sediments and the thickness of marine rocks led to widely divergent ages anywhere from one million

19. These locations do not represent uninterrupted deposition through time. Intervals of deposition and erosion are recognized, but preserved intervals of deposition include representative fossils from every geologic period.

20. Adapted from Morton, "The Geologic Column and its implications for the Flood," and Robertson Group, *Stratigraphic Database of Major Sedimentary Basins of the World*.

years to over a billion years. This technique was abandoned after realizing that the rock record included numerous time gaps of uncertain duration where rock had been exposed and eroded.

More promising attempts were made toward the end of the nineteenth century using calculations of salt accumulation in the ocean and the cooling rate of a molten sphere in space. Salt-accumulation estimates by John Joly were based on an assumption that the early ocean was fresh and became increasingly salty as rivers delivered dissolved material over time. Measurements of modern delivery rates by rivers globally led to an estimated age for the earth of approximately 90 million years. What was not recognized was that salt is removed from the ocean by a variety of mechanisms, including adsorption on marine clays and precipitation as thick evaporite sediments in shallow saline seas.

At roughly the same time, Lord Kelvin argued that the age of the earth could be determined by assuming an initial surface temperature of a hot, molten earth, and calculating the length of time for a sphere the size and mass of the earth to cool to its current temperature. His later estimates ranged from 24 to 40 million years. Unknown to Kelvin, the earth has its own heat source resulting in gross underestimates of age. Radioactivity, which generates heat with each decay reaction, was not discovered until 1896.[21]

The significance of radioactivity for geologic studies proved to be much more than the discovery of an internal heat source. When it was further discovered that each radioactive atom decayed at a predictable rate, unaffected by changes in temperature, pressure, or chemical reactions, it presented an unprecedented opportunity to determine the age of some rock types directly. Understanding how the various dating methods work requires an understanding of radioactivity, so we'll start with a brief primer on radioactive decay.

The nucleus of an atom is made up of protons and neutrons. Each possible combination of protons and neutrons is referred to as a *nuclide*. Some combinations are unstable, which makes them radioactive. Over the course of time, a portion of the existing unstable atoms decays. Radioactive decay does not mean atoms disappear; radioactive decay refers to the spontaneous restructuring of the nucleus. There are several ways the nucleus can be restructured, but all ways result in a change in the number of protons and neutrons in the

---

21. The history of early attempts to determine the age of the earth are drawn primarily from Levin, *The Earth Through Time*, 18–19, and Hallam, *Great Geological Controversies*, chap. 4.

nucleus and a release of energy. By changing the number of protons, the atom is changed from one element to another. The newly configured atom is called a *daughter product.*

The degree of radioactivity of any nuclide is determined by the relative instability of the nucleus. As an example, an atom with one proton and two neutrons (tritium: ^3H) is much more unstable than an atom with six protons and eight neutrons (carbon-14: ^{14}C). Tritium is thus more radioactive than ^{14}C, and decays at a much faster rate. The rate of decay for a specific nuclide is predictable, and is described in terms of a *half-life*: the time required for half of a set of atoms to decay.

A rough analogy for half-life can be drawn by filling a box with coins and shaking it. Each time the box is opened, all the coins with heads facing up are removed. If we start with 1,000 coins, we can predict that roughly 500 will turn up as heads when the box is opened. If we remove all the heads and shake again, roughly 250 of the remaining 500 coins will be heads. Each time, roughly half the coins will be removed until so few coins are left that it becomes difficult to predict how they will land. Each time the box is opened represents one half-life. Highly radioactive atoms can be compared to the box of coins shaken and opened to remove all the heads every few minutes. Less radioactive atoms can be compared to a box opened only once every few days, years, and so on.

If the original concentration of a radioactive nuclide is known, it is a simple calculation to determine how many half-lives (how much time) was required for the original concentration to decay to the current concentration.[22] If the original concentration is not known, the current concentration can be measured and compared with the concentration of accumulated daughter products. In ancient rocks, the original concentration is rarely known, so the latter technique is often used.

Many rocks are dated using ^{238}U or ^{235}U, two radioactive varieties of uranium with different half-lives. Both varieties produce unstable daughter products upon decay, which in turn decay into other unstable daughter products, eventually ending at stable varieties of lead (^{238}U decays to ^{206}Pb; ^{235}U decays to ^{207}Pb). A simple ratio of ^{238}U to ^{206}Pb cannot be measured in a whole rock to determine an age, however, for some ^{206}Pb was likely

---

22. The concentration of a radioactive nuclide is generally referred to as an *activity*, measured by counting the number of decay reactions in a given mass of sample over a particular period of time.

to be present at the start. Uranium and lead atoms will coexist and mix in a magma (melted rock), but will separate into different mineral phases during solidification. Uranium-bearing minerals like zircon do not readily incorporate lead into their crystal structure. A freshly solidified zircon is thus nearly lead-free and the radiometric clock "starts ticking." Lead atoms forming from uranium decay are trapped inside the crystal, so that over time, the number of uranium atoms in a mineral decreases and the number of lead atoms increases. A ratio of the two allows calculation of the time since solidification (mineral formation). The smaller the ratio of ^{238}U to ^{206}Pb, the older the material.[23]

Efforts to find the oldest rocks on earth focused on the massive crystalline bedrock typically found in the interior of each continent. The oldest samples have consistently yielded ages of around 4.1 to 4.2 billion years. Meteorites, thought to represent rock material that solidified during the initial formation of the solar system, yield maximum ages near 4.6 billion years. The age of the earth is thus thought to be somewhere in the neighborhood of 4.6 billion years old.[24]

Confidence in a calculated age is enhanced if more than one dating method can be employed to arrive at the same age. This is often possible in a single rock sample using more than one radioactive species with different half-lives, or by measuring the amount of radioactive decay independently of the ratio of parent-to-daughter atoms. Fission-track dating, for example, counts the tracks left behind from individual uranium decay reactions in a mineral compared with the number of radioactive atoms still left.[25] This method circumvents the problem of lead impurities that may have been present at the time of mineral formation.

Determining the age of specific geologic periods, such as the Cambrian or Jurassic, is not as simple as determining the age of a specific rock formation. Most radiometric techniques date the time since a crystal formed from a molten state, but geologic time periods were formulated from studies of fossil-bearing sedimentary rocks. Clastic sedimentary rocks (e.g., sandstone, mudstone, and shale) are made from preexisting

---

23. Young and Stearley, *The Bible, Rocks and Time: Geological Evidence for the Age of the Earth*, 388–443. This is an excellent source for how these methods work, including methods to account for complicating factors, such as sampled minerals that may have crystallized with some lead already present.
24. Levin, *The Earth Through Time*, 29.
25. When uranium decays, a high-energy alpha particle is emitted that damages the mineral along its trajectory and leaves a visible track.

mineral grains that have been transported, deposited, and buried. The minerals contained in a sediment are thus older than the age of deposition. Fossil-rich limestone does not share this problem because calcite (the mineral that forms limestone) precipitates directly from the ocean, though calcite does not typically contain sufficient long-lived radioisotopes to enable direct dating. Dating clastic formations requires association with contemporaneous igneous deposits such as volcanic ash or lava. If volcanic ash layers are found interspersed with sediment deposits, the ash layers can be dated and used to bracket the age of sedimentary rock lying between them (Fig. 13).

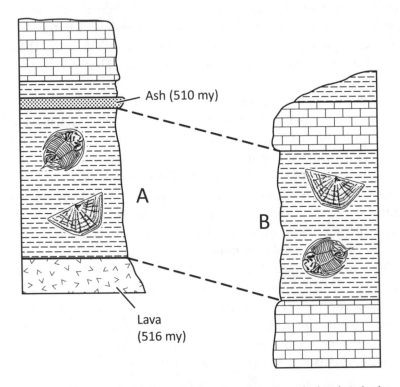

Ash (510 my)

A

B

Lava
(516 my)

Figure 13—The age of a fossil-bearing layer in outcrop A can be bracketed using radioisotopes to date the underlying lava flow and the overlying volcanic ash. If repeated measurements and observations in many other locations demonstrate these particular fossils are always of a particular age, they qualify as *index fossils* and can be used to say the fossil-bearing unit in outcrop B must be the same age, even if not directly radiometrically dated.

The ages and duration of each time interval in the modern geologic column were derived using techniques such as these. Refinements in the dates assigned to particular geologic time divisions are still occasionally made as new igneous/sedimentary rock sequences are discovered and dated.[26]

Testing Theories and Assumptions

Radiometric dating of rocks did more than just assign an age to a particular rock. As dates were acquired from around the world, they allowed testing of whether the *relative-dating* methods had put layers in the correct order of age. Even if decay rates varied in the past, older rocks should still exhibit more decay than younger rocks, and layers thought to be of the same age should exhibit equal degrees of radioactive decay.

Radioactive dates are indeed consistent with the order established by relative-dating methods. Layers assigned to each successively older geologic period contain fewer and fewer radioactive parent atoms, and more and more stable daughter atoms. Even most young-earth advocates today acknowledge that geologists have the *order* correct.[27]

Getting the order right is important, but what about the actual ages? Confidence in radioactive ages requires confidence that decay rates have not varied in the past. Fortunately, scientists don't have to just assume and hope they are right. There are two types of tests that have been carried out to confirm constant decay rates. The first is direct testing of atoms. Exposing radioactive nuclides to extremes of temperature, pressure, chemical reactions, electric fields, and magnetic fields demonstrates negligible changes in the rate of radioactive decay. The second approach is indirect, comparing two unrelated phenomena to determine if consistent results are obtained. To set up one of my favorite examples, we need some background on *plate tectonics*—the science of how continents move.

The crust of the earth is made up of a series of interlocking plates that move in response to convection currents far beneath the surface. The possibility that continents move relative to one another was hotly contested when first proposed by Alfred Wegener in 1915. If you look at the eastern border of North and South America, and the western border of Europe and Africa (Fig. 14), you can see that they look like they fit together, but until the 1960s, no

---

26. McKinney, "The age of things found in the earth."
27. Snelling, "Order in the fossil record"; Morris, *Scientific Creationism*, 2nd ed., 116.

mechanism was known that could move a continent. What convinced many geologists was the discovery of a ridge running down the middle of the Atlantic Ocean, aptly named the *Mid-Atlantic Ridge*, with parallel and matching bands of reversed magnetic orientation on either side. The only way this was possible was if crustal plates on opposite sides of the ridge were being pulled apart from each other, with fresh magma rising and iron-bearing minerals, such as magnetite, solidifying with a preferred orientation aligned to the earth's alternating magnetic field.

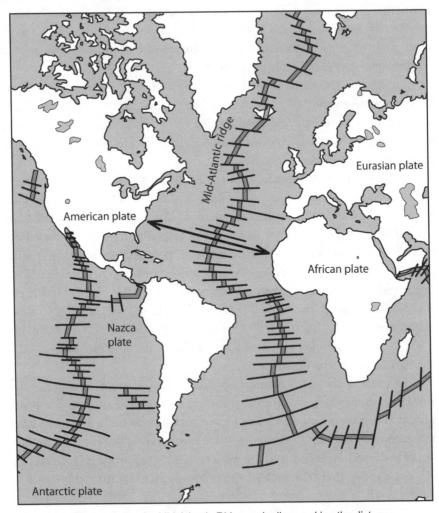

Figure 14—Map showing the Mid-Atlantic Ridge and a line marking the distance between North America and Africa in the direction of plate movement.

Periodic reversals in the earth's magnetic field had already been documented in layered lava flows on the continents, with radiometric dates determined for each reversal. Based on these dates, the oldest ocean crust in the Atlantic at the edges of the continents is roughly 180 million years. The distance between North America and Africa, along the direction of spreading, is about 3,500 miles (220 million inches). Dividing the distance by the time gives an average rate of spreading of 1.2 in/yr. That is an average value, which could have been considerably higher or slower in the past. We can check possible variability using the ages of ocean crust at intermediate distances from the mid-ocean ridge. Doing so yields a surprisingly consistent rate of 1.1 to 1.7 in/yr.[28]

Now for the test. We can measure the rate of movement in *real time* using the same GPS technology that tells you how fast you are driving. In your car, a signal is bounced off satellites to identify your location at a point in time. If your location moves 100 feet in 1 second, a calculation is made dividing distance by time to yield 100 ft/sec, or 68 mi/hr. If radioactive decay was much faster in the past or if plate velocity was much faster in the past (both claimed by young-earth advocates), we have no reason to expect our current *measured* rate to be anywhere near our *calculated* historical rate.

So what do we find? Current measured rates in the Atlantic are about 1.0 in/yr, remarkably close to our calculated range. And this is not an isolated test. The same measurements have been made for the Hawaiian Island chain and submerged Emperor Seamounts, but instead of using the age of magnetic reversals, rock samples from the islands have been directly dated. Using the radiometric ages of islands and seamounts and the distances between them yields faster plate speeds in the Pacific of 2 to 4 in/yr over the last 80 million years. The current measured rate of plate movement at the Hawaiian Islands averages (insert drum roll) … 3 in/yr!

The significance of these comparisons is profound. For radioactive methods to be grossly in error as young-earth advocates claim, it requires that two completely unrelated processes (tectonic-plate movement and radioactive decay) dramatically slowed down over time at exactly the same rate so that measurements today *falsely* appear to confirm the accuracy of radioactive dating methods.[29] And why, exactly, would God do such a thing?

---

28. Müller, et al., "Age, spreading rates, and spreading symmetry of the world's ocean crust."
29. Amazingly, organizations such as Answers in Genesis have made this exact claim, stating that God slowed radioactive decay rates and plate motion in "lockstep." Snelling, "Hawaii's volcanic origins—instant paradise."

9

EVOLUTION AND THE ORIGIN OF LIFE

Prior to the nineteenth century, little was known about the fossil record to suggest that life on earth had ever been different than it is today. Fossils had certainly been found at various times in human history for which no modern representative was known, but these had received little scientific attention.[1] It was not until William Smith and his contemporaries began to systematically catalogue the unique assemblages of fossils found in successive layers in Europe that it became apparent that there were times on this planet when life was remarkably different from today. As more formations were studied and fit into the developing geologic column, it also became apparent that life-forms fossilized in younger strata were increasingly complex and diversified. It is worth noting that strata were not considered younger because they contained more complex fossils; relative age was determined simply by observing the order of layers and noting that sequential deposition means that younger layers are deposited on top of older layers.

Given the apparent progression from simple to complex life-forms in the fossil record, it was inevitable that someone would eventually suggest that earlier life-forms gave rise to later forms. Indeed, though Charles Darwin is commonly known as the father of evolution, the first published record of his theories was presented at a hastily convened meeting in which very similar theories were put forward by a comparatively unknown naturalist named Alfred Wallace. Darwin published *The Origin of Species* the following year in 1859.

---

1. Legends of dragons and mythical beasts may have been inspired by chance discoveries of exposed dinosaur bones: Mayor, *The First Fossil Hunters: Dinosaurs, Mammoths, and Myth in Greek and Roman Times.*

Darwin and Wallace both postulated that change over time was driven by what Darwin termed *natural selection*. Individuals in any population exhibited variations that could increase or decrease the ability of that individual to survive and reproduce. Those traits enhancing the ability to survive resulted in more offspring with those traits, eventually leading to an entire population with the new trait.

Evidence supporting evolution and natural selection at the time was strong in some areas and weak in others. Strong support was found in *homologous* and *vestigial* anatomical studies of modern organisms. As an example of a homologous feature, it was noted that the skeletal structure of whales and bats are strikingly similar for such vastly different organisms. The flipper of a whale and the wing of a bat both have arm, wrist, and finger bones that are nearly the same in number and configuration, differing substantially only in size and shape. If whales and bats were created independently of one another, there is no apparent reason to give a whale indexed finger bones. On the other hand, if whales and bats were created through successive generations from the same stock, it makes sense that both would retain some of the same anatomical features adapted for use in different environments (Fig. 15).

Vestigial features are typically organs which have a necessary function in other animals, but not in the animal with the vestigial organ. We can use whales again as an example. Many whales have olfactory nerves that are not employed for smell, ear muscles with no external ears, a rudimentary pelvis and hind-limb bones, and even fetal hair that is lost before

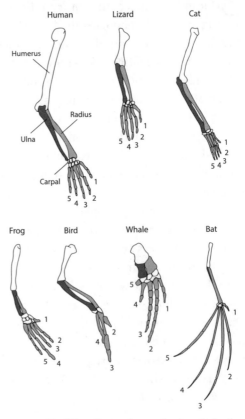

Figure 15—Homologous bone structure in the front limb of a variety of organisms with vastly different forms of locomotion. Similar shading denotes the same bone in each organism.

birth.[2] If the whale descended from terrestrial mammals, it makes sense that some whale species would retain vestiges of organs that had a critical function in their ancestors but are not necessary for survival in modern descendants.

Criticism of evolutionary theory attacked two points of weakness at the time: (1) lack of a known mechanism for causing beneficial changes in the anatomy or function of an organism, and (2) an absence of convincing intermediate or transitional features in the fossil record. Although both of these criticisms are voiced today, neither is justified. The mechanisms controlling mutations continue to be increasingly well understood, and fossil discoveries are now *overflowing* with transitional forms. We will start with the fossil evidence before addressing mechanisms.

FOSSIL ORDER

There is an obvious order of appearance of life-forms in the fossil record (Fig. 11). The oldest fossil-bearing strata contain only remnants of colonies of single-celled organisms that lacked a nucleus. Organisms with a nucleus only appear in younger, overlying layers. Above these we find shelled organisms and jawless fish. In successively younger deposits jawed fish appear, followed by amphibians and nonflowering land plants, then by reptiles and insects, then by dinosaurs, mammals, birds and flowering plants, and finally by primates in the youngest sediments.

Young-earth literature addresses this order, strangely enough, by simultaneously attacking and supporting it. Henry Morris, a founding father of the modern young-earth creationist movement, accused geologists of creating the composite geologic column based on the assumption of evolution,[3] but also confirmed that it is correct in its basic order of life-forms. The confirmation is explicit in his seminal work, *Scientific Creationism*:

> Creationists do not question the general validity of the geologic column, however, at least as an indicator of the *usual* order of deposition of the fossils.[4]

Young-earth leaders today continue in a similar vein of simultaneously attacking the geologic column as a construct of evolutionary assumptions,

2. Sutera, "Origin of whales and the power of independent evidence."
3. Whitcomb and Morris, *The Genesis Flood*, 136.
4. Morris, *Scientific Creationism*, 2nd ed., 116.

yet acknowledging the accuracy of the general order of fossils.[5] Fossils were certainly utilized to piece together a composite history for the earth, but without the claimed evolutionary assumptions. Much of the framework was worked out decades before Darwin's work was published (see dates in Fig. 10). Those developing the geologic column included men who *opposed* Darwin's ideas when they became public, including Darwin's former professor, Adam Sedgwick.[6]

As described earlier, different periods of earth history were identified by observing that certain sets of fossils always appeared above other specific sets of fossils and logically concluding that the underlying fossils were older than those above. It was only after repeating this exercise at myriad outcrops on multiple continents that it became apparent that life did not just change, but that there was a *logical order* in the arrangement of preserved life.

The order is not just in complexity or the appearance of novel functions. There is a logical sequence in the *environments* that were populated over time, with each environment presenting increasing challenges. The progression matches what would be expected if life began as simple one-celled organisms in the ocean and progressed to multicellular forms, still surrounded by water. Then adapting more complex physiology to be able to make forays onto land, followed by still more adaptations that allowed full-time existence out of water. Once terrestrial life was established, further adaptations allowed movement into the air with wings and migration into cold regions with the control of body temperature or the ability to hibernate during winter.

There is also an order to the *geologic setting* reflected in any sequence of fossil-bearing rocks. In many places, layers alternate between marine and terrestrial fossils. A relatively small number of beds contain both terrestrial and marine fossils, but they are not the norm.[7] This fits well with our understanding and observations of plate tectonics. At any given location, jostling plates alternately lift and lower large swaths of land, resulting in regions being shifted above or below sea level. This is not just speculated or assumed. We see it happen in real time today. As one example with human interest, a rupture at a plate boundary near New Zealand in 1931 produced a 7.9

---

5. Patterson, *Evolution Exposed: Earth Science*, chap. 6; Snelling, "Order in the fossil record."
6. Young and Stearley, *The Bible, Rocks, and Time: Geological Evidence for the Age of the Earth*, chap. 4.
7. Note that lakes are considered terrestrial in this context (part of the continental environment), so freshwater fish and turtles in the same layer as waterfowl or wading mammals is not mixing of marine and terrestrial.

earthquake and lifted fifteen square miles of seafloor above water. Today, it is the location of the Hawke's Bay Airport.[8]

Occasional mixtures of marine and terrestrial fossils are expected, and fall into three categories: (1) estuary, lagoon, and tidal-flat environments today have marine and terrestrial creatures coexisting, (2) flooding of rivers near the coast occasionally sweep terrestrial organisms out to sea, and (3) localized tsunamis toss marine organisms up onto shore. Examples of each of these are known in the fossil record, but they are the exception to the general rule.

In contrast, a violent global flood, with waters sweeping across continents, gives a very different expectation. We have firsthand knowledge of what the aftermath of a tsunami looks like. The 2011 tsunami that devastated the coastline of Japan left behind boats and shattered houses, along with ripped up coral and flattened fruit trees in the same layer. Mixed marine and terrestrial debris were swept to sea and carried in currents all the way across the Pacific Ocean. If the fossil record is characterized by a supersized, global rendition of this event, chaotic mixtures of marine and terrestrial should be *the norm*. Young-earth advocates frequently cite a handful of examples of mixed layers as evidence of a global flood, such as an isolated dinosaur in a marine bed, but these are the outliers. The vast majority of fossil-bearing layers fits the expectation of rising and falling land (or rising and falling sea levels) and life adapting to populate new environments.

We could end the description of the fossil order here, but young-earth writers make a secondary set of arguments to insist that the flood provides a better explanation of the fossil order than the evolutionary model. For those unfamiliar with the actual fossil evidence, the explanations can sound quite plausible, so it is worth spending a few pages considering their arguments.

Young-earth advocates acknowledge the basic order of the geologic column, often even accepting the nomenclature of the geologic divisions (such as Cenozoic and Ordovician), but compressed within the timeframe of a recent global flood. Assigning specific portions of the geologic column to the flood turns out to be problematic, for young-earth researchers cannot agree among themselves where the flood deposits end and post-flood deposits start.[9] This is a remarkable observation in its own right, for one would think that the dramatically different conditions during and after a global

---

8. McKinnon, *Bateman New Zealand Historical Atlas*, plate 87; additional information at https://en.wikipedia.org/wiki/1931_Hawke%27s_Bay_earthquake.
9. Johns, "Scriptural Geology, then and now"; Oard, "The geological column is a general flood order with many exceptions."

flood would make that boundary the most obvious demarcation in all of the geologic record. After reviewing dozens of young-earth articles arguing for and against differing positions on where the end of the flood should be, Phil Senter concluded that they had effectively eliminated all possible choices.[10]

One popular young-earth construct assigns the first 150 days of the flood roughly to the Paleozoic Era, the remainder of the flood (receding waters) to the Mesozoic Era, and the post-flood to the Cenozoic Era (Fig. 16).[11] Three mechanisms are suggested for the resulting fossil order (regardless of where the boundaries are specifically drawn): sequential flooding of unique biomes, the ability of more complex animals to flee to higher ground, and sorting of dead animals and plants by flood currents and earthquakes.

Era	Period	Young-Earth Division
Cenozoic	Quaternary	Post-Flood
Cenozoic	Neogene	Post-Flood
Cenozoic	Paleogene	Post-Flood
Mesozoic	Cretaceous	Late Flood
Mesozoic	Jurassic	Late Flood
Mesozoic	Triassic	Late Flood
Paleozoic	Permian Pennsylvanian Mississippian Devonian Silurian Ordovician Cambrian	Early Flood
Proterozoic		Antediluvian
Archaean		Creation Week
Hadean		Creation Week

Figure 16—Alignment of geologic column to a common young-earth view.

10. Senter, "The defeat of flood geology by flood geology."
11. Vail, *Grand Canyon: A Different View*, 36.

Flood Explanation 1: Sequential Burial of Unique Biomes

It is argued that the pre-flood world was divided into land masses with unique classes of organisms. After initial floodwaters buried exclusively marine communities, the first terrestrial organisms to be buried lived on immense, floating continents (analogous to modern floating bogs) with amphibians and nonflowering plants. Rising waters then swept away low-lying continents populated with reptiles, dinosaurs, and pterodactyls. Mammals, birds, and flowering plants were only found at high elevations, so they were the last to be buried.[12]

What is most striking about this model is the number of *classes* of organisms that should be found in the lowest flood layers but that are entirely missing. We should not just expect general marine organisms here, but a host of specific kinds of bottom-dwelling creatures. In deposits from the first weeks of the flood (Cambrian/Ordovician), we should find graveyards of oysters, lobsters, crabs, sand dollars, bottom-dwelling fish like halibut and rays, burrowing organisms like tilefish and weevers, and creatures like eels that inhabit cavities in reefs. At the same time, torrential rains at the start of the flood should have rapidly inundated the river valleys, sending floodwaters racing to the sea. Riverine organisms like trout and bass, beavers and muskrats, water lilies and cattails should also be common in these early flood deposits.

Remarkably, in layers said to represent the first 150 days of violent flooding (Paleozoic), there are no oysters, no crabs, no lobsters, nor even *sand dollars*. There are no river-swept mammals, birds, dinosaurs, or flowering plants. Even *pollen* from flowering plants is entirely absent. In the earliest of these deposits (Cambrian/Ordovician) not a single jawed fish, ray, or eel is found.

Moving up into the Mesozoic (late flood) layers, we finally start to see flowering plants, yet all the large mammals like gazelle, mammoths, bears, horses, cows, goats, and lions are still missing. Waterfowl like ducks and geese might have survived a global inundation, but we find no birds at all—not even ravens or doves (birds specifically identified as being on the ark). Yet birds are found in abundance in Cenozoic (post-flood) fossils.

Touring young-earth speakers frequently show pictures of fossilized boneyards or organisms caught in the midst of eating or giving birth as evidence of a sudden, catastrophic flood.[13] The bulk of these should naturally be found

---

12. Wise, *Faith, Form, and Time: What the Bible Teaches and Science Confirms About Creation and the Age of the Universe*, chap. 12; Snelling, "Order in the fossil record"; Garner, *The New Creationism: Building Scientific Theory on a Biblical Foundation*, 199–203.
13. Snelling, "What are some of the best flood evidences?" 283–85.; Brown, *In the Beginning: Compelling Evidence for Creation and the Flood*, 10–11, 61–62.

in the early-flood layers, when the flood was careening over the continents. Curiously, *none* are found in early-flood layers. In fact, most are not even in late-flood deposits, but *are* found in layers that leading young-earth proponents identify as *post*-flood (Fig. 17).

Figure 17—Fossil of fish eating another fish, Green River Formation, Fossil Butte National Monument. Eocene Epoch (post-flood in most young-earth models). Park Service photo (public domain).[14]

Flood Explanation 2: Animals of Greater Complexity Fled to Higher Ground

Animals of greater complexity are typically more mobile, and could potentially flee from rising floodwaters to higher ground.[15] Overlying layers would thus be expected to contain more complex fossils than underlying layers. If true, we should expect fossils of the more mobile dinosaurs to be found at the same level as elephants and giraffes, and at higher levels than slow mammals like sloths or moles. Sparrows and pterodactyls, both capable of flight, should share the highest layers. Since plants cannot run, flowering and nonflowering plants would be expected to be well mixed in layers at all pre-flood elevations (Fig. 18). Since marine creatures do not benefit from higher ground, marine reptiles and marine mammals should be found mixed, or at least in layers of the same age.

---

14. Young-earth *post*-Flood arguments for the Green River Formation: Whitmore, "Difficulties with a Flood model for the Green River Formation"; Brand, "Wholistic [sic] geology: Geology before, during, and after the biblical flood."
15. Morris, *Scientific Creationism*, 2nd ed., 118–20; Snelling, "Doesn't the order of fossils in the rock record favor long ages?"

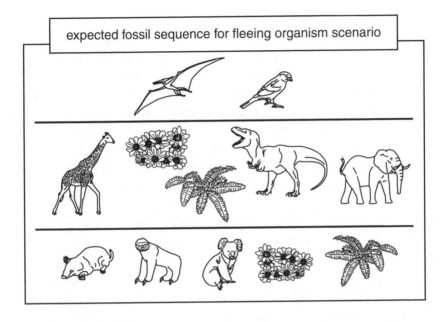

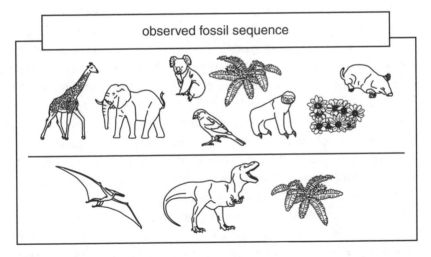

Figure 18—Expected fossil sequence if based on the ability to flee rising waters, and the sequence as actually found. Horizontal lines represent borders between lower/older layers and higher/younger layers.

What is actually observed is far different. In the oldest undisturbed layers containing plant fossils, flowering varieties are completely absent. Not just mostly absent, *completely* absent. Flowering plant fossils only appear in younger layers.

In layers containing dinosaur fossils, a few small mammal fossils can also be found (contradicting the separate biomes argument), but these layers are universally devoid of fossil elephants, giraffes, bears, kangaroos, hippos, gazelles, cows, whales, seals, dolphins, or *any* of the large-mammal species known today. Even sloths appear only in sediments that are above/younger than sediments containing the most agile dinosaurs. Still worse, the supposedly fleeing dinosaurs appear to have stopped to establish nesting grounds, complete with eggs that had time to hatch, not just once, but over and over again in successive layers. Flying reptiles are not mixed with birds, nor are marine reptiles mixed with marine mammals. Birds and mammals are found only in higher/younger layers.

Flood Explanation 3: Hydrodynamic or Vibrational Sorting

It has been observed that vibration of sediment can cause larger particles to migrate upward. It is thus suggested that intense earthquake activity following the flood could have caused buried organisms to be separated into different layers based on their size and density.[16] Following this reasoning, we should find midsized dinosaurs, mammoths, elephants, giraffes, and giant sloths in the same layers, or at least in contemporaneous layers, while flowering and nonflowering plants should remain well mixed since large and small varieties are common for both. The largest of the dinosaurs should be found in some of the uppermost layers (Fig. 19). By the same reasoning, we should not find clean breaks between coarse-grained deposits and overlying fine-grained deposits, since the vibrations should move coarse grains upward.

Hydrodynamic sorting—moving bodies around based on their shape, size, and density—should have nearly the same result as earthquake sorting.[17] The largest organisms might not be expected at the very top, but they should at least be found together. Large, streamlined, air-breathing marine reptiles and mammals should be commonly found in the same layers.

The fossil distribution looks *nothing* like this. The many large mammal varieties, including those alive and extinct, are always found in layers higher/younger than even the most massive dinosaurs. Flowering plants come in all sizes from towering oak trees to tiny duckweed, yet they are completely absent from the older fossil layers. And marine reptiles are always found in lower/older layers than marine mammals of similar size and shape.

---

16. Brown, *In the Beginning*, 169–82.
17. Morris and Morris, *Many Infallible Proofs*, 298–99; Snelling, "Doesn't the order of fossils in the rock record favor long ages?"

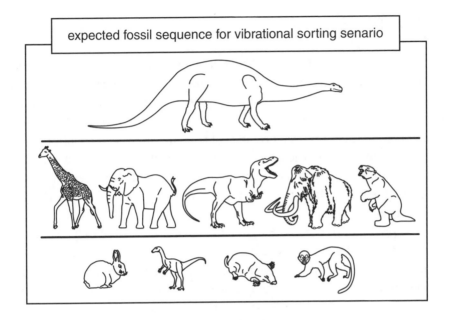

Figure 19—Expected fossil sequence for hydrodynamic or vibrational sorting, and the sequence as actually found. Horizontal lines represent borders between lower/older layers and higher/younger layers.

EXTINCTIONS

The vast majority of life that has existed on earth is now extinct. According to a literalist interpretation of the creation story, God created hundreds of thousands of plant and animal varieties that he promptly allowed to die out within human history, yet without any oral tradition or written record to account for the mass disappearance of so many species. The biblical flood story is *not* an extinction account, for Genesis 7:8–9 clearly says that *all* land-based creatures were represented on the ark (everything that creeps along the ground). The loss of so many species had to occur either shortly after the fall, or shortly after the flood.

The principal young-earth argument is that species were well adapted to environments before the flood, but exited the ark to a vastly changed environment and drastically changing climate that resulted in the failure of many species to survive.[18] Though an omnipotent God is certainly free to allow such an event, it makes little sense for God to have ensured the preservation of all terrestrial creatures *during* the flood only to allow their immediate failure *after* the flood. If we consider the possibility, nonetheless, what would we expect to find in the fossil record?

In pre-flood and flood sediments, evidence of all the types of terrestrial animals (amphibians, reptiles, birds, mammals, and insects) should be found in layers of equivalent age followed by an abrupt disappearance of now extinct organisms at roughly the same time (Fig. 20). The disappearance of dinosaurs, for example, should be concurrent with the disappearance of other extinct organisms such as mastodons and giant amphibians. Populations of organisms surviving for even a few generations in the post-flood environment were likely to survive to the present, meaning that most extinctions would have occurred well within a single century.

What is actually seen is difficult to reconcile with flood explanations. Rather than preserving evidence of a single extinction event, the disappearance of entire classes of organisms occurs at multiple places in the sequence of rock layers, followed by younger layers with brand-new organisms. As an example, as much as 95 percent of the life-forms found in Permian layers never appear again in overlying/younger layers. Not a single dinosaur, mammal, bird, or flowering plant is found in the older layers, but appear in

---

18. Wise and Richardson, *Something from Nothing: Understanding What You Believe About Creation and Why*, 173.

abundance afterwards. In those younger layers that contain remains of thriving dinosaur populations, not a single elk, horse, elephant, whale, seal, bear, or any other large mammal can be found, but these mammals appear in abundance after the disappearance of dinosaurs.

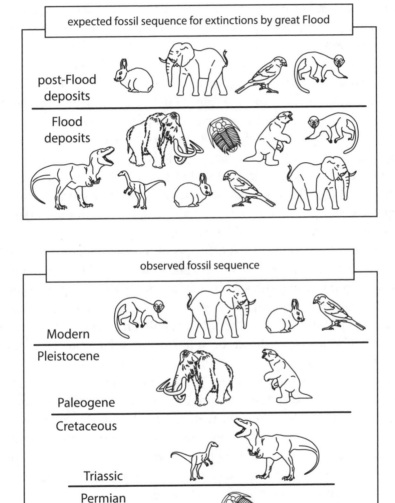

Figure 20—Expected fossil sequence if the majority of extinctions were caused by the Flood, and the fossil sequence as actually found. Horizontal lines represent extinction events at different times. (The Cretaceous-Paleogene line was formerly called the K-T boundary.)

TRANSITIONAL FORMS

If God created life through a long succession of generations, there must have been a plethora of transitional forms: organisms with traits intermediate between ancestor and descendant species. When Darwin published *The Origin of Species*, existing fossil collections provided strong evidence that very different life-forms existed during different periods of earth history, but fossils possessing clearly transitional features between older and younger species were not readily apparent. In the decades following, fossils were indeed found that were believed to represent transitional species, but the numbers remained small and the transitional nature was always contested. The perplexing paucity of transitional forms gave rise to theories such as *punctuated equilibrium*, which is still evolution, but with periods of rapid change interspersed with much longer periods of stability.[19] (Keep in mind a million years can be considered rapid to a geologist.) In this scenario, the vast majority of fossils would represent the longer periods of *stasis* (little or no change), with few transitional forms preserved due to the much shorter time period during which they would have lived.

So what is the current status? Many people remain under the impression that transitional fossils are rare at best, and at worst, based on hypothetical reconstructions starting with a few scattered bone fragments. Antievolutionist books repeatedly demand that "even one" genuinely transitional fossil be produced, and insist that none exist.[20] If evolution happened, even via punctuated equilibrium, there should be at least a few solid examples of transitional forms among our growing fossil collections.

In truth, there are now *thousands* of fossil specimens that are recognized as possessing transitional features, with intermediate specimens sufficient to fill books devoted to describing the richness of transitional forms.[21] This may seem odd, given the impression among many in the church that scientists are still scratching their heads looking for even one solid example in the fossil record. With evolution being such a hot topic in the media, why are these fossils not broadcast from the proverbial rooftops?

---

19. Eldredge and Gould, "Punctuated equilibria: an alternative to phyletic gradualism"; Gould and Eldredge, "Punctuated equilibrium comes of age."
20. Gish, *Evolution: The Fossils Still Say No!*, 42, 108, 112, 114, 128, 130, 148, 159, 188; Sarfati, *Refuting Evolution 2*, 130–43; Huse, *The Collapse of Evolution*, 3rd ed., 86–90; White, "Hasn't evolution been proven true?," 291–95.
21. E.g., Martin, *Missing Links: Evolutionary Concepts and Transitions Through Time*; Prothero, *Evolution: What the Fossils Say and Why It Matters*.

I believe the primary reason for the disconnect is that most people (not just young-earth believers) have expectations that are wedded to an outdated model of evolution. The outdated understanding of evolution is that adaptations giving rise to a new class of organisms happen in a single population through time. With this understanding, fossils that are argued to be transitional should fit in a lineage of direct ancestors between old and new. Subsequent fossil discoveries should begin to fill in gaps, moving toward a species-by-species reconstruction of the evolutionary pathway. If a fossil organism is determined not to be a direct ancestor of a modern organism, it is disqualified as a transitional form and, some would argue, no longer evidence for evolution.

In this light, consider the classic and much argued *Archaeopteryx*, a reptilian bird first discovered in Germany in 1861 (Fig. 21). *Archaeopteryx* fossils possess clearly reptilian features such as a long bony tail, conical teeth in a bony jaw, belly ribs (gastralia), and three separate clawed digits on each forearm, yet also clearly birdlike features such as a flexible wrist, a wishbone, and asymmetrical feathers capable of at least rudimentary flight. Notable features of modern birds missing in *Archaeopteryx* include alula feathers at the wing extremities that enhance flying skill, a fully opposable back toe, and a distinct keel on the sternum where flight muscles attach.[22] While *Archaeopteryx* was immediately touted as transitional, it was eventually thought to be on an evolutionary side branch, not a direct ancestor of modern birds. For one, older fossils were discovered that were *more* birdlike than *Archaeopteryx*, placing *Archaeopteryx* in the wrong evolutionary order for being a direct link between dinosaurs and birds. According to the popular view, it was dethroned from its transitional perch.[23]

A wealth of fossil discoveries beginning in the 1990s has blown this model out of the water. The built-in (God-given) propensity for life to adapt is far greater than once imagined. The expanding trove of fossils is revealing a consistent and repeated pattern of adaptations that do not appear in just one population, but across multiple related populations over a constrained interval of time. The evidence increasingly suggests that if one species has a body plan and underlying genetic structure that can give rise to a novel and beneficial adaptation, other closely related species with a similar genetic foundation

---

22. Martin, *Missing Links*, chap. 7; Kennedy, "Solnhofen limestone: home of *Archaeopteryx*"; Nedin, "All about *Archaeopteryx*"; Prothero, *Evolution*, 276–89.
23. Sample, "'Oldest bird' *Archaeopteryx* knocked off its perch in controversial new study."

are likely to manifest similar changes, resulting in a plethora of "cousin-species" with overlapping adaptive features or traits.[24] The result is that we now have abundant evidence of the intermediate features that accompanied the transition from one major class of organism to another, while at the same time, virtually no ability to precisely identify which of the many cousin-species were the direct ancestors of modern organisms.

Figure 21—Skeleton of *Archaeopteryx* (left) compared to a modern dove (right). Note the differences in the jaw/beak, forearms, tail, ribs, and sternum/keel.[25] Artist rendering of a living *Archaeopteryx* is based on fossilized feather imprints.[26] Antievolutionists dismiss *Archaeopteryx* as "just a bird," which is hard to justify when comparing its skeleton with the adjacent bird skeleton.[27]

If this sounds odd (or slippery), imagine a photo of a family reunion of Irish redheads. An outside observer could readily identify the shared origin of the individuals of this group, with all exhibiting variations of pale complexion, freckles, and vibrant hair. One could even pick out a child and reasonably argue there is a good chance that the photo includes the child's mother and possibly a grandmother or two. But now try to identify the child's actual ancestors (mother and grandmothers). This is probably not possible without tracking down everyone in the photo for a DNA test. The same principle is at work in a

---

24. *Cousin-species* is not a formal term. It is my nontechnical term for closely related species alive at the same time. Paleontologists use terms like *clade*, *sister taxa*, and *collateral ancestors*: Prothero, *Evolution*, 281.
25. *Archaeopteryx* skeleton drawing adapted from Prothero, *Evolution*, Fig. 12.9.
26. Romanes, *Darwin, and After Darwin*, 172.
27. Thomas, "Archaeopteryx is a bird ... again."

sampling of fossil cousins. Shared traits speak convincingly of a common ancestry, but picking out the exact lineage is a much more challenging task.

To illustrate the richness of transitional forms, I will highlight three
purported transitions: dinosaurs to birds, reptiles to mammals, and terrestrial
mammals to marine whales.

Dinosaurs to Birds

Theropod dinosaurs were a group of bipedal, agile, carnivorous dinosaurs
that first appeared about 230 million years ago. Early theropods had hollow,
thin-walled bones, sharp recurved teeth (arching backward) in a bony jaw,
three main fingers on the front limbs (fourth and fifth digits reduced), three
weight-bearing toes (first and fifth digits reduced), claws on each finger and
toe, belly ribs (gastralia), and a long, bony tail.

The earliest essentially modern birds first appeared 130 million years
ago. Some of the unique characteristics, relative to early theropods, include a
beak (not a bony jaw), no teeth, collarbones fused into wishbone (furcula), a
more flexible wrist (semilunate carpal), two fused finger bones and one shortened "thumb" (alula, allows more controlled flight), a short, fused tailbone
(pygostyle, anchors tail feathers), ribs that overlap, an enlarged sternum (keel,
anchors flight muscles), only four digits on the feet with digit 1 shortened and
reversed into an opposable toe (hallux, allows gripping a perch), and a wide
variety of feather types. Flight feathers are asymmetrical, with a hook and
barb structure that prevents separation while flying.

In the 100 million years between the theropods and first modern birds,
an amazing array of intermediate features is manifest in the fossil record.
The earliest feathers so far discovered date to roughly 160 million years ago,
followed by many variations in structure that provide a glimpse into the
likely steps of feather evolution, including single filaments, downy plumes,
and symmetrical feathers on clearly theropod dinosaurs.[28] Front limbs are
found in various stages of fused finger bones with reduced or missing claws.
Some fossils have a wishbone and flexible wrist, while also having teeth and
a long, bony tail. Later fossils exhibit an array of increasingly birdlike
features including increasing fusion of lower back vertebrae with the pelvis,
more porous vertebrae, smaller shinbone (fibula), fusion of tailbones to

---

28. Examples include *Sinosauropteryx, Protarchaeopteryx, Sinornithosaurus, Caudipteryx,*
    Beipiaosaurus, Microraptor. Prothero, *Evolution,* 283.

form the pygostyle, loss of teeth, fusion of finger bones, loss of belly ribs, enlarged bony keel, and alula.[29]

An example of the progression of the front limb is shown in Figure 22. The specific species shown are probably not in a direct ancestral lineage (note one is *Archaeopteryx*), but they are nonetheless representative of the adaptations that were occurring during this period of earth history—a period that falls right where expected if dinosaurs gave rise to birds. If it seems hard to believe that forelimbs could morph in this fashion over multiple generations, consider the fact that the South American hoatzin exhibits analogous morphological changes *within the same bird* as it develops from juvenile to adult.

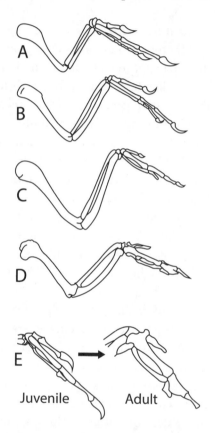

Young-earth proponents point out supposed out-of-order ages for transitional fossils to disqualify them as genuine transitional forms. To understand why this is no longer a valid argument, consider an idealized family tree with a focus on feather development (Fig. 23). Subgroups among a population of nonfeathered theropod dinosaurs begin to appear with simple hairlike feathers. Subgroups then begin adapting independently in various ways, with multiple appearances of different feather types, some lineages leading to asymmetrical flight feathers and other lineages dying out.

Figure 22—Forelimbs of (A) *Ornitholestes*, a theropod dinosaur, (B) *Archaeopteryx*, (C) *Sinornis*, and (D) *Dendragapus* (modern grouse). (E) Morphological changes between juvenile and adult digits of the modern South American hoatzin.[30]

29. Examples of fossils with a mosaic of dinosaur-bird traits (in approximate order of exhibiting more birdlike traits): Rahonavis, Confuciusornis, Iberomesornis, Sinornis, Gobipteryx, Enantiornis, Vorona, Patagopteryx, Hesperornis, Ichthyornis. Prothero, *Evolution*, 285–86.
30. Adapted from Carroll, *Vertebrate Paleontology and Evolution*, 340.

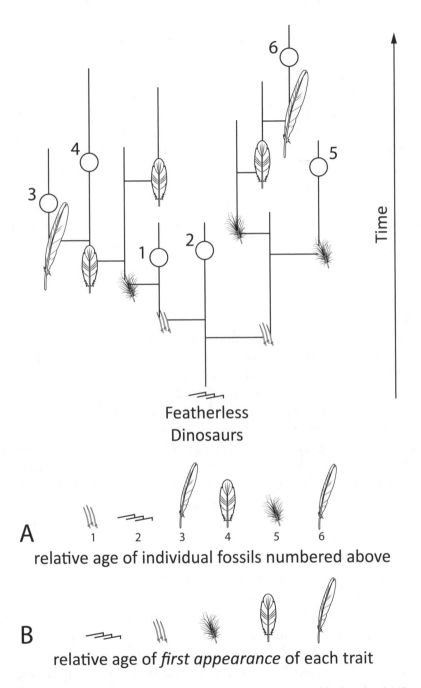

Figure 23—Idealized lineages showing simultaneous adaptations of feathers in related populations, starting with a single population of theropod dinosaurs. Numbers in sequence A match the numbers in the lineage diagram above. See text for discussion.

Now suppose that we have just a few individual fossil specimens, shown in Figure 23 as numbered circles. If arranging the fossil feathers by age (sequence A), they seem out of order for an evolutionary explanation. As more fossils are discovered, however, three important observations are made. (1) The transitions are all occurring within a narrow window between the first appearance of theropod dinosaurs and the first appearance of modern birds. (2) Less derived populations (those retaining more theropod features) did not immediately die off. They continued to live alongside their more derived (more birdlike) cousins, resulting in mixing of organisms with greater or lesser adaptations. (3) With additional fossil discoveries, the *first* appearances of types of feathers fall increasingly in the expected order (sequence B).

Reptiles to Mammals

We could stop with birds, but the claim that there are no transitional fossils is made so frequently and with such apparent confidence that it is important to demonstrate that the birdlike dinosaurs are not a fluke of the fossil record. There are many other examples of well-documented major transitions. One that has actually been known for decades is the reptile-to-mammal transition.

The first reptiles appear in rocks dated to 320 million years ago. Some characteristic features include a wide body stance with legs extending to the sides, undifferentiated teeth, a lower jaw made of at least four bones, a single ear bone, birth from eggs, skin with scales, and a three-chambered heart. The earliest mammals appeared 160 million years ago. Features unique from reptiles include legs directly beneath the body, specialized teeth (like canines and molars), a different jaw joint, a lower jaw made of a single bone, three middle-ear bones, live birth, skin with hair, a four-chambered heart, and mammary glands.

Hearts and mammary glands do not fossilize easily, but there is a wealth of fossil evidence for the transition from reptiles to mammals in fossilized skeletons. These are the early synapsids, often referred to as "mammal-like reptiles," first appearing 240 million years ago between the first appearances of reptiles and true mammals. As with dinosaurs, adaptations appeared in multiple cousin-species at overlapping times, expressing varying combinations of leg position, teeth specialization, and shifting jaw structure. Of particular note, a stepwise sequence is found in the lower jaw with the front-most bone growing larger and the other bones diminishing in size to their current position as inner-ear bones in mammals (Fig.

24).[31] Jaw hinges in reptiles can be seen in transition to a distinctly different mammalian hinge, with some fossils possessing both hinging mechanisms at the same time (this sounds less improbable when realizing snakes have a dual hinging mechanism today). Teeth transition from a standard reptilian conical shape to the variable mammalian shapes (e.g., cusped molars, serrated cutting teeth, and incisors). In successive species, a small opening behind the eye socket of reptiles can be seen growing in size and merging with the eye socket to form the characteristic cheekbone of mammals.

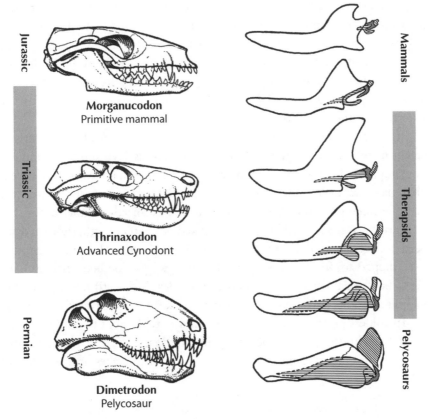

Figure 24—Generalized diagrams showing the transition of bones in the lower jaw of reptiles (synapsids) to a configuration found in mammals (from Prothero, 2007, *Evolution: What the Fossils Say and Why it Matters*, Columbia University Press, pg 277; used with permission).

---

31. Inner-ear bones found in a transitional position in an early mammal (*Yanoconodon allini*): Luo et al., "A new eutriconodont mammal and evolutionary development in early mammals"; Perkins, "Catching evolution in the act."

The positioning of the legs likewise migrates from the outward-protruding stance of reptiles to a mammalian positioning under the body.[32]

In any illustration of the transitions, the species shown are not necessarily ancestral to one another, but are nonetheless representative of the types of adaptations appearing in related populations. The *first* appearance of many of the traits found in the mammal-like reptiles also fits with the expected evolutionary sequence.

Terrestrial Mammals to Marine Whales

Perhaps the most audacious of all evolutionary claims is that a terrestrial quadruped—a mammal with four legs and a wolflike body—took to the water and, over many generations, became a whale. Not just one species of whale. *All* of them—toothed whales, baleen whales, killer whales, unicorn-horned narwhals, dolphins, and porpoises. One hardly needs to list the characteristics distinguishing terrestrial and marine mammals, but we will follow the pattern set in the previous examples.

The first mammals appeared 160 million years ago, with characteristics already mentioned in the previous section. The first whales belonging to modern groups appeared around 36 million years ago. Unique characteristics relative to other mammals include hearing that channels vibrations from the jaw to the ear, a unique configuration of the tympanic bulla (specialized chamber in the skull for hearing), a streamlined body, an elongated head and mouth, shortened and fused neck vertebrae, flukes on the tail, nostrils on the top of the cranium (blowhole), flippers for front legs, and no external back legs. Toothed whales (Odontoceti) have sonar capabilities, and baleen whales (Mysticeti) feed by straining out krill and other small marine life using hairlike oral fibers (instead of teeth).

The oldest proto-whale fossils are found in rocks about 50 million years old. In that window between 50 and 36 million years ago, transitional features are found in dozens of different cousin-species (62 species and counting).[33]

---

32. A continuum of skeletal features can be seen starting with the fully reptilian *Hylonomus* of lower Middle Pennsylvanian age, through the successively younger *Archaothyris*, *Haptodus*, *Sphenacodon*, *Eoarctops*, *Pristerognathus*, *Procynosuchus*, *Thrinaxodon*, *Probainognathus*, and *Morganucodon*, to the fully mammalian *Amphitherium* and *Asioryctes* of upper Cretaceous age. (Synapsids with dual jaw hinge: *Sinoconodon* and *Morganucodon*): Cuffey, "The fossil record: Evolution or 'scientific creation'"; Hopson, "The mammal-like reptiles: A study of transitional fossils."
33. Ryan Bebej, a paleontologist at Calvin University, has compiled a list of identified and published species. Example genera can be found in Marx, Lambert, and Uhen, *Cetacean Paleobiology*, and Uhen, "The origin(s) of whales."

Various species have additional vertebrae extending the body length, elongated heads, detached pelvises, smaller hind legs, shortened necks with varying degrees of fused vertebrae, and nostrils positioned farther and farther up on the cranium. Baleen feeding was a later adaptation, with some intermediate fossil species going through a suction feeding stage with neither teeth nor baleen, and some possibly possessing teeth and baleen at the same time. Suppressed DNA for tooth building is still present in modern baleen whales.[34]

Figures 25 and 26 show abbreviated sequences of transitional fossils leading to modern whales. Figure 25 focuses on fossils with well-preserved skulls, used here to draw attention to the stepwise migration of the nostrils from the end of the snout to the position of a modern blowhole. Figure 26 shows fossils with more of their skeleton preserved. Looking at the earliest proto-whales, one could be forgiven for wondering if a few terrestrial mammals were arbitrarily selected as so-called transitional fossils. Significantly, all have the unique configuration of the tympanic bulla that is found *only* in whales today. *Pakicetus*, the oldest known proto-whale, lived in a coastal environment, with a cranium and body plan well suited for catching fish in shallow waters (Fig. 27). The first appearance of the specialized tympanic bulla in a semiaquatic mammal like *Pakicetus* is likely an adaptation that resulted in improved hearing in water, leading to subsequent generations with still more adaptations for life beneath the waves. Other remarkable intermediate features from these examples include the greatly reduced hind limbs of *Dorudon* detached from the vertebrae, and the paddle-shaped hind limbs of *Maiacetus* and *Rodhocetus* with digits that end with tiny *hooves*.[35]

If 14 million years (or less) seems like too short a period of time to transition between a wolflike creature to a whale, it doesn't make the sixty transitional fossil species go away. They display the full range of transitional features and lie in sediments of the expected age if intermediate between first mammals and first modern whales.[36]

---

34. Peredo, Pyenson, Marshall, and Uhen, "Tooth loss precedes the origin of baleen in whales"; Deméré, McGowen, Berta, and Gatesy, "Morphological and molecular evidence for a stepwise evolutionary transition from teeth to baleen in Mysticete whales."

35. Yet another proto-whale with tiny hooves, *Peregocetus pacificus*, was reported in 2019: Lambert et al., "An amphibious whale from the Middle Eocene of Peru reveals early South Pacific dispersal of quadrupedal cetaceans."

36. Much more can be said about these fossils also being in the expected *geologic environments* and *paleogeographic settings* if evolution actually occurred.

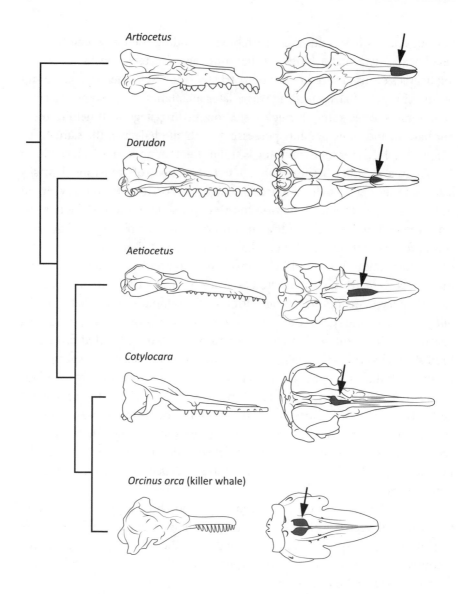

Figure 25—Skulls of proto-whales and a modern killer whale. Arrows point to the position of the nostrils (blowhole).[37]

37. Drawings adapted from: Gingerich et al., "Origin of whales from early artiodactyls: hands and feet of Eocene Protocetidae from Pakistan" (*Artiocetus*); Uhen, "The origin(s) of whales" (*Dorudon*); Barnes et al., "Classification and distribution of Oligocene Aetiocetidae (Mammalia; Cetacea; Mysticeti) from western North America and Japan" (*Aetiocetus*); Geisler et al., "A new fossil species supports an early origin for toothed whale echolocation" (*Cotylocara*); Orca bone atlas, https://ptmsc.org/boneatlas (killer whale).

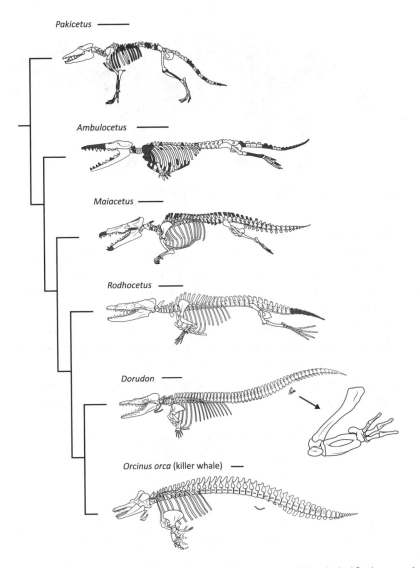

Pakicetus ——————

Ambulocetus ——————

Maiacetus ——————

Rodhocetus ——————

Dorudon ——————

Orcinus orca (killer whale) ——

Figure 26—Transitional features of proto-whales and a modern killer whale (*Orcinus orca*). Shaded bones are inferred (missing in fossils). Scale bar after each name is 1 ft. The tiny hind limb of *Dorudon* is enlarged, showing all the bone structure of a complete leg detached from the vertebrae.[38]

---

38. Drawings adapted from: Thewissen, *The Walking Whales: From Land to Water in Eight Million Years* (*Pakicetus* and *Ambulocetus*); Gingerich et al., "New protocetid whale from the middle Eocene of Pakistan: birth on land, precocial development, and sexual dimorphism" (*Maiacetus* and *Dorudon*); Gingerich et al. "Origin of whales from early artiodactyls: hands and feet of Eocene Protocetidae from Pakistan" (*Rodhocetus*); Orca bone atlas, https://ptmsc.org/boneatlas (killer whale).

Figure 27—Artist rendition of Pakicetus. Illustrator: Roman Yevseyev. Used with permission.

Transitions and Timing

As a closing note on transitional fossils, I will revisit the timing and position in the geologic column. In each of the examples, the ages of the earliest transitional fossils fall exactly where expected if one class of organisms evolved into another. Figure 28 shows parallel timelines for the three examples. The first birdlike dinosaurs appear between the first dinosaurs and the first modern birds. The first mammal-like reptiles appear between the first reptiles and the first true mammals. And the first proto-whales appear between the first mammals and the first modern whales. Why would God allow such an order, over and over again, if he was not actively fashioning new creatures from old?

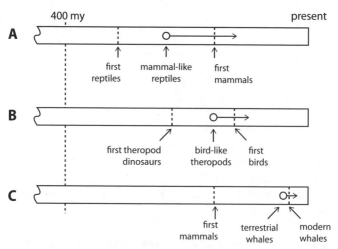

Figure 28—Timelines for transitions of (A) dinosaurs to birds, (B) reptiles to mammals, and (C) terrestrial mammals to whales. Circles designate the first appearance of fossils with transitional features. Horizontal arrows represent the approximate time of existence of creatures that continued to display intermediate features.

MECHANISMS

At the time when *The Origin of Species* was published, there was no knowledge of genetics or DNA, so any proposed mechanisms were highly speculative. With the discovery of Gregor Mendel's work on genetics and the later discovery of DNA by Watson and Crick,[39] it was finally possible to propose a mechanism. Mutations in the genetic code could, in theory, result in a new function or trait that could be passed on to offspring. Acceptance of mutations as a mechanism for biological change was limited, at least among the general populace, because recognizable mutations appeared to be uniformly deleterious. The rare beneficial mutation seemed too improbable to occur with enough frequency to account for the vast changes required by evolutionary theory.

Our understanding of molecular genetics has advanced light-years in the last few decades, and advances continue at a rate that ensures that descriptions and explanations provided today will be only a small part of the explanation tomorrow. Mutations remain part of the vocabulary, but with a very different understanding. Old ideas of external forces—such as radioactivity or ultraviolet rays—causing damage to DNA that results in an occasional improvement have been largely abandoned. Instead, it is becoming increasingly apparent that change is built into the very design of DNA, and occurs by several different processes.[40]

DNA is the programming from which organs are constructed, physiochemical processes are regulated, and instinctive behaviors arise. The information is written in a code made up of a series of four different molecules, called *bases*, in an exact sequence. The sequence is often compared to a computer code, where a series of ones and zeros in a precise order can be used to convey information, send signals to initiate specific actions, and respond to external input. The entire DNA sequence is not used at all times, but sections are periodically accessed based on the physiochemical environment in and around a cell, and the coding instructions. The significance of any changes to this code will depend on how and when the code is accessed.

---

39. Gregor Mendel's work was not widely read or accepted when first published in 1866. Acceptance required rediscovery of his work many years later in 1900.
40. Those claiming there is no mechanism focus on what we don't know concerning the details of how changes are implemented and then declare it cannot happen by natural means, e.g., Matti Leisola, "Evolution: A story without a mechanism"; Tyler, "Evidence from embryology challenges evolutionary theory."

One way that the DNA code can change is through random copying errors during cell division. When a cell divides, the DNA splits and an exact copy of each side is made for the new cells. Or at least an *almost* exact copy. With millions of bases to copy, and millions of cells dividing, it is inevitable that copying errors occur. The smallest error is a change at a single point where one base is substituted for another.

Here is where our familiarity with computer codes actually gets in the way of our understanding of genetic change. Our experience with computers conditions us to think that any random change to a software code will cause the program to fail, or at least will introduce glitches that will interfere with its proper function. But DNA turns out to be much more pliable. The same function can be carried out by more than one variation of base pairs. This is readily apparent by looking at the same genes in different species. Genes found in the same place on chromosomes that carry out the same basic function are nearly the same in different species, but frequently vary by several base pairs.[41] At the very least, this tells us that there are multiple configurations of DNA that can potentially give rise to a particular function. This means there is room for variation without harm, and possibly for novel development.

Another way DNA can change is by copying a sequence of base pairs twice. In some cases, the entire genome may be replicated, with each successive generation faithfully reproducing double the genetic coding. Entire genome duplication is not just a hypothesized occurrence. There are many closely related species with identifiable duplications in the genome of one species. Consider frogs. One can imagine that the size of the genome required to produce a frog should not vary greatly from one frog species to the next. But the size of the largest known frog genome, that of the ornate horned frog (*Ceratophrys ornata*) from Argentina, is seven times larger than the genome of its remarkably similar-looking cousin, the Columbian horned frog (*Ceratophrys calcarata*), and *fourteen times* larger than that of the frog with the smallest recorded genome, the Australian ornate burrowing frog (*Platyplectrum ornatum*).[42] The entire genome of the ornate horned frog was replicated multiple times in one or more horned-frog ancestors, and the redundant DNA passed on to each subsequent generation.

---

41. Venema and McKnight, *Adam and the Genome: Reading Scripture after Genetic Science*, 24–33.
42. Gregory, *Animal Genome Size Database*, http://www.genomesize.com.

A doubly copied sequence of DNA is a veritable playground for genetic experimentation without risk of disabling a critical gene. We can find direct evidence of such events from our growing database of sequenced genomes, such as the highly studied fruit fly (genus *Drosophila*). Among three species of fruit flies (*D. melanogaster, D. sechellia, D. simulans*), all have the same gene call Éclair. Only *D. melanogaster*, however, has an extra gene right next door (called *p24-2*) that looks nearly the same as Éclair. The other two flies exist fine without the extra gene, yet *D. melanogaster* dies without it. At some point in the ancestry of this fly, a mutation not only doubled this particular gene, but its current necessity means subsequent mutations eventually resulted in a novel function that that fly now depends on.[43]

A third way DNA can be altered is by the insertion of genetic code from one organism directly into the DNA of another. This is most common where a single-celled organism or virus invades a foreign cell. There are many sections of DNA even within the human genome that are direct matches with known viruses, some that may harken back to historical viral plagues.[44]

Finally, and perhaps most amazing, there are DNA sequences, called *mutator genes*, where the primary function appears to be to create changes in other sections of the DNA sequence. It may seem odd that an organism would contain programmed instructions to change its own operational code, but it is features like this that make it possible for subsequent generations of a population to survive in rapidly changing environments. This is precisely what made the AIDS virus so deadly.[45] Rapid, programmed mutation of the AIDS virus results in a suite of closely related offspring. The adaptations may be fatal to most of the offspring, but a few end up having the right configuration to circumvent the latest drug. The new strain rapidly reproduces to repopulate its human microenvironment. Life appears designed with change in mind.

Realizing all this, it may still seem that mutations that enable drug resistance in bacteria remain insufficient to turn a dinosaur into a bird, but that is likely due to the misperception that alterations to the DNA need to somehow transpose an entire arm-building sequence into an entirely new wing-building sequence. The actual changes are not so revolutionary. The protein-building

---

43. Chen, Zhang, and Long, "New genes in *Drosophila* quickly become essential"; described in more detail in Venema and McKnight, *Adam and the Genome*, 70–77.
44. Wildschuttea et al., "Discovery of unfixed endogenous retrovirus insertions in diverse human populations."
45. Many viruses use RNA rather than DNA, but the same principles of mutation and adaptation apply.

instructions for arm and wing production are largely the same. What differs is the regulation of those protein-building sequences: regulation governing the timing, duration, and orientation of bone and tissue construction. Subtle changes in these regulatory genes may change the length or thickness of a bone, the position of a joint, whether individual digits developing in a fetus remain separate or fuse, or whether coding for a particular feature may be suppressed altogether. Successive changes in the regulatory genes over multiple generations could result in large changes in body form enabling improved function in new environments or an ability to take advantage of an open niche.

Figure 29—Female humpback whale captured in 1920 with rudimentary hind legs (bones shown on facing page). The appendage in the photo extends 4.2 ft from the body of the whale.[46]

Evidence of genetic code existing for features that are suppressed is readily evident in examples such as a humpback whale discovered with partially developed external hind legs. Young-earth literature is remarkably quiet on this subject, and where addressed, generally dismisses such examples as undifferentiated bony growths.[47] Yet the photographs speak for themselves. Figure 29

---

46. Andrews, "A remarkable case of external hind limbs in a humpback whale."
47. Wieland, "The strange tale of the leg on the whale"; Sarfati, *Refuting Evolution*, 77–78.

shows a photograph of a whale with visible appendages over four feet in length.[48] Figure 30 shows the bones dissected from one appendage. A cartilaginous femur and tarsal element, and a bony tibia and metatarsal are easily identified. In this particular whale, a regulatory gene probably failed to suppress coding for legs in the whale DNA.

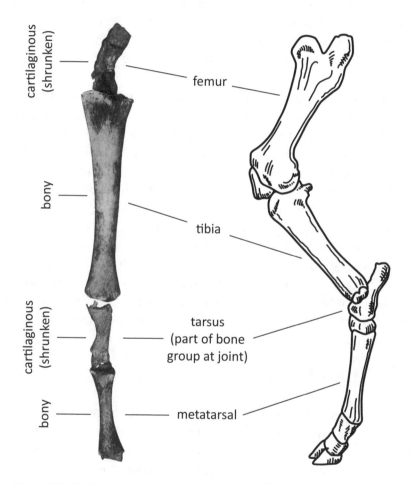

Figure 30—Hind appendage from the humpback whale shown in Fig. 29. The cartilaginous sections were already shriveled when photographed, and were approximately three times larger when first removed from the whale. A cow's hind leg is drawn to the right of the whale leg for comparison.

48. An example of a sperm whale with external hind limbs is reported in Ogawa and Kamiya, "Case of the Cachalot [sperm whale] with protruded rudimentary hind limb."

Why would coding for legs be in whale DNA at all? If whales descended from ancestors with legs, it makes perfect sense that some residual coding for legs could remain that normally is not activated by the whale's regulatory genes during fetal development. Some argue that if natural selection is really active, suppressed coding should be jettisoned because resources are being wasted on the creation of unused code,[49] but if the suppressed code does not inflict harm on the organism, there is no driving force to get rid of it. Mutations in successive generations within that sequence may ultimately destroy the code, but the organism does not have to get rid of it entirely to thrive.

Residual coding for legs in whales, and the occasional expression of partially formed legs are examples used by atheistic writers as evidence against an intelligent creator.[50] Hearing this, the most typical reaction from religious people is to deny the evidence altogether. But if we stop and think about this, a different reaction should prevail. God, the ultimate Creator, did not just make cookie-cutter creations. He designed life in such a way that his creation would express in a brilliant array of forms, filling every conceivable environmental niche, and even some inconceivable niches where it seems too hot or too caustic. It is as if, imagine this, the Creator knew what he was doing when the master plan was developed. Why should it seem incredible to the Christian that God could implant the seeds of diversity within the very design of life? Imagine the artistry and engineering that can imbue a single cell with the capacity to give rise to the incredible array of life past and life present.

EVOLUTION IN A BOTTLE

Fossil order and a whale with legs may all be consistent with evolutionary theory, but has anyone ever actually *witnessed* evolution of a novel function? With complex organisms that reproduce slowly, truly novel changes in body plan or function can be difficult or impossible to detect over a human lifetime, but what about organisms like bacteria that can reproduce several generations in a single hour? If evolution is real, surely scientists would have observed it inside a flask by now.

---

49. Gish, *Evolution*, 317; Wise, *Faith, Form, and Time*, 129.
50. E.g., Dawkins, *The Blind Watchmaker*, 174 and throughout the book.

In fact, it has been observed—multiple times.[51] A frequently cited example studied a phage-lambda virus that specifically infects *E. coli* bacteria.[52] The virus gains entry using a protein, *J*, that binds with a specific protein, *LamB*, on the surface of many *E. coli*. After binding, a series of additional reactions are required to open up the bacteria for injection of viral DNA that then replicates until the bacterial cell bursts.

The researchers set up experiments where most of the *E. coli* were missing the *LamB* surface protein in order to see if the virus could evolve a new way to attack the bacteria. If no *E. coli* had *LamB*, the viruses died. Keeping a small percentage of *E. coli* with *LamB* allowed the viruses to live and replicate, and potentially develop a novel way to attack the larger population of *E. coli* that *lacked LamB*. Solutions were set up in replicate, with portions of the bacteria-virus mixtures extracted at regular intervals and frozen to preserve a "fossil record" of transitions if something interesting should eventually be found. Not only did the viruses evolve to attack *E. coli* at a different protein site (*OmpF*), the adaptation proved reproducible. In replicate experiments, adaptations arose no less than *twenty-five times*.

Analyses of the genome of viruses in solutions prior to and after adaptation revealed that genetic mutations were required at four separate sites in order to bring about the novel function of binding to OmpF. Viruses with one, two, or three of the mutations did not have the new function. The fact that replicate experiments observed the sequential accumulation of these mutations indicates that each conferred some benefit, which may have been as simple as stronger bonding to the original *LamB* protein. All four were required, however, before binding to a *new protein* site on *E. coli* was possible, giving the virus access to the much larger population of bacteria lacking *LamB*.

In addition to the obvious significance of evolution witnessed in real time, such findings also show that evolution does not require extremely low-probability "all-at-once" mutations at multiple sites. The research demonstrated that sequential accumulation of mutations employed for other purposes eventually led to the novel function. The fact that these mutations were reproducible in separate experiments suggests that the genetic structure of life is *designed* to adapt.

---

51. E.g., Duffy, Burch, and Turner, "Evolution of host specificity drives reproductive isolation among RNA viruses"; Hall, Scanlan, and Buckling, "Bacteria-phage coevolution and the emergence of generalist pathogens"; Blount, Borland, and Lenski, "Historical contingency and the evolution of a key innovation in an experimental population of *Escherichia coli*."

52. Expanded description in Venema and McKnight, *Adam and the Genome*, 78–80; original study: Meyer et al., "Repeatability and contingency in the evolution of a key innovation in Phage Lambda."

ORIGIN OF LIFE

Life in its simplest form is complex. Herein lies the controversy over life's origin. How could it have been possible for a random grouping of nonliving molecules to join in such a way as to initiate the first life-form? The simplest cells contain a protective cell membrane, complex organelles, and genetic information that seemingly defies the odds of any random assembly of nonliving molecules to re-create. There are several theories about how this assembly may have occurred, but there is no proven mechanism currently known. Is this the silver bullet in the heart of evolution?

To answer this, we will look at the big picture first. The belief that life originated from nonliving materials is not derived exclusively from a commitment to materialism (recall that Scripture tells us that the *earth* brought forth life at God's command). Rather, the belief rises from the observation that the earth contains a distinct pattern of life-forms through time. This pattern starts with very simple, single-celled organisms that did not even have a cell nucleus. Given this clear record of developing and adapting life over time, it is logical to believe that there were likely natural (God-ordained) processes at work to bring the simplest life-forms into existence.

So what is known? For one, we do know that the conditions on earth prior to life were considerably different than they are today. We have an oxygen-rich atmosphere now that rapidly attacks cell tissue. Oxygen was largely absent in the early atmosphere. We can tell this by looking at iron oxide deposits in ancient rocks. Iron readily oxidizes in the presence of oxygen and produces reddish colored deposits.[53] We see this routinely in the form of rust. Iron oxides are common in deposits less than about 2.5 billion years in age, but are rare or intermittent in older rocks. The oldest fossils come from rocks more than 3 billion years old.[54] The timing of the appearance of oxygen and the age of the oldest known fossils suggest that the increase in oxygen in the earth's atmosphere was actually produced by these organisms. Photosynthesis produces oxygen as a by-product of using the sun's energy to convert carbon dioxide and water into useable organic molecules. Photosynthesis is common in many single-celled organisms today, including varieties recognized in

---

53. Turner, "The development of the atmosphere," 121–36; Wiechert, "Earth's early atmosphere."
54. Schopf and Packer, "Early Archean (3.3-billion to 3.5-billion-year-old) microfossils from Warrawoona Group, Australia"; Sankaran, "The controversy over early-Archaean microfossils"; Dodd et al., "Evidence for early life in earth's oldest hydrothermal vent precipitates."

some of the most ancient fossils. Stromatolites are communities of single-celled, photosynthetic organisms that continue to exist today.

Organic molecules had a much better chance of staying intact in an oxygen-deficient environment. Simple organic molecules are routinely generated by inorganic processes,[55] though all known processes fall far short of producing even the smallest strand of DNA. This is where probability arguments generally appear. The chances of randomly grouping these organic molecules in such a way to yield the DNA found in even the simplest single-celled organism are said to be profoundly small. If one starts from a soup of dispersed molecules and expects an accidental alignment at one moment to produce functional DNA, the odds would indeed be impossibly small. But no one exploring the origin of life thinks this way. For life to become a possibility, the only thing required is that a single organic molecule begin to replicate in a way that allows infrequent substitutions to be preserved in subsequent replications. These simple molecules do not need to be "alive" in order to replicate.

To understand this conceptually, let's say we have a small variety of simple organic molecules known to be naturally created—we will identify these by the letters A, B, C, and D (Fig. 31). Strong bonds form between A and B molecules, allowing chains of varying length to form (e.g., A-B-A or B-B-A). The same is true for C and D molecules, which also form chains. In this scenario, *weak* bonds form between A and C molecules, and between B and D molecules.

- If a simple chain of A-B-A exists, C and D molecules bumping into the chain will tend to stick in a particular sequence of C, D, C (aligned with A, B, A).

- Strong bonds then form between the aligned C and D molecules, forming a new C-D-C chain when it breaks away from its weak bonds to the A-B-A chain.

- Critically, the same process *can work in reverse*, with an existing C-D-C chain facilitating the generation of a new A-B-A chain. This sets up the basis for self-replication of these paired chains.

---

55. One example of hydrocarbon molecules thought to be generated by inorganic processes is discussed in Perkins, "Seafloor chemistry: Life's building blocks made inorganically."

- Now suppose that at some point in time an extra A group attaches to a simple A-B-A chain to yield A-B-A-A. As C and D groups bump and bond, C-D-C-C molecules are formed that can in turn generate new A-B-A-A molecules.

- If these are easily degraded, the new configurations may eventually be lost. If the new configurations result in stronger bonds more resistant to degradation, then they will persist and increase in numbers.

- With increasing numbers, many different combinations of A, B, C, and D occur, most of which are degraded and disappear, but a small number prove more resistant to degradation and persist.

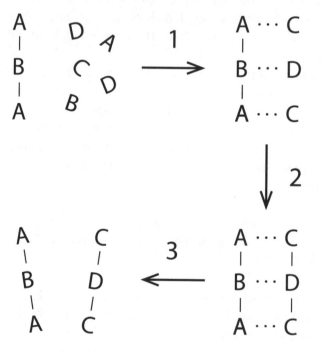

Figure 31—Conceptual example of replicating organic molecules designated by letters A, B, C, and D. Prior to step 1, an ABA molecule floats in solution among other unassociated organic molecules. Step 1: weak bonds form between A and C, and between B and D molecules. Step 2: strong bonds form between the C and D molecules. Step 3: the weak bonds break leaving a new CDC molecule which can in turn make new ABA molecules in a likewise fashion—replication.

From this point forward, a perpetual march toward more and more complex configurations is enabled by the simple principle that any change that increases the ability of the molecule to generate matching molecules before being degraded will result in an increase in the abundance of this variety. Changes that decrease the ability of the molecule to produce replicates before being degraded will result in the eventual (or abrupt) disappearance of this variant.

But how can we go from a replicating molecule to a cell? Cells have so much more than a replicating molecular chain. There is a cell membrane that protects that chain and organelles inside the cell with complex functions. Further, the replicating chain (DNA) does not just reproduce itself, but controls the growth, repair, and function of all the organelles and surrounding membrane. If requiring all this in a single step from replicating organic molecule to fully functioning cell, it does indeed represent an impossible chance combination of atoms. Here again, however, an "all-at-once" step is neither likely nor required.

Continuing our example using combinations of smaller organic molecules with letters A through D, let's say a stable, replicating chain develops with a sequence of 100 A, B, C, and D groups. Rather than always producing a complete replicate, groups often align along shorter sections where they bond and are released. One particular arrangement of groups produces a sticky substance that adheres to and coats portions of the original molecular chain, setting the stage for eventual alteration to a protective barrier, the cell membrane, around the replicating chain. Note that the replicating chain both produces this material and is protected by it. Once a protective shield becomes common, other organic molecules produced by shorter sections of the replicating chain may behave in many different ways, such as filling in certain holes in the membrane (first step in regulating what passes into and out of the membrane) or bonding with other molecules or atoms in potentially beneficial ways when struck by light (first steps of photosynthesis).

If any of this actually happened, one might expect that we could reproduce such behavior in the laboratory. It may well be, however, that the original encounter of molecules leading to the first nonliving, replicating organic molecule was indeed an improbable event that happened only a few times (or even just once) over a period of hundreds of millions of years. If this is true, then it is even more improbable that laboratory experiments, using only approximately known water and atmospheric conditions for the early earth, would produce these same molecules.

But if we still see examples of the first known life-forms like stromatolites alive today, shouldn't we also see examples of these hypothesized replicating, nonliving molecules today? The answer may sound slippery, but a truthful response is both yes and no. No, because these early molecules would have first appeared in an oxygen-deficient atmosphere where they could persist for some time without a protective cell membrane. Once complexity increased to the point of photosynthesis and oxygen accumulated in the atmosphere, less advanced, unprotected molecules still in existence would have been chemically attacked and degraded, leaving only the more advanced, protected forms to further replicate and adapt. On the other hand, there should be some protected forms that fall short of "life" that should still be replicating and found in nature.

In fact, there are many such molecular structures that are candidates. We considered one variety in the previous section. They are known as viruses. Viruses are a thousand times smaller than single-celled organisms such as bacteria and are not considered to be technically alive, yet they are extraordinarily proficient at replicating themselves in ways that keep medical researchers constantly searching for ways to interrupt the process.

10

ORIGIN OF MAN

A mong those who have reconciled their faith and the evolution of life-forms, many remain uncomfortable with the possibility of human evolution. Humans have a unique place in God's kingdom, so surely God's creation of our kind is unique. It is thus worth reminding readers here that the intent of this chapter is not to disprove the Bible. On the contrary, the authority of the Bible was used as the starting point for this book, and scientific theories were laid on a scriptural template to identify any areas of concern. Having noted the remarkable similarity between God's creation of man, "of dust from the ground," and God's creation of animals, "let the earth bring forth," it seems reasonable that what makes humans special is not the manner of creation, but the endowment of a soul and God's choice to focus his love and attention on our humble frame.

COMMON ANCESTRY WITH EARLIER HOMINIDS

Controversy over the evolution of humans typically focuses on the veracity of individual fossil remains, but what is the big picture? Is the theory of human evolution built on a few fragmentary fossil pieces and a strong desire to make them be what scientists want them to be? Even those who accept human evolution are sometimes surprised to learn that there are now fossil remains from over 6,000 different individual creatures that exhibit features intermediate between modern humans and ancient apes.[1] The oldest of these come from Africa and southeastern Europe from layers up to seven million years in age. Fossil remains of the very oldest are fragmentary and

---

1. Richard Potts, director of the Human Origins program at the Smithsonian Institution, personal database.

relatively rare; bones from more recent species are more abundant and often more complete. Fossils of *Australopithecus afarensis*, in sediments three to four million years in age, have been found from more than 300 individuals, corporately covering most of the bones in the species' skeleton. Though more apelike than human, *A. afarensis* had the body plan that made it an obligate biped (always walked upright), and several cranial features that differ from apes. Multiple fossil footprints from the area where *A. afarensis* remains are found show deep heel prints and no handprints, typical for creatures with an upright posture.

Describing the features that distinguish ape from hominid or ancient hominid from modern human is a formidable task because of the existence of many distinct skeletal features that pass unnoticed by most of humanity and the technical jargon employed by specialists. As an example, one of the differences between *A. afarensis* and African apes is that the roof of the supraorbital torus slopes evenly up the frontal squama, rather than being separated by a sulcus. Such descriptions do little to aid most readers in their personal assessment of the evidence. In nontechnical language, a few of the features used to differentiate species include:

- size of jaw relative to skull
- size of canine teeth
- shape of the arch made by the teeth (i.e., do side teeth run parallel or arch outward)
- protrusion of mouth in front of the face
- position and angle of cheekbones
- thickness or existence of brow ridge over the eyes
- slope of the forehead
- size of braincase
- size (or absence) of ridge on top of skull where large jaw muscles attach

More than a dozen different hominid species have now been identified that represent a broad spectrum of transitional forms. Transitions can be seen in a reduction in the protrusion of the face and jaw, a change toward a more vertical slope of the forehead, an increase in the size of the braincase, and a decrease in the size of the brow ridge, the canine teeth, and the cranial ridge where chewing muscles attach. (Species names have intentionally been left off the skulls in Figure 32 to focus attention on the obvious changes rather than on names.) Note that this does not mean that each fossil species represents an ancestor of modern humans. Several of these species existed at the same time, and all but one lineage became extinct.

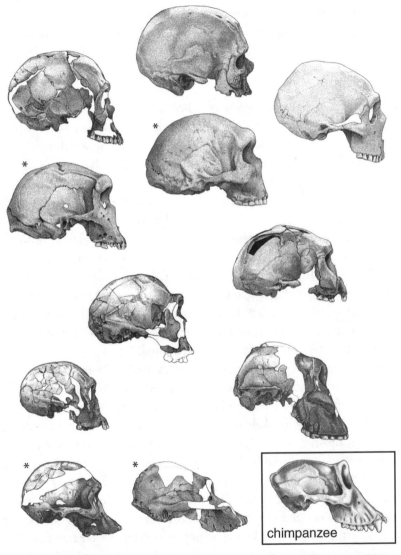

Figure 32—Hominid craniums, positioned in increasing age toward the bottom. White areas depict missing fossil material. Asterisks identify drawings rotated 180° from originals. A modern chimpanzee cranium is shown for comparison. (Hominid skulls from Ian Tattersall, 2009, *The Fossil Trail*, Oxford University Press; used with permission.)

One may argue that the earlier hominids assigned to the genus *Australo-pithecus* or *Paranthropus* are simply extinct apes with coincidentally more humanlike body forms.[2] This could be, but it becomes more difficult to explain away the increasingly humanlike appearance of later forms such as *Homo habilis, ergaster,* and *erectus.* Members of the *Homo* genus have skulls with a clear human likeness due to small canine teeth, a larger braincase, and a more vertically sloped forehead, but retain features that are clearly apelike as well. Features include thick brow ridges, a protruding jaw, and a braincase of intermediate size. These are clearly not extinct apes, yet they are also clearly not what we know as human.

Some accuse paleontologists of fabricating these creatures based on a few bone fragments.[3] In most cases, what is being referred to is a *reconstruction.* Reconstructions of the missing pieces of a skull or skeleton are created using several methods. The first method assumes that the left side looks like the right. Thus, if the left brow ridge is missing on a skull, a left brow ridge is crafted as a mirror image of the right to complete the skull. If both brow ridges are missing, but pieces of the brow ridge from another skull of the same species from the dig site are found, these are used as a model for brow ridges on the reconstruction. In cases where only a few fossil fragments were known, especially during the early history of hominid fossil excavations, reconstructions were more speculative and sometimes inaccurate. Most reconstructions today, however, have sufficient fossil material to eliminate the need for speculation. As a general practice, reconstructed pieces are cast in a different color so the original pieces can be easily differentiated.

Of the hominids overlapping in time with modern humans, the most well known are the Neanderthals (*Homo neanderthalensis*). These hominids coexisted with *Homo sapiens* for several thousand years throughout Europe and the Middle East. Neanderthal skeletons are very similar to those of modern humans, but differ in distinct ways (Figs. 33 and 34). As a few examples, Neanderthal features include a longer skull (front to back), a more sloping forehead, a jutting forward of the nose and jaw, a small but distinct bulge at the back of the skull, a thick brow ridge, no chin, a wider nasal opening, unique dimensions of the pelvis and hip joints, and proportionally shorter arm and leg bones. When only a few Neanderthal fossils were known, many believed they were humans who had suffered from some deforming disease. This notion was dispelled, however, with

---

2. Gish, *Evolution: The Fossils Still Say No!,* 279; Wise, *Faith, Form, and Time,* 238.
3. Huse, *The Collapse of Evolution,* 3rd ed., chap. 7; Sarfati, *Refuting Evolution 2,* 188.

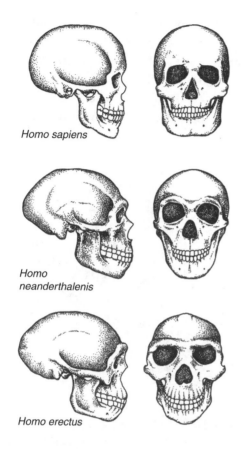

Homo sapiens

Homo neanderthalenis

Homo erectus

Figure 33—Comparison of ancient hominid skulls (lower two pairs) with human skulls (top pair) (from D. R. Prothero, 2007, *Evolution: What the Fossils Say and Why It Matters*, Columbia University Press, pg 341; used with permission).

additional discoveries (now over 300 skeletons) and recognition that habitation sites with multiple skeletons, or layers within a habitation site, contained either Neanderthal or human remains, but not clear mixtures of both together.[4]

The similarities between Neanderthals and modern humans are substantial enough, however, that a long-standing debate ensued over whether the Neanderthals were really a separate species, if they interbred with contemporaneous *Homo sapiens*, or if modern humans evolved from a subpopulation of Neanderthals. The relatively young age of these fossils presents a unique opportunity to link fossil studies directly with genetic analysis. In most genetic studies, only modern organisms can be analyzed because no DNA remains in ancient fossils. Relatedness among living creatures can only be used to *infer* past relationships and evolutionary pathways.

However, Neanderthals lived recently enough that some specimens still contain surviving DNA. It is highly fragmented, but advanced analytical and data-processing methods allow overlapping sequences to be aligned and the original DNA mapped to compare with the DNA of living humans. The results have been intriguing. Current research shows no evidence of

---

4. Martin, *Missing Links: Evolutionary Concepts and Transitions Through Time,* 243–45; Wood and Constantino, "Human origins: life at the top of the tree"; Fagan, *The Journey from Eden: The Peopling of Our World*, chaps. 7 and 11.

interbreeding between sub-Saharan Africans and Neanderthals, but the rest of humanity has 1 to 4 percent Neanderthal DNA. The explanation is that human subpopulations migrating out of Africa encountered established populations of Neanderthals in the Middle East and Europe. The two populations did not merge, but interbreeding was frequent enough to distribute Neanderthal DNA widely through the non-African human population.

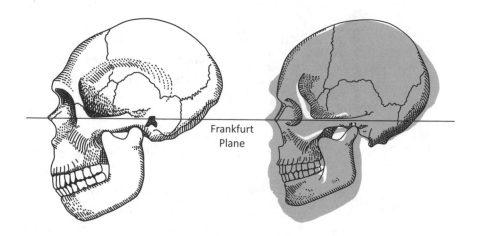

Figure 34—Neanderthal skull (left) and overlay of Neanderthal skull over a human skull (right), drawn at the same scale. The Frankfurt plane is a line from the lower eye socket to the upper margin of the ear canal.

This realization is pertinent for the question of whether humans and Neanderthals were different species or variants within a single species. When a population splits and begins to adapt in different directions, the two populations will remain similar enough that interbreeding is still possible for many generations. During this time, the dividing line between *species* or *subspecies* is fuzzy. Regardless of what Neanderthals are called, their physical characteristics and genetic makeup were clearly distinct from their human neighbors.

Genetic studies now indicate that there were other hominids around at the time and in the same regions that also contributed in small ways to our genetic makeup. DNA from fragmentary bones found in the Denisova Cave in the Altai Mountains in Siberia do not fit neatly into either the Neanderthal or human groups.[5] No one yet knows what these Denisovans looked like, but their DNA shows up in Melanesian and Aboriginal Australian human populations.[6] Fossils have also been found with DNA demonstrating interbreeding between Neanderthals and Denisovans.[7]

Skeptics of human evolution simply declare all these hominids to be humans, with differences in appearance functionally equivalent to differences observed today between a hulking, fair-skinned Dutchman and a petite, dark-skinned African pygmy.[8] The differences are known to be greater than these, however, from genetic, anatomical, and paleocultural studies. Genetic comparisons place common ancestry between Neanderthals, Denisovans, and all living humans well before "Mitochondrial Eve." Anatomical studies note distinct differences in skeletal structure, including cranial differences linked to cognitive function. Neanderthal skulls exhibit enhanced brain development in areas of visual acuity, but reduced development of areas thought to be critical to self-awareness and abstract thought.[9] Archaeological evidence yields similar conclusions. In spite of coexisting in the same regions, Neanderthals never picked up on the advanced toolmaking skills, jewelry making, artwork, or more sophisticated burials practiced by their human neighbors.

Some explain away the later observations by arguing that evidence of less advanced culture among Neanderthals is simply a result of isolation of a subpopulation of humans (after sin or after the flood) and loss of technological knowledge. Modern "backwards" tribes are cited as examples of how different populations living at the same time may have vastly different levels of *apparent* cognition.[10] This argument requires long-term isolation, yet Neanderthals and humans were clearly *not* isolated from each other during their period of overlap. In fact, they appear to have even shared an occasional bed!

---

5. Krause et al., "The complete mitochondrial DNA genome of an unknown hominin from southern Siberia."
6. Callaway, "First Aboriginal genome sequenced."
7. Slon et al., "The genome of the offspring of a Neanderthal mother and a Denisovan father."
8. Menton, Purdom, and Upchurch, "Cavemen...really?"; Luskin, "Missing transitions: human origins and the fossil record."
9. Wilcox, "Updating human origins"; Pearce, Stringer, and Dunbar, "New Insights into differences in brain organization between Neanderthals and anatomically modern humans."
10. Huse, *The Collapse of Evolution*, 3rd ed., 139–40; Sarfati, *Refuting Evolution 2*, 191–92.

COMMON ANCESTRY WITH OTHER LIFE

To address claims of shared ancestry with other life-forms, we don't really need to tackle the whole animal kingdom. The big hurdle for most people is shared ancestry with *any* other creature, so if we can demonstrate common ancestry with other primates, the difficult work is done. Our ability to address questions of kinship has been revolutionized not just by the capacity to sequence DNA, but also by the ever-increasing ease with which it can be done. It took thirteen years and nearly three billion dollars to *mostly* decipher the first human genome. As I write this, it can be done in a day for about $1,000, and the time and cost continue to drop.[11]

We have an interesting societal disconnect, at least in Western culture, in how much we trust DNA evidence. If the question is whether Joe is the father of Jane's baby, or whether Sarah and Cindy share the same grandparent, most implicitly trust the conclusions returned by a genetic analysis. If we make use of the same methods to infer familial relationships between different kinds of organisms, the results are often met with skepticism or outright disbelief. Yet the science behind these applications is fundamentally the same.

So what is it that geneticists see that makes them think there is no reasonable doubt left that humans share a common ancestor with other primates? There are many ways DNA can be brought to bear on this question. One example draws on our growing knowledge of the genes involved in smell.[12] On average, mammals have about 1,000 genes that have been linked to the ability to smell. Not all mammals are equally proficient. Relative to creatures like wolves or pigs, humans are olfactory lightweights. We can differentiate only a tiny fraction of the airborne chemicals that a dog smells. Sense of smell for chimps, gorillas, and monkeys is better than that of humans, but not as good as that of canines.

When comparing the genomes of wolves and primates (including humans), an interesting discovery was made. The genes giving canines superior smelling abilities also appear to be present in primates, but with alterations that have degraded or deactivated them. Deactivated genes are one example of what geneticists refer to as *pseudogenes*. This discovery

---

11. Herper, "Illumina promises to sequence human genome for $100—but not quite yet."
12. Venema and McKnight, *Adam and the Genome: Reading Scripture after Genetic Science*, 19–42.

provided (one of many) opportunities to shed light on the question of shared ancestry.

In general, the presence of genes that are deactivated in some mammals but that work fine in others makes sense if primates and canines shared a distant ancestor with working olfactory genes. Over time, populations leading to primates depended less and less on smell, such that a reduced ability to smell did not result in diminished reproductive success. Causing no direct harm, the degraded genes got passed on through the subsequent generations up to the present.

Looking more closely at the individual alterations (mutations) in these sections of DNA allows more specific tests. The number of mutations found in the same positions in different organisms serves as both evidence of shared ancestry and a way for determining which groups of creatures shared a more recent common ancestor. As an example, consider the hypothesis that humans share a common ancestor with chimps, the two share a more distant common ancestor with gorillas, and the three share an even more distant common ancestor with monkeys. If true, we should expect to see a greater number of mutations shared between chimps and humans, a lesser number between gorillas and humans/chimps, and a still lesser number between monkeys and humans/chimps/gorillas.

To assist in understanding how this would work, consider the conceptual model illustrated in Figure 35. The bottom vertical line identifies a single mammal population hypothesized to be ancestral to all humans, chimps, gorillas, and monkeys. Any mutations (represented by a white circle) at this stage get passed on to all future generations. At some point, the population is divided, with one branch giving rise to monkeys, and the other giving rise to more apish creatures. Mutations in this apish population (represented by a gray circle) will be shared by later gorillas, chimps, and humans, but not by monkeys. A later split within the apish population produces two distinct groups (still apish), one leading to gorillas, and the other leading to chimps and humans. Mutations in the latter population (represented by a gray square) will be shared by chimps and humans, but not by gorillas or monkeys. In the final split, one population gives rise to chimps and the other to humans. Subsequent mutations are unique to each group.[13]

---

13. Venema and McKnight, *Adam and the Genome*, 33–37, provide examples with the actual sequence of DNA for humans, chimps, gorillas, and orangutans (rather than monkeys).

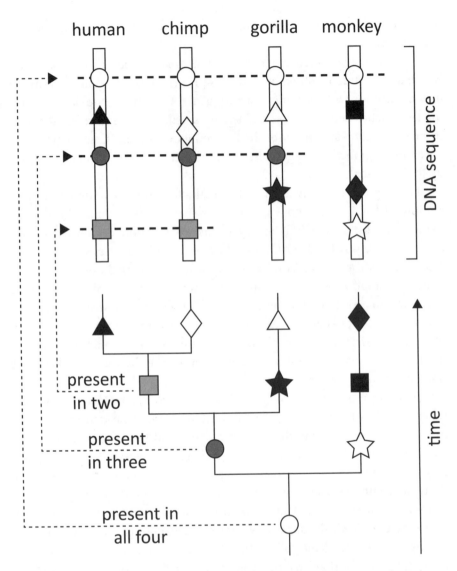

Figure 35—Conceptual representation of divergence from a common ancestor and the collection of mutations in a sequence of DNA. Each symbol represents a specific mutation in a specific gene or pseudogene. Dashed lines represent mutations shared by different species. See text for explanation.

So what do we find in the genomes of humans, chimps, gorillas, and monkeys? Many point mutations (change of a single base-pair) are positioned in exactly the same place, with humans and chimps sharing the greatest number in common. A fewer number are shared by humans, chimps, and gorillas, and the least are shared by humans, chimps, gorillas, and monkeys.[14] Exactly as expected for the specified hypothesis of common ancestry.

While this is considered by most scientists to be powerful evidence of evolution, others contend that the best explanation of similar genetic structure is not because of shared ancestry (*common descent*), but because God used similar genetic coding to build organisms with similar body plans and physiology (*common design*). The common-design model requires that most of the variations found between unrelated organisms were designed for a function unique to each kind of organism. We will consider this claim generally for pseudogenes and then for the specific positions of mutations.

Design advocates argue that pseudogenes are misnamed, having functions that are simply not yet known. When a function is discovered for a pseudogene, design advocates believe it to be undermining the evidence for evolution.[15] There are two reasons why this makes no sense. First, common-design advocates generally believe that once sin entered the world, perfectly crafted genes were subject to decay and degeneration. This model should thus expect pseudogenes to be *common*—with unabashed claims that Adam and Eve's sense of smell was probably better than ours is today. Second, the evolutionary model does not require pseudogenes to remain functionless forever. In fact, pseudogenes are thought to be one of the playgrounds for genetic experimentation that periodically gives rise to a new function. Discoveries of function for so-called pseudogenes are interesting, but irrelevant to this discussion.

The more pertinent question, for the above example, is how similar these non-olfactory genes are, in sequence and in position in the genome, to genes for smell in nonprimates. If coding for a different function than smell, there is no reason why these genes need to be positioned exactly where the genes for smell are found in other mammals.[16] Why would God place these genes in a position where it would appear to lend support to evolution—where they look just like disabled or altered olfactory genes?

---

14. With much less frequency, some genetic variants are shared more between humans and gorillas than between humans and chimps. To understand why this is expected within evolving and diverging populations, see Venema and McKnight, *Adam and the Genome*, 53–55.
15. Rana, "Pseudogenes and the origin of humanity: A response to the Venema critique of the RTB Human Origins Model."
16. Gene expression is influenced by position, but if a gene has a different function, it doesn't need to be in the same position found in another creature's DNA: Takizawa, Meaburn, and Misteli, "The meaning of gene positioning."

In the same line of reasoning, consider the matching mutations between various primates. The design model requires that these are not mutations, but reflect necessary tweaks in the underlying common genetic code for the particular needs of each organism. But recall that DNA is remarkably plastic. There is more than one combination of base pairs that can produce the same result. Why would God place specific base-pair variants in the same places in the DNA of unrelated species in a manner that coincidentally matches the expectations of the evolutionary model?

To summarize, the special-creation (design) argument requires that God (1) made non-olfactory genes to look nearly the same as olfactory genes, (2) placed them intentionally in positions in the primate genome where olfactory genes are found in other mammals, and (3) among many workable options, selected the same variant base pairs to place in the same genes of unrelated organisms, such that (4) it *falsely* provides support for common descent. Does this sound like the God of Romans 1:20?

ADAM AND EVE REVISITED

For those thinking that Adam just got swept under the rug, nothing written above is an argument against Adam and Eve being actual people. Nor is any of this an argument against a single couple being progenitors of all living humans today. A return to Chapter 6 will provide a reminder of how modern genetics can potentially be reconciled with both an ancestral population of evolved hominids and a real first human couple. If sufficiently intrigued and wanting to know how a lineage could be traced from all living humans back to both a common couple and a larger population, additional information with visual illustrations, designed for nonspecialists, can be found in publications cited in the footnote. [17]

---

17. Davidson, "Genetics, the Nephilim, and the historicity of Adam"; Swamidass, "The overlooked science of genealogical ancestry"; Swamidass, *The Genealogical Adam and Eve: The Surprising Science of Universal Ancestry.*

PART 5

WAR OF WORDS

11

CREATION SCIENCE—BEHIND THE CURTAIN

When I was a kid, we didn't have movies available at the tap of a finger on a smartphone. We actually had to wait—often an entire year—for classic movies to be replayed on TV. One of my favorites was *The Wizard of Oz*. I loved the climax of the film, where Dorothy and her motley crew cower before the giant face of the great and powerful Oz. Smoke and fire billow as Oz berates the supplicants for their impertinence, until the little dog Toto tugs at a curtain. "Pay no attention to that man behind the curtain!" Oz frenetically commands, but it is too late. All can suddenly see that the fearsome countenance of the great wizard is an illusion. An old man with a microphone and mechanical levers is the real Oz.

Those steeped principally in young-earth literature are likely to have the impression that the natural evidence for a massive global flood and recent creation is "great and powerful." Young-earth arguments seem *at least* as strong as old-earth arguments, with people swayed to one side or the other only by their presuppositions—their purported worldview. Some go even further to claim that the evidence for a global flood and young earth is overwhelming, far *greater* than the paltry evidence trotted out by those who have chosen to believe "the words of man over the words of God." [1]

Is the natural evidence for a young earth as strong as claimed, overlooked simply because of spiritual blinders? After reading hundreds of young-earth articles and books over the last thirty years, I have observed a disturbing

---

1. Ham, *The Lie: Evolution*, 46–47; Mortenson, "Why shouldn't Christians accept millions of years?", 27; Snelling, "Doesn't the order of fossils in the rock record favor long ages?", 342; Otis, *Theistic Evolution: A Sinful Compromise*, 94.

pattern. In every case where the argument appears compelling, it is an illusion. A partial list of the "microphone and mechanical levers" includes:

- false options given from which to choose
- critical opposing data or information left out
- scientific terms misdefined
- scientific understanding misrepresented
- scientists quoted out of context
- outdated science portrayed as if current
- informative evidence buried in superfluous "data"
- significance of young-earth literature grossly overplayed
- alternative explanations claimed with no evidentiary support
- evidence categorically dismissed based on an isolated error
- statements of purported fact that are simply untrue

I recognize that these are strong claims, which will require examples to support. That is the purpose of this chapter. I hope to serve in the humble role of Toto, pulling back the curtain so you can see what lies behind.

Though the content of this chapter is critical of young-earth and antievolution arguments, the objective is not principally to dissuade belief in a recent creation or miraculous interventions in nature. If you choose to disbelieve evolution or deep time, but do not think poorly of others for holding a different view, I feel no urgency to convince you of my own perspective. Some of my closest friends believe the earth is young, and we have prayed and worshiped together for many years with minimal conflict (one can hardly call someone a friend if there is *never* conflict). It is a fellowship possible because of a mutual recognition that there is more than one Bible-honoring understanding of the creation story. For those personally wrestling with the evidence or who have been using young-earth arguments as an apologetics tool, I *do* hope to convince you that the purported evidence for a young earth is not what it seems. Young-earth arguments far too often serve as a barrier rather than a gateway to faith in Christ.

In the examples that follow, the purpose is not just to explain what is wrong with a particular young-earth argument, but to shine light on the various tactics employed to make something likely true sound ridiculous or something likely false sound quite plausible. I have broken the examples into categories, each highlighting a different young-earth practice. This is not an exhaustive coverage, but it is broadly representative of what is found in the young-earth message.

As we begin, I expect that some readers have already raised a brow at the brazenness of my characterization of the work of men and women who have devoted their lives to what they believe to be Christian ministry—the defense of the Word of God. That is an understandable reaction, which I do not take lightly. At the end of the chapter, I will attempt to address that very concern.

POLARIZE TO PREVAIL—BUILDING FALSE DICHOTOMIES

A core tactic of young-earth leaders is to draw the perceived chasm between their position and all others as wide as possible. This tactic insists that it is the young-earth view that accepts God at his word, operates under a biblical worldview, and understands the true role of science. All others accept man's word over God's, operate under a humanistic worldview, and elevate science above the Bible. Such polarization makes it much easier to discount any opposing argument by placing it in the camp that refuses to honor God. In fact, such characterizations are false dichotomies, and serve to muddle rather than enhance understanding. Two examples follow.

Biblical Worldview vs. Humanistic Worldview
The debate is repeatedly framed in these terms. Those who have a biblical worldview observe the world and natural evidence through the lens of Scripture, causing them to see the abundant evidence supporting a young earth and a global flood. Those with a humanistic worldview observe the world through the lens of human reason and see the same evidence as supporting evolution and great age.[2] But this is an utterly false dichotomy, for there are many who are firm believers in the truth of Scripture who fall between these choices. These are Christians who find the scriptural arguments for a young earth to be riddled with modern cultural bias, and who find the scientific evidence of great age and adapting life to be so overwhelming that denial might as well include denying the existence of atoms (we can't see atoms, after all).

There are certainly people with a humanistic worldview who disavow all things spiritual or divine, but given disagreements among Christians on the subject of origins, what exactly does it mean to have a biblical worldview? The most common mistake in defining such a view is failure to recognize the

---

2. Ham, The Lie, 73; Kelly, Creation and Change: Genesis 1.1–2.4 in the Light of Changing Scientific Paradigms, 15–28; Oard, "Landslides win in a landslide over ancient 'Ice Ages'", 111; Reed, Plain Talk About Genesis, 77–98.

difference between interpretation of the Bible and the Bible itself. To simply say that I believe the Bible and therefore have a biblical worldview is effectively declaring my particular understanding of God's Word to be perfect, inspired, and infallible.

If two groups of Christians believe the Bible is true, but disagree on the intended meaning of a passage, both are at least attempting to hold to a biblical worldview. The choice is not biblical versus humanistic, but which version of the competing "biblical" worldviews is most representative of what the Bible actually teaches. There are real dichotomies, though not ones that need to divide the church into warring tribes.

The first genuine dichotomy is on the intention of Scripture when touching upon nature. Does it intend to instruct on the function and structure of nature? Or does it draw on humanity's common experience at the time of writing to illustrate eternal truths about the kingdom of God? Should Christians hold to *comprehensive inerrancy* or inerrancy that acknowledges *divine accommodation*? Both views seek to honor the Bible and its Author. While one understanding must be wrong, it does not mean that all who err on this question are undermining the mission of the church or dishonoring the Bible.

The second genuine dichotomy is whether nature can be trusted to reveal a truthful story. Does nature reflect its Creator, revealing a consistent story open to all? Or has nature been so corrupted by sin that only those who know its real story in advance can understand the evidence preserved in its layers? Thoughtful Christians fall into both camps, though I find that those trying to reconcile natural evidence with a young-earth view must increasingly call upon actions of God that cross into deception, with myriad independent natural processes tweaked by God so that they now falsely align with conventional scientific expectations.

History vs. Myth

The 2017 film *Is Genesis History?* exemplifies a closely related polarization strategy. The subtitle, *Two Competing Views…One Compelling Truth*, presents viewers with only two choices. Either the creation story is *history*, argued to mean creation in six consecutive days and a global flood, or it is *myth*. There are no other options. One must choose between the secular/scientific view or the biblical view.

This is another false dichotomy, for it makes the unjustified assumption that the creation story is historical only if events happened as they appear in a superficial, literalistic reading of the text. All who disagree must believe the creation story is a myth. The Bible and modern science are set against each other as mutually exclusive choices.

This view is nonsensical, for it boils down to a belief that real history can only be told in literalistic prose, never in poetic or even semi-poetic form. There is no inherent reason why this should be true, and, in fact, Scripture speaks boldly against such a position. Consider the poetic songs of Moses after crossing the sea on dry land (Exodus 15), or of Deborah after God gave Israel victory over its Canaanite oppressors (Judges 5). In both examples, the historical reality of the events is not undermined by relating the events in poetic form. The relevant Scriptures are poetic *and* historical.

The same can be said of the creation story in the Bible. Real history—an actual, supernatural creation of the universe—is related in poetic language. Language that is so much *richer* than a sequence of days.[3]

SLEIGHT OF HAND—TWISTING THE MEANING OF TERMS

"I do not think that word means what you think it means."[4]

An often-employed tactic is to twist the meaning of scientific terms in ways that make evolution or earth history appear weak or speculative. Two terms in particular repeatedly fall prey to this twisting: *uniformitarianism* and *theory*.

Uniformitarianism: All Things "Slow and Steady"

This term was already introduced in Chapter 8, but it is worth revisiting here. Those listening to the young-earth message are repeatedly told that evolution and deep time are based on the untestable principle of uniformitarianism, which stipulates that ancient processes occurred at the same *rates* and *magnitudes* observed today.[5] Geologists reject a global flood, we are told, because it doesn't fit the uniformitarian principle of all things slow and steady.

Now consider for a moment a few widely known theories proposed and defended by conventional geologists. (1) A giant meteorite struck the earth sixty-six million years ago, creating virtually instantaneous global havoc and

---

3. Miller and Soden, *In the Beginning…We Misunderstood: Interpreting Genesis 1 in its Original Context*, 137–38; Martin and Vaughn, *Beyond Creation Science*, 275–79.
4. Iconic line spoken by the fictional character Inigo Montoya from the 1987 film *The Princess Bride*.
5. Morris, *Scientific Creationism*, 2nd ed., chap. 5; Reed et al., "Beyond scientific creationism"; Snelling, "Doesn't the order of fossils in the rock record favor long ages?," 346.

leading to the mass extinction of dinosaurs. (2) Over the same time period, massive volcanic eruptions belched layer after layer of lava over land masses the size of Texas, at rates never observed today. (3) The Mediterranean Sea was once dry land and flooded several million years ago when rising sea levels in the Atlantic began to pour over and erode the Strait of Gibraltar, rapidly inundating nearly a million square miles of land. (4) An abrupt environmental perturbation at the end of the Permian period wiped out over 95 percent of all marine species. (5) Bursting glacial dams at the end of the last ice age catastrophically carved enormous channels out of solid rock in the state of Washington.

Where in these examples does one find commitment to all processes in the past proceeding at the same rates and magnitudes as observed today? Young-earth writers and speakers are aware of these and many other examples of processes in the past argued to be faster or bigger than anything observed today, yet persist in the false assertion that conventional geologists naively believe geologic processes have been constant.

Fundamentally, uniformitarianism simply means that the same physical laws governing natural processes today have been in effect since the formation of the universe. As such, if we see mud cracks forming today in fine-grained sediments as they are exposed to air and dry, we can reasonably assert that mud cracks preserved in an ancient shale were formed by the same processes. Uniformitarianism does not mean everything happens slowly, nor does it mean that if we can't see it happening today, it never happened.

Ironically, young-earth advocates employ uniformitarian principles whenever they attempt to explain how a feature in the earth's layers could have been formed by a flood. In their own words, "The universe is logical and orderly because its Creator is logical and has imposed order on the universe.... We can trust that the universe will obey the same physics tomorrow as it does today because God is consistent. This is why science is possible."[6]

This *is* uniformitarianism.

Evolution Is "Only a Theory"

Young-earth advocates take advantage of nuances in the English language where a word can have different meanings depending on the context. In common usage, the word *theory* is typically used to mean a hunch, an educated guess, or even a wild idea someone dreams up with no supporting evidence

---

6. Lisle, "Can creationists be 'real' scientists?," 147–48.

at all. Nearly every book attacking evolution notes that evolution is *merely* a theory, insinuating or explicitly claiming that it is a wishful idea with little or no actual evidence in its defense.[7]

In the practice of science, however, *theory* has a very different meaning. According to the National Academies of Science, a theory is

> a comprehensive explanation of some aspect of nature that is supported by a vast body of evidence. Many scientific theories are so well-established that no new evidence is likely to alter them substantially. For example, no new evidence will demonstrate that the earth does not orbit around the sun (heliocentric theory), or that living things are not made of cells (cell theory), that matter is not composed of atoms, or that the surface of the earth is not divided into solid plates that have moved over geological timescales (the theory of plate tectonics).[8]

Direct evidence for how the first cells evolved is genuinely sparse, but evolution from single cells to the diversity of life today is supported by such "a vast body of evidence" in multiple scientific disciplines that most scientists now consider evolution to be a fact. New discoveries continuously tweak our specific understanding of genetic processes, specific relationships between ancient and modern species, and the timing of particular events, but the adaptation of organisms over millions of years is now considered to have an equivalent level of evidential support as matter being composed of atoms.

MISAPPLY SCIENTIFIC PRINCIPLES—SQUARE PEGS IN ROUND HOLES

This tactic misuses fundamental scientific principles to give a false impression that they undermine the possibility of scientific claims. In each case, a general principle is accurately described, but then applied in a nonsensical manner—a square peg in a round hole. As an analogy, suppose I argue that materials become denser as they change from gas to liquid, and liquid to solid. The explanation is the well-known phenomenon that the spacing between atoms decreases as the temperature decreases. If I drop a block of

---

7. Gish, *Evolution: The Fossils Still Say No!*, 2–4; Morris, *Scientific Creationism*, 2nd ed., 5–9; Sarfati, *Refuting Evolution 2*, 23–26; Huse, *The Collapse of Evolution*, 3rd ed., 17–22.
8. National Academy of Sciences, *Science, Evolution, and Creationism*, 11.

solid wax into a pot of hot liquid wax, the solid is more dense and sinks, as expected. So far, so good. But now suppose I blindly apply this reasoning to water. Ice cubes obviously cannot float in water because solid water should be denser than liquid water. *Scientific law disproves floating ice cubes!* Yet ice cubes clearly *do* float. When we include unique bonding angles and crystal structure in the discussion, we discover why ice ends up less dense than water—without defying any scientific laws.

As examples for this section, we will consider the often cited principles of thermodynamics and spontaneous generation.

The Second Law of Thermodynamics Makes Evolution Impossible
The second law of thermodynamics can be stated in many different ways, but the general principle is that all spontaneous transformations result in a net increase in disorder. In practical terms, this means that no increase in order can be achieved without consumption of energy and that a localized increase in order will be accompanied by a larger decrease in order in the surrounding system. The universe as a whole is thus ever increasing in disorder.

To most opponents of evolution, this observation is a decisive and fatal blow to evolution.[9] Evolution, which requires increasing biological complexity over long periods of time, is viewed as a blatant contradiction of the second law. The apparent contradiction, however, arises only with a faulty understanding of thermodynamics.

If the second law of thermodynamics forbids increases in order over time, how does a single-celled embryo increase in complexity to produce a fully developed human being with eyes, arms, and internal organs? How does a majestic cave formation grow from disordered ions dissolved in dripping water? How does a volcano grow from the ocean floor to add a new island to the Hawaiian chain? How do people defy the second law to achieve the erection of a building from raw earth materials? Clearly, increases in complexity occur all around us at every moment. The second law in no way forbids an increase in order or complexity, but simply states that each increase in order will be accompanied by a greater decrease in order somewhere in the system.

As a simple example of how this works, consider the formation of crystals from evaporating saltwater. The dissolved salt exists as dissociated Na^+ and Cl^- ions (sodium and chloride) distributed through the water. As sunlight warms the

---

9. Morris, *Scientific Creationism*, 2nd ed., 40–42; Huse, *The Collapse of Evolution*, 3rd ed., 112–16; Kelly, *Creation and Change*, 60–66.

water, evaporation increases the concentration of the dissolved salt. Eventually, the capacity of the remaining water to hold dissolved salt is exceeded, and Na^+ and Cl^- ions begin to join and build salt crystals on the bottom. An increase in complexity has just occurred, somehow without defying the second law of thermodynamics (Fig. 36). The reason is clear when we expand our view to include what happened to the water. A large number of water molecules went from a closely associated arrangement in the liquid to a highly dispersed distribution in the gaseous (evaporated) state. There was more disorder in the water than order in the salt, but we are left with highly ordered salt crystals in the beaker.

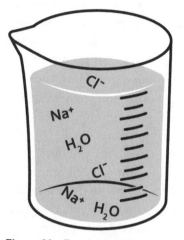

Figure 36—Evaporating salt water results in water distributed through the air and highly organized salt crystals sitting in the beaker.

Now consider a biological system. Increasing complexity within biological systems is constrained by the second law of thermodynamics in much the same way as evaporating saltwater. Increasing order within one organism or within a group of organisms can be sustained by the addition of energy and will be accompanied by a net decrease in order in the system as a whole. This process can be seen in the development of a human from embryo to birth. The energy required for human development comes from breaking down consumed plant and animal tissue. A significant fraction of this energy is lost to the environment as heat, requiring consumption of more material than is actually used. In the span of time between embryo and birth, far more ingested tissue will be broken down during digestion than will be built up as new tissue in the human body. The net result is a localized increase in complexity in the human body and an overall decrease in order for the plant-human-earth system as a whole.

From a thermodynamic perspective, increasing complexity of life-forms over time is no different than increasing complexity within a single organism as it develops from its embryonic state. If energy is available to sustain increases in order, and overall entropy (disorder) increases with each transformation, no thermodynamic laws are violated.

Some antievolution writers acknowledge the discussion above, but seek to undermine it in one of two ways. First, it may be argued that development of an embryo to a mature adult is not a true increase in complexity, but is simply an unfolding of information already contained within the first cell.[10] This is a game of words with no merit, for the development of hair, bones, muscle, and other tissues from a single, undifferentiated cell is clearly an increase in complexity.

A second approach is to claim that energy can be added to generate increases in *order*, such as crystal formation, but energy has no power as a *creative* force to convert energy into increases in *complexity*.[11] Much could be said about the legitimacy of distinctions between order and complexity, but there is a simple question in this context that is of greater importance: What does this have to do with thermodynamics? Thermodynamics deals with the role and fate of energy in physical and chemical transitions without regard to whether a given transition was initiated by a random or intelligent force. Those using this argument start with the science of thermodynamics and subtly shift to a philosophical discussion of whether organisms are designed, while leading the audience to believe the subject is still thermodynamics.

Life Developing from Nonliving Materials Is Belief in Spontaneous Generation, Which Was Proven False 150 Years Ago.

In ancient times, maggots were observed to appear almost magically on rotting meat and mice could be found in places where there seemed to be no entry point.[12] The belief that the right mix of materials could spontaneously develop these life-forms came to be known as *spontaneous generation*. This belief was enhanced by the discovery of microorganisms that seemed to appear spontaneously even in a cup of clean water left on the counter a few days. It was not ultimately proven false until Louis Pasteur conducted a famous experiment in 1859 in which he boiled meat broth in flasks and bent some of the narrow necks

---

10. Morris, *Biblical Cosmology and Modern Science*, 146; Huse, *The Collapse of Evolution*, 3rd ed., 112–16.
11. Morris, *Scientific Creationism*, 2nd ed., 43–44; Sarfati, *Refuting Evolution 2*, 159.
12. Lamont, "Louis Pasteur, outstanding scientist and opponent of evolution (1822–1895)"; Etinger, *Foolish Faith*, chap. 3; Bergman, "Why abiogenesis is impossible."

into a loop (Fig. 37). Microbes only appeared in flasks with straight necks, where airborne particles could settle into the broth. It was thus recognized that microbes were floating in from the air. Spontaneous generation was proven false.

So how does this relate to the evolution of life? Marginally at best. Spontaneous generation addressed the routine appearance of intact, fully functioning organisms in essentially a single step. The experiments testing spontaneous generation did not address the possibility that the right mixture of raw

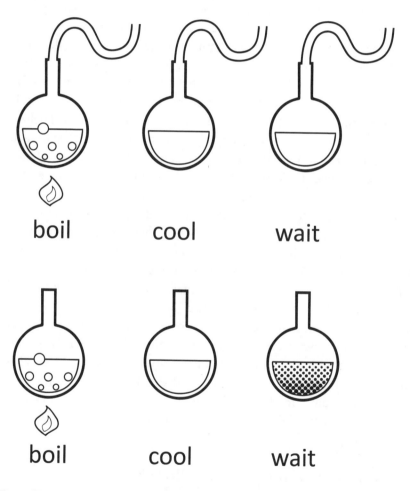

boil   cool   wait

boil   cool   wait

Figure 37—Pasteur's flask experiment. Boiled broth killed all microorganisms. After cooling and sitting for a time, living microorganisms only reappeared in the broth in the straight-necked flasks (stippled pattern). This demonstrated that the microbes had to have settled out from the air rather than being spontaneously generated in the broth.

materials and energy could give rise to an organic molecule with a tendency
to replicate itself in ways that could eventually lead to living cells.

TELL HALF A STORY—HOW TO MISLEAD USING NOTHING BUT TRUTH

Students often come up with clever ways of telling their parents a "truthful" story that diverts attention from their actual misdeeds. At my home institution at the University of Mississippi, students have been known to assure parents concerned about poor academic performance that they have been spending many evenings and long hours at the library. At face value, the statement is true. They have indeed spent many nights and hours just as they have claimed. What they fail to mention is that The Library is the name of a local *bar*. The words used are technically true, but by leaving out one critical piece of information, an utterly false impression is given of their actual behavior.

This tactic is pervasive in young-earth literature. The greatest challenge in writing this section was culling the myriad half stories down to a few representative examples to describe. I ultimately decided to pick four to describe in some detail (two related to age, two related to evolution), and I will follow with a table of additional examples in more bullet-point form (Table 14).

Each of the four examples starts with a brief description of a young-earth "half story," followed by the critical information that is routinely left out—the *untold* story. For all of these, young-earth advocates will protest that they do, in fact, address the information I claim is left out. This objection is itself a half-truth, for the critical information is typically addressed in a separate venue. Rather than present the full story to unsuspecting audiences, the young-earth assessment of the critical counterinformation is often shunted into organizational magazines and web archives, allowing them to claim that they have, in fact, addressed these issues (though I find these contain the same litany of errors identified at the start of this chapter). The majority of the young-earth audience remains unaware that the counterstory exists.

"Millions of Years" Was Invented to Exclude God

The young-earth half story
Frequent mention is made of prominent men in the development of "millions of years," including Comte de Buffon, Pierre-Simon Laplace, Jean-

Baptiste Lamarck, Abraham Werner, James Hutton, Georges Cuvier, William Smith, and Charles Lyell. All are documented or suspected of being atheists, deists, or at best "vague theists." On occasion, a "compromising" Christian, such as William Buckland, is also mentioned as contributing to the acceptance of long ages of earth history.[13]

The stated implication is that the idea of millions of years did not originally derive from physical evidence, but from a desire to come up with an explanation for life that excluded God. The only alternative to special creation was lots of time to allow life to evolve from nonlife by random natural processes, hence the *invention* of "millions of years" of earth history. The underlying motivation is evident by looking at the worldview of the men responsible.

The untold story

What is left out is the fact that ancient geologic history was promoted just as vigorously by an equal or greater number of men who *professed to be Christians*, some of whom even opposed evolution at the time. How can one be accused of inventing millions of years to allow for evolution if one *doesn't believe* in evolution?

Names include Isaac Newton, who used science as an apologetics tool against atheism, and Thomas Burnet, John Playfair, John Fleming, William Conybeare, and Adam Sedgwick, who were ministers and clergymen as well as accomplished scientists. Louis Agassiz argued convincingly that ancient continental glaciers in Europe explained surface geology better than a global flood, yet he also opposed evolution, mostly on theological grounds. William Buckland, an early paleontologist who discovered one of the first dinosaurs, made arguments for Intelligent Design. Even Cuvier, included in the young-earth list of those antagonistic to the gospel, was vice president of the Bible Society of Paris, and opposed evolution.[14] One may choose to question the legitimacy of the faith of any particular individual, but to simply leave them out of the discussion is unconscionable.

---

13. Mortenson, "Where did the idea of 'millions of years' come from?," 111–21; Otis, *Theistic Evolution*, 63–76; Ham and Lisle, "Is there really a God?," 29.
14. Young and Stearley, *The Bible, Rocks, and Time: Geological Evidence for the Age of the Earth*, 91–95.

The Earth's Declining Magnetic Field Clearly Limits the Age of the Earth.

The young-earth half story

The earth's magnetic field is on the decline. With well over a century of measurements in hand, we can back-calculate and project what the earth's magnetic field must have been in the distant past. If projecting backward by 10,000 years, earth's magnetic field approaches that of the strongest magnetic star. The earth clearly must be younger than 10,000 years.[15]

The untold story

So what part of this story is left out? A well-documented record of *reversals* in the earth's magnetic field throughout geologic history. During each cycle, the magnetic field diminishes, reverses, and increases again. We are currently in a *phase* of decreasing magnetic strength. Knowledge of magnetic fields cycling up and back down *totally* changes the significance of currently declining magnetic strength.

In order to claim they are not telling half a story, some young-earth writers *mention* the idea of reversals, but dismiss it as an unproven hypothesis invented by evolutionists.[16] In fact, the reversals are readily recognized in volcanic rock and on the ocean floor. The process was already described in Chapter 8, but it is worth adding some detail here. When magma solidifies, some iron minerals form crystals that are oriented to the earth's magnetic field. Once cooled, the orientation is preserved unless the rock is reheated to near melting or experiences physical upheaval. Studies of volcanoes have found that the orientation of these iron minerals repeatedly flip between current and reversed orientations in a stacked sequence of lavas (Fig. 38). Further, the radiometric ages of lavas at each reversal match the ages of reversals in other volcanoes around the world.

Where reversals (or magnetic fluctuations) are acknowledged as real, young-earth writers simply attribute it to the chaos of the flood.[17] They fail to add that if they themselves believe the strength of the earth's magnetic field has been higher and lower in the past, they are agreeing with old-earth observations that the current declining strength is *irrelevant* for limiting the age of the earth.

---

15. Morris, "Earth's magnetic field"; Kelly, *Creation and Change*, 151–52; Humphreys, "Earth's magnetic field is decaying steadily—with a little rhythm."
16. Huse, *The Collapse of Evolution*, 3rd ed., 67–68.
17. Snelling, "Can catastrophic plate tectonics explain flood geology?," 194–95.

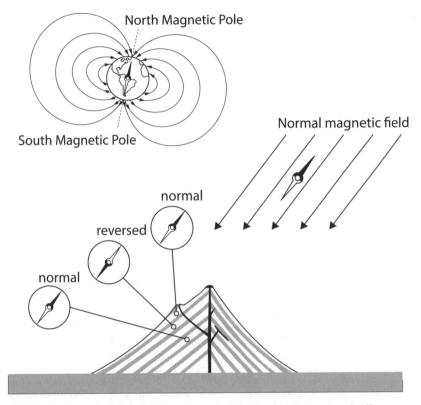

Figure 38—Iron minerals in solidifying lava orient to the earth's magnetic poles like a compass needle. Alternating layers in many volcanoes have iron minerals with a reversed orientation, indicative of times in the earth's past when the magnetic poles flipped.

Soft Tissue in Dinosaur Bones Proves They Are Much Younger Than Evolutionists Claim

The young-earth half story

In 1990, while working in the lab of paleontologist Jack Horner, Mary Schweitzer made her initial discovery of preserved soft tissues in *Tyrannosaurus rex* and other dinosaur bones said to be over 65 million years old. Since that time, more discoveries of soft tissues have been made, including proteins and flexible blood vessels, now all claimed by young-earth advocates as proof that these bones cannot be as old as evolutionists assert.[18]

---

18. Snelling et al., "What are some of the best evidences in science of a young creation?," 117–19; Ross, "Those not-so-dry bones."

The untold story

Shortly before entering her PhD program at Montana State University, Mary Schweitzer was a committed young-earth creationist, intent on learning all she could to overturn the evolutionary paradigm.[19] Given this starting point, one might reasonably think that her subsequent discovery of soft tissues in a *T. rex* femur would have confirmed her initial convictions. The *opposite* happened. Dr. Schweitzer is still an outspoken Christian, yet it was the very same studies, and a greater awareness of the actual evidence for evolution, that resulted not just in the acceptance of evolution, but that turned her into a *leading advocate* of the evolution of birds from dinosaurs. The molecular structure of those preserved proteins shows a closer relationship to birds than to reptiles,[20] and the bone structure she observed was stunningly similar to birds when ovulating, enough so that she could peg the *T. rex* as a pregnant female.[21]

No one actually knows how long organic tissues can be preserved. There is no decay law for biological materials. Prior to Dr. Schweitzer's work, no one thought to break open a precious dinosaur femur and look for surviving proteins. More to point, however, is that the degree of preservation (or lack of preservation) actually works *against* the young-earth paradigm. Part of the story left out is that we don't find equal levels of preservation/degradation in the bones of all creatures of similar size or character. If the majority of fossils represent organisms killed in the same year, we should find organic tissues preserved *equally well* in a Mesozoic dinosaur as we do in a Cenozoic reptile, bird, or mammal. Organic tissues are common in Cenozoic fossils tens of thousands of years old, but only trace amounts appear in dinosaurs. This makes sense only if dinosaurs, as an entire class of organisms, are much, much older.

Fossils That Appear in the Same Layer but Are Supposed to Be Different Ages Invalidate Evolutionary Theory.

The young-earth half story

Fossils that evolutionists say were separated by millions of years are sometimes found in the same layers, and footprints of modern creatures

---

19. Service, "'I don't care what they say about me': Paleontologist stares down critics in her hunt for dinosaur proteins."
20. Service, "Scientists retrieve 80-million-year-old dinosaur protein in 'milestone' paper"; Schweitzer et al., "Biomolecular characterization and protein sequences of the Campanian hadrosaur *B. canadensis*."
21. Yeoman, "Schweitzer's dangerous discovery"; Schweitzer, Wittmeyer, and Horner, "Gender-specific reproductive tissue in ratites and *Tyrannosaurus rex*."

are sometimes found in layers said to be millions of years old. It is argued that this is expected for the flood model, but exposes the lie of evolution.[22]

The untold story

Most claims of mixed-age fossils are based on unverifiable stories, though it is indeed true that fossils that are supposedly separated by millions of years have on occasion been found together in the same layer. The half of the story left out is that the earth is a dynamic system. There will be occasions when rock will be eroded, reworked, or moved in ways that can alter

Figure 39—Cartoon example of how two creatures that lived at very different times can be found represented in the same layer.

---

22. Brown, *In the Beginning: Compelling Evidence for Creation and the Flood*, 12; Sarfati, *Refuting Evolution 2*, 130–32.

the original record of deposition. A lighthearted example is shown in Figure 39. Evolution opponents typically discount such explanations as a convenient excuse for sweeping away data that does not fit the evolutionary model. This essentially demands that earth processes be neat and tidy, where sediment always rests permanently and quietly where first deposited.

If the earth is so dynamic and fossils can end up in the wrong place, how can fossils be used with any confidence at all? The answer is that there are reliable methods for distinguishing disturbed and undisturbed rock sequences. As an example, suppose we find fossils that are believed to be separated by millions of years all together in one spot (Fig. 40). Is this conclusive evidence that evolution is a hoax, or have we simply overlooked something? As we move laterally in our example environment, we find layers with fossils in the expected sequence. The fossils are mostly buried in ancient volcanic ash deposits, indicat-

ing both the cause of death and the means of rapid burial. Sand and silt layers between the ash layers are fossil-poor. Where the fossils are found mixed together, there is mostly sand and silt with little ash. This sand-silt deposit snakes through the area and cuts through the ash deposits, indicating we are looking at an ancient stream channel. Upon closer examination, we discover the fossils in this mixed deposit bear evidence of abrasion and bleaching. Thus, there is strong evidence that the stream eroded through the ash deposits, unearthed fossils from multiple layers, exposed them to air and light, and tumbled them in stream flow before redepositing them mixed together in a sandbar.

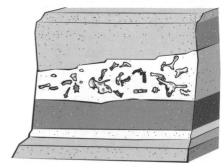

Figure 40—Bison and triceratops fossils exposed in an eroding cliff face. In undisturbed deposits (upper figure), the bison clearly sits in more recent deposits than the triceratops. In eroded, transported, and redeposited sediments (lower figure), the bones are mixed and show signs of bleaching and abrasion.

TABLE 14—ADDITIONAL COMMONLY USED YOUNG-EARTH HALF STORIES, AND WHAT INFORMATION IS LEFT OUT

Young-earth half story [23]	The untold story
Too little sediment in oceans if the earth is billions of years old.	Plate tectonics opens and closes ocean basins. No ocean is more than about 200 million years old (less than 5 percent of the total age of the earth).[24]
Organisms thought to be extinct for millions of years have been found living today (Lazarus fossils, or "living fossils")—argued to invalidate evolution.	*Lots* of creatures that lived millions of years ago have similar relatives still living today (like bacteria and sharks). Lazarus fossils are fascinating, but are irrelevant to whether life evolved.
Large folds are found in rock layers with little evidence of fracturing. Rock does not bend without breaking, so these must have been soft and wet, and bent during/after the flood.	Under high *confining* pressures (pushing in from all sides), lab studies demonstrate that rock can deform in a plastic manner. Old limestone tables have even been found bending under their own weight.[25]
Recent lava from Mt. St. Helens yielded radiometric dates of 300,000 years.	Indiscriminate sampling of lava can easily include fragments of ancient wall rock incorporated as the lava rises from great depth. The resulting date is an average of old and young.
There is not enough salt in the oceans if billions of years old.	Shifting tectonic plates can close up ocean basins, precipitating and isolating vast amounts of salt.
Helium produced by radioactive decay slowly diffuses out of minerals. Based on measured diffusion rates, minerals supposedly millions of years old have too much helium.	The laboratory-measured diffusion rates did not simulate the high pressure and external helium concentrations at the sampling depth.[26] Both can significantly reduce helium loss over time.

23. Snelling et al., "What are some of the best evidences in science of a young creation?"
24. Database of ocean crust age: http://www.ucmp.berkeley.edu/tectonics/atlantic.html.
25. A 200-year-old marble table in Westminster Cemetery, Baltimore, MD, is visibly bent under its own weight.
26. Henke, "Dr. Humphreys' young-earth helium diffusion 'dates.'"

CREATE DISTRACTIONS—HOW TO HIDE A FOREST BEHIND TREES

If you don't want people to see how vast a forest is, get their attention focused on trees sitting only at the forest edge. This is how opponents of evolution typically address fossils. In order to obscure the obvious change-over-time message of the fossil record as a whole (the forest), attention is distracted by focusing on the nuances of individual fossils, internal disagreements among paleontologists, the significance of forgeries, or nonsensical claims of what a transitional fossil should look like. We will consider four examples.

Disagreement among Evolutionists over the Origin of a Class of Organisms Is Evidence the Organisms Did Not Evolve at All.

A decade ago, a lively debate was going on among evolutionists over whether birds originated from theropod dinosaurs or from an earlier set of reptiles. One point of contention was the development and suppression of digits on the forelimb. During gestation, birds begin to form five digits in their wings, but two are then suppressed, resulting in three fused digits. Theropod dinosaurs also had only three digits, though there was uncertainty if they were the same three found in birds. Those arguing for an earlier origin of birds noted that one of the suppressed digits appeared to be different in birds and dinosaurs.[27] Young-earth writers latched onto the disagreement among evolutionists as evidence that birds did not evolve at all.[28] No attention was given to the widespread *agreement* on evidence supporting evolution of birds from reptiles in general, including facts such as bird embryos beginning to develop five digits and then suppressing two. Initiating five digits makes sense if derived from ancestral stock with five digits, but makes no sense if specially created as a three-fingered class of organisms.

This is a distraction that intentionally draws attention away from the primary evidence. As an analogy, imagine a reporter sitting in the courtroom for a murder trial. Two forensic experts, after reviewing the available evidence, disagree over the specific cause of death. The reporter, ignoring

---

27. Burke and Feduccia, "Developmental patterns and the identification of homologies in the avian hand."
28. Gish, *Evolution,* 129; Sarfati, *Refuting Evolution 2,* 159.

the agreement on the identity of the body in the morgue, writes his news story saying, given the disagreement between the supposed experts, he doesn't believe the victim is dead!

This is not very different from the bird-reptile-dinosaur debate of a decade ago. At the time, there was widespread agreement on a host of evidence linking birds to reptiles in general, with disagreement over the more specific relationship to dinosaurs or to an earlier set of reptiles. Since that time, the accumulation of evidence has largely put the debate to rest (just as new discoveries in a criminal case often do). Fossil dinosaurs with feathers, preserved dinosaur proteins similar to birds, and advances in gestational research predominantly lend support to the origin of birds from dinosaurs.[29] A recent study even found that by doing nothing more than restricting leg movement inside an egg, chicken embryos grew the normally downward-facing back toe with a reversed orientation, just like the back toes found in theropod dinosaurs.[30]

If an Organism Was Capable of Survival, It Can't Be Transitional.

As odd as this sounds, it is a standard argument in the rhetoric of evolution opponents. Duane Gish, in *Evolution: The Fossils Still Say No!*, describes the hypothetical development of flight among reptiles with this statement:

> At some stage, the developing flying reptile would have had about 25% wings. This strange creature would never survive, however. What good are 25% wings? Obviously, the creature could not fly, and he could no longer run, as he would be forced to drag those useless appendages along as, presumably, his hind limbs could still function.[31]

The only acceptable transitional fossil between land and airborne reptiles is thus one that has 25 percent wings (or some other fraction) that serve no purpose other than to ensure the untimely death of its unfortunate owner. The lack of such a discovery must be viewed as a remarkable triumph. Declare that only an organism incapable of survival can qualify as a transitional form,

---

29. An interesting case for how digits 1, 2, and 3 develop into digits 2, 3, and 4 in modern kiwis is made in Wagner and Gauthier, "1, 2, 3 = 2, 3, 4: A solution to the problem of the homology of the digits in the avian hand."
30. Botelho et al., "Skeletal plasticity in response to embryonic muscular activity underlies the development and evolution of the perching digit of birds."
31. Gish, *Evolution*, 103.

and accurately proclaim that no such fossil has ever been unearthed! Any fossil that appears transitional can be immediately discredited because it is a complete, fully formed organism without halfway developed, *unusable* organs. If this sounds as if it is stretching what evolution opponents actually think, consider this additional statement from Gish:

> Some evolutionists insist that since *Archaeopteryx* had characteristics of both reptiles and birds, it does represent an intermediate between reptiles and birds, but whatever features it had were complete, not part-way or transitional.[32]

This expectation that fossils can only be transitional if possessing useless, partway organs reverberates through young-earth literature, with every purported intermediate fossil disqualified because it abruptly appears "fully formed."[33] Aside from the obvious problem of circular reasoning (transitional organisms could not have survived; fossils were living organisms so they can't be transitional), the argument is a complete misrepresentation of what evolution should look like (creating the distraction).

If evolution really occurred, transitional forms lived to give rise to other forms precisely because newly derived features were *well suited* for a particular niche. In a transition from dinosaurs to birds, each stage in a land-bound to airborne transition had to be fully functional or the process would have abruptly ended. That's the whole idea of natural selection. A creature ill-suited for survival or reproduction gets weeded from the gene pool. Game over. While it's not always obvious how a particular intermediate trait provided an advantage, the presence of these traits in fossil after fossil is clear. The many dinosaurs being discovered with feathers yet incapable of flight provides one of many examples. We may not know for certain if the benefit was for insulation, brooding, locomotion, or attracting a mate, but the presence of feathers is undeniable. And these creatures appear in the fossil record right where expected if dinosaurs gave rise to birds (Fig. 28).

Require Transitional Forms to Be Halfway Between Modern Organisms.

If cows and whales share a common ancestor, then opponents of evolution insist that a fossil must exist somewhere that is half cow and half whale (Fig. 41).

---

32. Gish, *Evolution*,138.
33. Gish, *Evolution*, 53, 70, 75, 81, 91, 95, 103, 108, 109, 119, 123, 161, 178, 187, 191, 321, 341;
    Sarfati, *Refuting Evolution*, chap. 3; Williams, "Kingdom of the plants: Defying evolution."

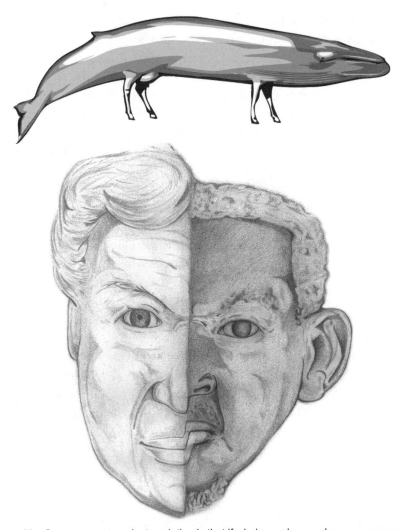

Figure 41—One argument against evolution is that if whales and cows share a common ancestor, there must be a cow-whale somewhere with halfway features. Using the same logic, if African pygmies and Dutch farmers share a common ancestor, there must be "Afridutchmies" somewhere with halfway features as well.

This particular example is the basis for Gish's widely promulgated pun that such a lineage would certainly result in "udder failure."[34] To understand why this claim is nothing more than a tactical distraction, consider the changes that have taken

---

34. Gish, *Evolution*, 198.

place within the human race since Adam. Christians and atheists alike currently believe that all modern humans can trace their origins back to the same mother (or at least the same small population). This means that the modern large-boned Dutch farmer and the diminutive African pigmy share a common ancestor. Following the reasoning of evolution opponents, proof of this shared ancestry requires discovery of an individual somewhere that is half white and half black, half tall and half short, with a nose that is half pointy and half flattened, and hair that is half long, blond, and straight, and half short, black, and curly (Fig. 41). As absurd as this requirement would be, it is equally absurd to look for a half cow, half whale as a common ancestor of cows and whales.

Keep in mind that if evolution actually occurred, *all* life shares a common ancestor. The whale-cow relationship is somewhat odd only in the sense that our intuition biases us to expect seals to be closer cousins to whales than cows are, but DNA and fossil evidence increasingly point to the opposite. So what *should* a common ancestor for cows and whales look like? Based on ancient whales discovered with various types of appendages, it was likely a four-legged, land-dwelling mammalian carnivore (see Chapter 9). Some members of this group began adapting toward a more aquatic existence leading to whales, while others adapted to a more herbaceous, land-based existence leading to the ungulates (e.g., cows, pigs, and camels).

What, then, does an antievolutionist do when a fossil whale (e.g., *Ambulocetus*) is found with small *hooves* on the digits of its hind legs? Answer: that person notes that fossils of *Ambulocetus* have been found in deposits that are a few million years younger than other fossils that are *more* whale-like and dismisses it.[35]

Equate Any Isolated Error or Fraud with Failure of Evolution as a Whole.

This distraction is most commonly employed with the few fossil forgeries. A relatively recent hoax was a cleverly disguised combination of two separate fossils to make them appear as one. Fossil tail feathers were cemented to the posterior of a dinosaur fossil. The initial "discovery" made the front page of the November 1999 issue of *National Geographic*, only to be rescinded in a much publicized "egg on their face" apology for being too quick to go to press. The forgery is now another weapon in the arsenal of evolution opponents to "prove" that evolution is false. What is never mentioned, however, is that it

---

35. Gish, *Evolution*, 202–3.

is always other evolutionists who identify the forgeries for what they are. If evolution was just a flimsy attempt to explain away God, no such self-purging would be expected. The existence of a few forgeries also does not change the legitimacy or significance of the vast number of genuine fossil finds. And since when does the appearance of a forged Rembrandt mean that Rembrandt himself never painted?

CHERRY-PICK QUOTATIONS—GAMES PLAYED WITH WORDS

When building a case for a particular scientific, political, or philosophical position, it is common and appropriate to quote those who hold an opposing position. There are three simple rules that we expect to be followed when calling attention to what someone else has said:

1. Quotations should be accurate.
2. Quotations should not be taken out of context in such a way that it alters the author's intended meaning.
3. Quotations should accurately represent contemporary thought or understanding.

Writers opposing evolution generally do well with the first rule. Quotations are rarely misprinted or intentionally altered. The remaining rules, however, are routinely violated.

Violation of Rule 2: Twisting Meaning by Quoting out of Context
Jean-Jacques Hublin is the director of the Department of Human Evolution at the Max Planck Institute for Evolutionary Anthropology in Leipzig, Germany. In 2000, he wrote a review of the second edition of the book *The Human Career: Human Biological and Cultural Origins* by Richard G. Klein. According to antievolutionist Daniel Jappah, Hublin made a telling admission about the classic image of human evolution from ape to primitive hominid to man:

> The once-popular fresco showing a single file of marching hominids becoming ever more vertical, tall and hairless now appears to be a fiction.[36]

---

36. Jappah, *Evolution: A Grand Monument to Human Stupidity*, 183–84.

This is remarkable. Here we have a highly respected evolutionist openly admitting that human evolution is a hoax—*fiction!* Or do we? What if we just added the next two sentences from that book review? Hublin's next words are:

> Humankind did not simply pass through successive stages, eventually leading to the emergence of anatomically and behaviourally modern humans. For most of the past four million years, several species of hominids coexisted, sometimes in limited geographical areas.[37]

Hublin's actual words communicate the *antithesis* of what he seems to be saying in Jappah's out-of-context quote. Hublin does not call human evolution "fiction." What is labeled as fiction is an out-of-date model of evolution, where we were conditioned to envision a single population changing over time from one species to the next. The fossil evidence, Hublin notes, reveals a *bushy* lineage, with multiple hominid cousin-species alive at the same time.

Violation of Rule 3: Quoting Out-of-Date Statements as if Current

Young-earth advocates frequently quote prominent evolutionists "admitting" transitional fossils are absent or rare.[38]

> The extreme rarity of transitional forms in the fossil record persists as the trade secret of paleontology.[39] *Stephen Jay Gould, Harvard paleontologist*

> The absence of fossil evidence for intermediate stages between major transitions in organic design, indeed our inability even in our imagination, to construct functional intermediates in many cases, has been a persistent and nagging problem for gradualistic accounts of evolution.[40] *Stephen Jay Gould*

> The record of evolution is still surprisingly jerky and, ironically, we have even fewer examples of evolutionary transition than we had in Darwin's time.[41] *David Raup, University of Chicago paleontologist*

---

37. Hublin, "An evolutionary odyssey."
38. One or more of the quotes that follow are found in: Menton, "Are there transitional forms in the fossil record?," 164–66; Otis, *Theistic Evolution*, 98; Blievernicht, "Transitional fossils?"
39. Gould, "Evolution's Erratic Pace."
40. Gould, "Is a new and general theory of evolution emerging?"
41. Raup, "Conflicts between Darwin and paleontology."

In any case, no real evolutionist, whether gradualist or punctuation, uses the fossil record as evidence in favor of the theory of evolution as opposed to special creation.[42] *Mark Ridley, Zoologist, Oxford University*

Gould and the American Museum people are hard to contradict when they say there are no transitional fossils.[43] *Colin Patterson, British Museum of Natural History*

Aside from such quotes often being taken out of context (Rule 2), when do you suppose these statements were made? Sometime in the 2000s, surely? Starting at the top, those dates would be 1977, 1980, 1979, 1981, and 1979. The most recent is nearly *four decades* old. If the apparent dearth of transitional fossils is real, we should find *current* paleontologists to be equally as forthcoming. The absence of such statements is not an accident. The wealth of fossil discoveries beginning in the early 1990s, and the resulting improvement in our understanding of evolutionary development, has dramatically changed the paleontological landscape. The old quotes serve no purpose now other than as diversions from genuine understanding.

ARM-WAVING AS A FORM OF ARGUMENT

The Oxford Dictionary defines *arm-waving* as "the use of insubstantial, unsupported, or sensational arguments or claims, especially in scientific discourse." The expression derives from the use of body language, such as dramatic hand gestures, and the use of volume or confident tone of voice to make up for a lack of evidential support for one's position or argument. Two examples follow.

Overplayed Significance of Young-Earth Literature
On any particular scientific subject, young-earth writers frequently lament that the errors in conventional understanding were already addressed in previous young-earth articles, and complain that others are not reading or keeping up with the young-earth technical literature. All such statements are designed to make the reader believe that young-earth investigations have been

---

42. Ridley, "Who doubts evolution?"
43. Letter reportedly sent to Luther Sutherland in 1979, reprinted in Sunderland, *Darwin's Enigma: Fossils and Other Problems*, 88–89.

thorough and their conclusions defensible, yet unjustly ignored or dismissed by conventional scientists.[44]

I will draw on personal experience for a pertinent example. Ken Wolgemuth and I wrote articles in 2010 and 2012 demonstrating how we can combine tree rings, annual sediment layers (varves), and carbon-14 to test and verify conventional geologic assumptions.[45] Data on the varves was drawn from intensively studied lake-sediment cores collected from Lake Suigetsu in Japan.[46] In 2016, a young-earth team produced a rebuttal paper that included a statement about the supposed annual laminations found in Lake Suigetsu:

> However, when one considers Lake Suigetsu's geological setting, creation scientists can plausibly account for this number of patterns. In fact, creation scientists have already addressed the claim that laminations in this particular lake prove an old earth.[47]

Few people go to the trouble of looking up such references to assess their significance or validity. In this case, the manner in which old-earth claims were "already addressed" by Oard turns out to be speculations on a series of improbable events that *could* have happened to produce layering that only coincidentally aligns with conventional scientific expectations. The most substantive statement in the cited work is a remarkable one:

> Unfortunately, there is very little literature on these [Lake Suigetsu] varves in English, and so it is difficult to analyze them.[48]

Young-earth writers are not wrong when they say their work is not being read or taken seriously by conventional scientists. Given the representative nature of my own experience, that is not likely to change any time soon.

---

44. Jeanson and Tomkins, "Genetics confirms the recent, supernatural creation of Adam and Eve," 324–28.
45. Davidson and Wolgemuth, "Christian geologists on Noah's flood: Biblical and scientific shortcomings of flood geology"; Davidson and Wolgemuth, "How old is the earth? What God's creation professes."
46. Lake Suigetsu website: http://www.suigetsu.org.
47. Hebert, Snelling, and Clarey, "Do varves, tree-rings, and radiocarbon measurements prove an old earth?," 341.
48. Oard, "Do Varves Contradict Biblical History?," 131.

Just-So Stories Sold as "Better" Explanations

A *just-so story* refers to a fanciful explanation, devoid of evidential support, to explain the origin of some feature or phenomenon. A commonly offered example is a mythological tale of "how the leopard got its spots." Young-earth explanations for what we find in nature frequently boil down to just-so stories. Note that I am not referring to Genesis as a just-so story. Rather, it is the natural explanations employed in defense of a faulty interpretation of Genesis that bear the hallmarks of mythology.

When radiometric dates of the Hawaiian Islands and Emperor Seamounts yield plate-spreading rates that match current GPS rates, the "better" young-earth explanation is that God first sped up radioactive decay and plate speeds during the flood, then slowed them down in tandem so it falsely looks as though radiometric dating works. Or when fossils with intermediate traits are found in abundance between the first appearance of earlier and later classes of organisms, the "better" explanation is that God specially created creatures with intermediate traits and allowed them to be sorted and buried in a sequence to falsely look like evolution. There is no evidential support for these explanations other than the unjustified claim that the Bible tells them so. They are *just-so* stories.

For an expanded example, I will revisit my experience writing about tree rings, varves, and carbon-14. It turns out that there is a very narrow window of carbon-14 values expected in tree rings and in varves *if* the trees grew one ring per year, *if* lake sediments deposited one varve per year, and *if* radioactive decay rates have been constant, even allowing for a fairly generous range of atmospheric carbon-14 concentrations in the past (Fig. 42). Alternatively, if any of these assumptions is not valid, the carbon-14 content of tree rings and varves should fall outside the expected range (in predictable ways).

Hundreds of carbon-14 measurements made on tree rings in Europe and varved sediments in Lake Suigetsu, Japan, fall right inside the expected range. No set of improbable events must be conjured to account for the results. Just normal processes of tree growth, sediment deposition, and carbon-14 uptake from the air.

The "better" young-earth explanation is that God (1) manipulated ultra-low initial atmospheric carbon-14 levels during the flood, (2) kept the decay rate of carbon-14 nearly constant while speeding up the decay rates for longer-lived isotopes, (3) allowed carbon-14 to seep quickly from the ground after the flood to modern levels (in time to allow accurate radiocarbon dating of biblical artifacts), (4) introduced wild climate swings after the flood to cause trees to grow tens of rings per year in Europe, (5) sent innumerable pulses of dust clouds over Japan to induce hundreds or even thousands of laminations per year on the lake floor, and (6) providentially orchestrated these independent processes such that the carbon-14 content of tree rings and sediment layers would *falsely* appear to confirm the validity of the conventional geologic model.[49]

In what way, exactly, is any of this glorifying to God?

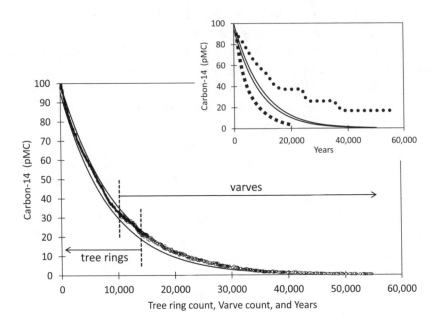

Figure 42—Top graph: Solid lines represent the window of expected carbon-14 levels in tree rings and varves today if conventional geologic understanding is correct. Multiple tree rings or sediment layers deposited in the same year should plot above the window (circles). Faster radioactive decay rates or much lower atmospheric carbon-14 in the past should plot below the lines (squares). Bottom graph: The actual data fall firmly in the window of conventional expectations (plotted data represents more than 4,800 samples).[50]

49. Hebert, Snelling, and Clarey, "Do varves, tree-rings, and radiocarbon measurements prove an old earth?"
50. Adapted from Davidson and Wolgemuth, "Testing and verifying old-age evidence: Lake Suigetsu varves, tree rings, and carbon-14."

FLAT-OUT WRONG

A great deal of what passes for young-earth reporting or research is just wrong. Three examples follow.

Operational Science vs. Historical Science

So-called *operational science* is defined by young-earth advocates as the kind of science you do in the lab, where experiments can be performed and observations can be made in the present. This, we are told, is how we get our medicines and rockets and cell phones. Historical science is defined as *speculation* about what happened in the unobserved past. Since you can't go back in time and replicate an event, there is no way to truly know what happened without an eyewitness. According to most young-earth literature, hypotheses about the unobserved past can never be tested, and thus fall outside of the bounds of science.[51]

This could have been used earlier as an example of a false dichotomy, but it is so wrong, it is more fitting to use it as an example of a widely accepted assertion for which there is no truth at all. To illustrate what is going on, imagine speaking with a city prosecutor who is presenting the case for a murder charge. A man was found dead in his living room. No one was present to see him die. No one saw anyone enter or leave the house prior to the body being found. And no one knows of anyone who wished the man dead. Yet the prosecutor is confident regarding when the man died, how the man died, how long the body lay before being found, and who killed him!

Wounds in the man's chest matched the blade of a kitchen knife found in the corner of the living room. Shoe prints outside a bedroom window matched the tread of shoes found in the closet of a man the victim had recently fired. This suspect had stopped at an ATM three blocks from the murder victim's home 30 minutes before the estimated time of death, which was determined based on the temperature of the victim's body when found by police. The former employee had scratches on his arm when arrested, and the dead man had skin cells under his fingernails with DNA that matched the DNA of the suspect. Aside from the suspect, who isn't talking, not a single person witnessed the event, yet there is virtually no doubt what happened.

Scenarios like this are played out nightly across the country on any number of television crime shows where the heroes are known as *forensic scientists*.

---

51. Patterson, *Evolution Exposed: Biology*, 19–32; Cosner, "What distinguishes origins and operational science?"; Ham, *The Lie*, 45–52; Otis, *Theistic Evolution*, 34–50.

These intrepid investigators recognize that physical processes observed in the present, like how fast a body cools after death, can be used to decipher what happened in the unobserved past. Fresh scratches on a suspect's arm lead to a hypothesis that, prior to death, the victim scratched the assailant during a struggle. As a test of this hypothesis, material is collected from beneath the victim's fingernails to see if cells are obtained with DNA that matches the suspect's. If the DNA matches, the hypothesis is supported. If it doesn't, the hypothesis is shown to be false. Even though no one was there to see it!

In cases where there are multiple plausible suspects, there may be competing hypotheses about who committed the crime. Finding support for one hypothesis may require the chance discovery of a cast-off murder weapon, a fragment of the victim's clothing, or tire tracks from a suspect's car in a suspicious location. Alternatively, one hypothesis (guilt of suspect 1) may eventually be found false only as evidence accumulates in favor of the competing hypothesis (guilt of suspect 2).

The study of the history of the earth operates in the same fashion as forensic crime investigations, and is, in fact, a type of forensic science—a study of what happened in the unobserved past. Earth scientists develop some hypotheses that are directly testable and readily found true or false. Other hypotheses are made that may only be supported by the chance discovery of particular fossils or shown false by the long-term accumulation of evidence supporting an alternative hypothesis. Examples of both types of hypotheses are given below to demonstrate how the *science* of earth history and evolution works.

Hypothesis: The oxygen content of the earth's early atmosphere was very low.

Test: Iron is abundant in sedimentary rocks of all ages and is readily oxidized by oxygen. If oxygen has always been present in high concentrations in the atmosphere, iron oxides should be found in the same abundance in ancient and recent sedimentary rock.

Result: The (mostly) oxygen-free atmosphere hypothesis is supported by the absence of pervasive iron oxide in the oldest rocks. (Note that the rocks are not considered old because they lack oxidized iron. They were independently dated first.)[52]

---

52. Turner, "The development of the atmosphere"; Wiechert, "Earth's early atmosphere."

Hypothesis: If whales trace their ancestry through four-legged terrestrial mammals, then modern whales should retain some genetic traces of this ancestry either in the form of inactive DNA that codes for hind legs or actual remnants of hind legs. Sharks, though designed for an existence similar to many whale species, are not thought to have derived from any four-legged predecessor, so no remnants of hind legs should ever be found in a shark.

Test: Testing this hypothesis requires the long-term accumulation of discoveries and analyses of whale and shark remains. It only takes one shark with partial hind legs to show at least part of the hypothesis false.

Result: Because whales and sharks were and are actively hunted, there have been ample opportunities to study their anatomy. No shark has ever been found that bears evidence of residual hind legs, nor has any shark DNA been linked to leg building. Several whale species have a pelvis, right whales have the bones for hind legs tucked in under the flesh, and humpback and sperm whales have been found with leg bones extending outside the body. The data support the hypothesis.[53]

Hypothesis: If birds evolved from nonflying organisms, feathers must have evolved initially for purposes other than flight.

Test: This is an example of a hypothesis that requires the chance discovery of fossilized flightless feathers to confirm it, or the accumulation of evidence for an alternative hypothesis to show it false.

Result: In this case, the requisite fossils have been discovered in the form of dinosaurs with many versions of feathers. With no use for flight, these feathers must have served a different purpose such as insulation, brooding, modest gliding ability, or attraction of mates. (Note that the specific creatures need not be direct ancestors of

---

53. Andrews, "A remarkable case of external hind limbs in a humpback whale"; Ogawa and Kamiya, "Case of the Cachalot [sperm whale] with protruded rudimentary hind limb"; Struthers, "The bones, articulations, and muscles of the rudimentary hind-limb of the Greenland right-whale (*Balaena mysticetus*)."

modern birds. They merely document that feathers could have evolved for use unrelated to flight.)[54]

Geologists Employ Circular Reasoning to Date Rocks and Fossils.

A frequent charge is made that geologists use the age of fossils to date the rocks where they are found and they use the ages of rocks to date the fossils. The entire dating enterprise is thus based on circular reasoning, built upon an underlying assumption of evolution.[55]

This description of circular reasoning could be labeled as *Two Truths and a Lie*. Two independently truthful statements are made, but inappropriately coupled to produce a false assertion. To understand the logic, imagine for a moment that a builder uses a wooden yardstick to measure out a series of ropes of different lengths. Later, at a project site, the ropes are used to measure the lengths of several boards in tight places where the yardstick doesn't easily fit. Someone watching then accuses the builder of circular reasoning, insisting that none of the measurements can be trusted. The builder used wood to measure ropes, and he used ropes to measure wood!

Was circular reasoning employed? Of course not. It only *sounds* that way because of the particular way the charge was worded. Two *technically* truthful statements were made (wood to rope, rope to wood) but oversimplified and combined in such a way to make a logical method appear stupid or sinister. There was no circular reasoning—all measurements were ultimately tied back to the calibrated yardstick.

The young-earth charge of circular reasoning is functionally the same. Our yardstick in this case is radiometric dating. Because most sedimentary rock cannot be directly dated (grains in the sediment eroded from some older rock), the radiometrically determined ages of underlying or overlying igneous rocks are used to constrain the age of the associated sedimentary layers and fossils (Fig. 13. At this point, one may accurately say the rocks are used to date the fossils.

After applying this method repeatedly, at many places around the world, *some* fossil species (or groups of species) have been found to consistently fall into a narrow range of ages. These are eventually recognized as *index fossils*,

---

54. Monastersky, "Feathered dinosaurs found in China"; Qiang et al., "Two feathered dinosaurs from northeastern China"; Prothero, *Evolution: What the Fossils Say and Why It Matters*, 276–89.
55. Hebert, "Deep core dating and circular reasoning"; Kelly, *Creation and Change*, 147–48; Vail et al., *Your Guide to the Grand Canyon: A Different Perspective*, 159.

because they "index" a particular time interval of earth's history. Index fossils then become a secondary method of identifying the age of rock layers in newly studied outcrops where radiometric dates cannot be made. Using these fossils to date rocks follows the same reasoning as using ropes to measure wood in our yardstick-rope analogy. The reasoning is logical and *linear*. It only sounds circular when worded to confuse.

Conventional Scientists Have No Explanation for ...

Young-earth and Intelligent Design writers repeatedly claim that data or observations or phenomena in nature are a "mystery" to conventional scientists.[56] I would agree, as most scientists would, that nature represents a virtually unlimited repository of things yet to be discovered or fully understood. Some scientific subjects that are currently a mystery include *what* is making expansion of the universe accelerate, *how* the very first cells came into existence, and *why* matter exerts a gravitational force. Note that "mystery" here is not equal to "no evidence it is real." We can directly measure gravity, for example, even if we can't explain why it exists.

When addressing fundamental subjects in geology or evolution, however, the claim that scientists have no explanation for observed data is rarely ever true. Such claims are typically based on sweeping statements that are wrong from the outset, followed by bold assertions that scientists cannot account for the made-up problem. Take the so-called "Cambrian Explosion" as an example. Anti-evolution writers describe this as the abrupt appearance of representatives of all modern phyla, fully formed and without predecessors. And, of course, this fits perfectly with young-earth (or Intelligent Design) expectations, but is a serious problem for evolutionists, who have "no explanation."

Nothing could be further from the truth.[57] (1) There are many fossils now known from Precambrian rocks around the world that are not as complex as those found in the Cambrian layers. (2) Transitional forms have been identified and described. (3) Cambrian fossils represent the proliferation of *shelled* organisms. Shells are far more resilient than soft tissue, and much more likely to be preserved. There is thus a built-in bias for the preservation of fossils

56. Vail et al., *Your Guide to the Grand Canyon*, 162–63; Bechly and Meyer, "The fossil record and universal common ancestry," 343–44; Ham, "What really happened to the dinosaurs?"; Oard, "Where does the Ice Age fit?," 216.

57. Stearley, "The Cambrian Explosion: How much bang for the buck?"; Miller, "The fossil record of the Cambrian 'Explosion': Resolving the tree of life"; Gramling, "Newfound fossils in China highlight a dizzying diversity of Cambrian life."

after hard parts appear. What is observed in the fossil record is in full accordance with evolutionary expectation. (4) The claim that most phyla appear in Cambrian rocks is misleading, for phyla are very large taxonomic groupings only one step below *kingdoms*. There are many *classes* of organisms (one more step down) and a vast number of *orders* and *families* that are entirely absent in Cambrian rock. Fossils in Cambrian (and Precambrian) deposits include no lobsters, sand dollars, bottom-feeding fish, reef-dwelling eels, or oysters. Nor can we find a single insect, amphibian, reptile, mammal, bird, fern, conifer, or flowering plant.[58] These layers look nothing like what should be expected from a violent global flood but fit an evolutionary model quite well.

HOW IS THIS POSSIBLE?

If this chapter felt a bit disturbing, it should have. The list of tactics designed to persuade rather than communicate truth is long, with many examples of how such methods are employed to dissuade people from acceptance of legitimate science. This raises an unsettling question. How is it possible for people to proclaim Jesus as Lord, to devote their lives to the defense of the Bible, and yet routinely employ methods inconsistent with Christian character?

I believe the answer involves two steps. The first step is a failure to recognize the difference between God's Word and one's interpretation of that Word (recall Chapter 1). Young-earth proponents start with the presupposed truth, not of the Bible but of their belief that the days in Genesis 1 were intended as a literal rendering of the creation events. As such, evolution *must* be false and the earth *must* be young. All examination of evidence *must* demonstrate this position. No effort is invested in the *discovery* of natural history. Natural history is *presumed*, and studied only for evidence that can be shoehorned into the accepted model.

This step has negative consequences (as all error does), but it is not enough by itself to prompt the use of the tactics described above. There are many Christians who are convinced the earth is young who do not knowingly twist truth to persuade others to their view. I respect their integrity while disagreeing with their reasoning and conclusions. There are some even among the leaders of the young-earth movement whom I would place in this category,

---

58. Stearley, "Fossils of the Grand Canyon and Grand Staircase"; Duff, "Tiny plants—big impact: Pollen, spores, and plant fossils."

such as Todd Wood of Core Academy of Science,[59] or my friend Marcus Ross, a paleontologist at Liberty University.[60] Todd and Marcus acknowledge the strength of evidence for evolution and vast ages, while also looking for plausible explanations to fit within a young-earth, global-flood paradigm.[61]

The second, more insidious step couples the perceived infallibility of a human interpretation of Scripture with a sense that it is of such importance that all methods available to persuade are justified if they draw people to the ultimate truth. Distortions of evidence or scientific principles may start small, but lead inextricably down a path of ever-increasing deception. As worship shifts from the Creator to the *mode of creation*,[62] hearts are blinded to the ability to recognize departures from truth or to realize that explanations, supposedly in defense of Scripture, march further and further from orthodox Christian faith. That young-earth organizations explicitly embrace the mission of *creation evangelism* is telling.[63] Creationism has become its own religion, with missionaries seeking converts to its unique tenets. In the next chapter, we will see how the young-earth movement has come full circle, embracing much of the science once mocked and advocating positions antithetical to traditional Christian understanding.

59. Todd Wood's website: http://www.coresci.org.
60. Marcus and I have adjacent opposing essays on the fossil record in the *Dictionary of Christianity and Science*: Davidson, "The fossil record (evolutionary creation view)"; Ross, "The fossil record (young-earth creation view)."
61. If I fault these men, it is in their partnering with those who take the second step (e.g., collaboration with the 2017 film *Is Genesis History?* The problem is not in working with unbelievers (I have coauthored many manuscripts with non-Christians), but in collaborating with those who twist truth.
62. Romans 1:25: "For they exchanged the truth of God for a lie, and worshiped and served the creature rather than the Creator, who is blessed forever. Amen." Worship of the *mode of creation* is functionally the same as worship of the *creature*.
63. Institute of Creation Research: H. Morris, "Creation Evangelism"; J. Morris, "Creation Evangelism"; Answers in Genesis: Ham, *Creation Evangelism for the New Millennium*; Creation Ministries International, "Creation Evangelism: Sharing Your Faith."

12

DAWN OF THE YOUNG-EARTH EVOLUTIONIST

After decades of insisting there is no evidence that supports a mechanism that can create beneficial mutations or that one kind of organism can turn into another,[1] it comes as some surprise that most of the leading young-earth proponents now argue not just for evolution, but evolution at hyperspeed. It is not called evolution, of course, for *evolution* has been declared to be inherently godless. *Adaptation* and *speciation,* though also used in the language of evolution, have not been so declared, so these are the terms that are used to describe what might aptly be called "evolution on steroids."[2]

The current young-earth understanding stems from the realization that all the terrestrial animals known from the past and today could not have fit on the ark, even if taken as juveniles.[3] The solution has been to note that the Hebrew word *min,* translated as "kind" in Genesis 1, can be interpreted to mean *types* of organisms rather than individual species. Thus, God may have created a single antelope-like creature during the first week of creation, which later gave rise to the varied types of antelopes known in living and fossil form (e.g., gazelles, pronghorns, giraffes, impalas, elands, bongos, waterbucks, dik diks, duikers, kudus, klipspringers, sables, springboks, addax, oryx, gemsboks, and myriad extinct varieties). Groups of related

---

1. Morris, *Scientific Creationism,* 1st ed., 13 and 54–57; Huse, *The Collapse of Evolution,* 1st ed., 87–92; Gish, *Evolution: The Fossils Still Say No!,* 3, 37.
2. Sarfati, *Refuting Evolution 2,* chap. 4; Gish, *Evolution,* chap. 2 (note: Gish argues for *and* against evolution in this book); Morris, "The microwave of evolution"; Catchpoole and Wieland, "Speedy species surprise."
3. Recognition that not all known living and extinct species could fit on the ark predates the earliest young-earth publications that acknowledge that fact. Examples of more recent citations include: Woodmorappe, *Noah's Ark: A Feasibility Study;* Sarfati, "How did all the animals fit on Noah's ark?"

organisms with a single, specially created ancestor are referred to as *baramin* (created from two Hebrew words—*bara*: created; *min*: kind).[4]

The flood is said to have transfigured the environment so drastically that rapid adaptation was required for organisms to survive. God, knowing what was to come, designed each of the original organisms with a built-in propensity for change that would allow subsequent adaptation to a changing environment. Populations experiencing different environmental pressures in different locales after the flood adapted in different ways to eventually produce a suite of unique species within each *baramin*, all within a period of a thousand years—or even a few hundred years—following the flood.[5]

Much of the evidence for evolution that has been ridiculed and declared to be wholly without merit for half a century is now embraced as evidence supporting the rapid adaptation of organisms leaving the ark. Long-standing evidence for evolution now included in the young-earth argument as evidence for rapid adaptation and speciation includes:[6]

- the presence of some imperfections in design;[7]
- organs without an apparent function (vestigial);[8]
- the occasional birth of a genetic "throwback" such as a modern whale with dangling hind limbs or a horse with three toes (atavism);[9]

---

4. Term coined in 1941 by Seventh-day Adventist, Frank Lewis Marsh in the book *Fundamental Biology*; Frair, "Baraminology: Classification of created organisms"; Wise and Richardson, *Something from Nothing: Understanding What You Believe About Creation and Why*, 73–83.
5. Wise, *Faith, Form, and Time: What the Bible Teaches and Science Confirms About Creation and the Age of the Universe*, 218; Criswell, "Speciation and the animals on the ark."
6. For the bullet list, references are provided that historically argued *against* each phenomenon and references that now argue *for* them. Not all young-earth proponents have embraced the change in thinking, though this does reflect the current views of organizations such as Answers in Genesis and the Institute for Creation Research.
7. Against imperfection: Huse, *The Collapse of Evolution*, 1st ed., 71–82; Wieland, "Seeing back to front: Are evolutionists right when they say our eyes are wired the wrong way?" Now expecting a degree of imperfection: Wise, *Faith, Form, and Time*, 131, 219.
8. Against vestigial features: Morris, *Scientific Creationism*, 1st ed., 75–76; Huse, *The Collapse of Evolution*, 1st ed., 107. Now expecting vestigial features: Wise, *Faith, Form, and Time*, 132, 219–20; Garner, *The New Creationism: Building Scientific Theory on a Biblical Foundation*, 173–76.
9. Against genetic throwbacks: Wieland, "The strange tale of the leg on the whale." (Earlier citations are difficult to find because young-earth proponents generally would not acknowledge the existence of genetic throwbacks in print.) Now expecting genetic throwbacks: Wise, *Faith, Form, and Time*, 132, 219–20; Sarfati, "The non-evolution of the horse: Special creation or evolved rock badger?"

- punctuated equilibrium;[10]
- greater similarity of DNA between island and mainland species that would not be expected if all modern species were specially created;[11 (1)]
- recognition of natural selection as a driving force both for the preservation of traits in a stable environment and for speciation in the presence of changing environmental conditions;[11 (2)] and
- recognition that there are multiple ways in which mutations occur and that they can produce *beneficial* traits in offspring.[12]

Apparent imperfections in design are allowed because changes that occurred since the fall are subject to the curse, and some flaws are thus now expected. Vestigial organs are allowed for the same reason. The original created organisms would have been perfect, but later offspring might have unused organs or features since genetic information that controlled their function was damaged or lost. In some cases, mutations may have resulted in the loss of genetic information for an entire body form such as legs. A rarity of transitional forms is expected because adaptation occurred so quickly that only a few generations of transitional forms existed before a completely new species was established. Island and mainland species are expected to be more genetically similar than species occupying similar niches in geographically

---

10. An apparent paucity of transitional fossils prior to the 1990s gave rise to a theory that organisms remained largely unchanged (*stasis*) for long periods interrupted by much shorter periods when evolutionary change occurred more rapidly (*punctuated equilibrium*). The short time span resulted in few transitional fossils being preserved. Now young-earth evolutionists argue that change was slow prior to the flood and fast after, and that transitional forms within baramins have not been found because the diversification was too rapid.

Against punctuated equilibrium: Morris, *Scientific Creationism*, 2nd ed., 90; Huse, *The Collapse of Evolution*, 1st ed., 45. Now supporting punctuated equilibrium (renamed *saltation*): Wieland, "Speciation conference brings good news for creationists"; Wise, *Faith, Form, and Time*, 124; some have gone so far as to argue for large morphological changes in a single generation (eerily similar to the once-mocked "chicken hatching from a dinosaur egg"), e.g., Wise, "Step-down saltational intrabaraminic diversification."

11. Against speciation and natural selection: anonymous, "To make a snake"; Huse, *The Collapse of Evolution*, 1st ed., 38–41; Morris, *Scientific Creationism*, 2nd ed., 51–54. Now arguing for rapid speciation and significant role of natural selection: Sarfati, *Refuting Evolution 2*, chap. 4; Wise, *Faith, Form, and Time*, chap. 14; Morris, "The microwave of evolution"; Catchpoole and Wieland, "Speedy species surprise."

12. Against beneficial mutations: Morris, *Scientific Creationism*, 2nd ed., 54–57; Huse, *The Collapse of Evolution*, 1st ed., 89–92. Now for beneficial mutations (through loss of genetic information): Sarfati, *Refuting Evolution 2*, 79, 90, and chap. 5; Wieland, "Beetle bloopers: Even a defect can be an advantage sometimes"; Jerlström, "Jumping wallaby genes and post-flood speciation."

remote islands because organisms migrating from the ark reached islands directly from adjacent continents and adapted to their new environments.

All this sounds suspiciously like evolution, yet young-earth advocates of this position are vehement in their expressed opposition to evolution. So how can someone believe that organisms can change from one species into another through a succession of generations, even to the point of a four-legged, whale-like creature giving rise to a modern legless whale, and still claim to deny evolution?

It's all in how the terminology is spun. Technically, *evolution* simply refers to change over time. When applied to life-forms, change over time through a series of generations is worded as *descent with modification*, a phenomenon now advocated and taught by many young-earth proponents. Thus, young-earth advocates of rapid speciation are in fact *evolutionists*. The distinction between traditional evolution and the young-earth variety is not whether evolution occurred, but the *extent* to which it occurred and the *manner* in which it is described.

CONVENTIONAL VS. YOUNG-EARTH EVOLUTION

Young-earth evolutionists claim two major distinctions between their view and that of mainstream science.

Limited Scope of Common Ancestry
Traditional evolutionists argue that all life shares a common ancestry, starting with single-celled creatures. Young-earth evolutionists argue that many species today share a common ancestor, but that no major group of modern organisms derived from any other. By way of analogy, evolutionists will speak of the "tree of life," where the trunk represents some original single-celled life-form, while young-earth proponents speak of the "orchard of life," where each tree trunk represents a specially created kind (*baramin*) that gave rise to many variants.[13]

Speciation tthrough Loss—Rather Than Gain—of Genetic Information
Conventional evolutionists believe that myriad alterations in the genetic code of simple organisms through a succession of generations resulted in a systematic increase in complexity that gave rise to new forms and functions in

---

13. Sarfati, *Refuting Evolution*, 38–39; Batten, "Natural Selection."

later offspring. Young-earth evolutionists believe that all adaptation and specia-tion has arisen from either rearrangement or impairment of the genetic code originally found in each specially created ancestor kind. Changes in the genetic code through point mutations, incorporation of duplicate sections of DNA during cell division, gene transfer between different organisms, and recombina-tion during sexual reproduction are all recognized as legitimate processes that can give rise to new species, but it is insisted that all such alterations produce no new information and usually represent a loss of information.[14]

The rise of poisons, thorns, parasitic behavior, and carnivory are attributed to mutations after the fall that eliminated the genetic coding that originally inhibited these expressions. Perhaps a plant produced an array of chemicals that worked together in a benign way before the fall. After the fall, a muta-tion disabled the production of one of these chemicals, resulting in a chemi-cal mix that was poisonous to many insects. All subsequent offspring of this plant carried this beneficial (to the plant) mutation that arose through a loss of genetic information. Bacteria and viruses may develop immunity to a new drug as mutations turn off production of proteins. A legged creature could even conceivably give rise to a legless species through the loss or disabling of the leg-building genetic code. Some dramatic changes are thus allowed within the young-earth model, but never ones that require an increase in information.

THEOLOGICAL ASSESSMENT

I will address the scientific shortcomings shortly, but I believe the bigger issue for the church is the violence done to the biblical text.

Young-Earth "Kind" Undermines the Biblical "Kind"

This issue was already addressed in Chapter 6, so I will add just a summary here. The repeated statement in Genesis that organisms were created or repro-duced "after their kind" was an encouragement to God's people that nature is not a chaotic outgrowth of capricious or warring gods, but is orderly, reflect-ing the character of its Author. In the human experience, sheep will give rise to sheep and goats to goats. Young-earth evolutionists eviscerate this theo-logical understanding, now arguing that people had no idea what to expect nature to kick up. A young-earth *baramin* could be as large as all ruminants,

---

14. Sarfati, *Refuting Evolution 2*, 79; Ham and Lisle, "Is there really a God?," 13–15; Jerlström, "Jumping wallaby genes and post-flood speciation."

meaning that a sheep might well give birth to a goat.[15] Mankind from Adam to Noah may not have even known what a cow or a sheep looked like, for these may not have arisen until after their ruminant-kind ancestor left the ark. Ironically, in an effort to preserve one aspect of a traditional interpretation of the creation story (the number of days), another part of equal or greater importance (the consistency of kinds) is sacrificed.

Increased Information Is Falsely Equated with Improvement

In the young-earth evolution model, all speciation must derive exclusively through a reshuffling of existing genetic information or through degradation of the genetic code—a loss of information. Increases in genetic information to produce novel features or physiology are not allowed. The reasoning is that the initial creation was perfect. Any increase in information or complexity would represent an improvement on perfection, which is obviously not acceptable

All this is based on the belief that information is inherently good, and increases in information lead to improvement. Following this logic, when Adam and Eve gained information about good and evil, their situation must have improved. Except that it didn't. In this earliest recorded instance of an increase in information, perfection took a serious hit.

There is no verse in Scripture and no logic that says that increases in information are universally good. We can identify many occasions where advances in information, often leading to increases in complexity, have had both good and bad consequences. An often-used example is the discovery of dynamite. Dynamite greatly improved our ability to extract minerals and build roads, but also our ability to mar the environment and kill fellow humans in greater numbers.

Information by itself is neither good nor bad, and increases in information have no direct relationship with improvement or impairment of the creation. Efforts to explain why one type of information increase is allowable after creation (growth of technological information) while another is not (growth of genetic information) are pointless.

Creation after Day 6 Attributed to Another God

This subject was addressed in Chapter 5, and so this will be another brief summary. Insistence that God's creative expression was complete on Day 6 runs into logical inconsistencies, and perhaps even heretical postulations. In

---

15. Lightner, "Mammalian ark kinds," 192. A good critique of this article is Duff, "Are ruminants derived from a common ancestor? Ruminating on the meaning of Noahic 'kinds.'"

the young-earth model, God created all the genetic information in the first six days, and then natural processes subsequently sorted those genes to produce many new species. The logical conclusion has to be that God may have been the creator of some initial monkey-kind, but is *not* the creator of the many modern species of gibbons, squirrel monkeys, baboons, tamarins, marmosets, capuchins, spider monkeys, macaques, and guenons.

In what way is this a more biblically consistent view of creation than a view that says God continues to create today? In fact, the notion that nature, or perhaps even Satan, is the creator of these wonderfully adapted creatures is a fundamentally heretical notion either by virtue of requiring that God is no longer in control over his creation or by ascribing the ability to create good things (organisms better suited to a particular environment or more disease resistant) to Satan or some other god.

SCIENTIFIC ASSESSMENT

Rapid Speciation after Release from the Ark

Organisms exiting the ark are said to have faced conditions radically different from those when they entered the ark and had to quickly adapt to survive. If the environmental conditions had changed over several generations, say from very warm to very cold, one might envision a series of successive births where long- and short-haired varieties were born and only the long-haired varieties lived to reproduce. But the environmental changes following a global flood would have been immediate. Organisms had to be capable of surviving in the new environment the moment they stepped off the gangway. The flood model offers no time for generational adaptation. If organisms were capable of surviving away from the ark for more than a few years, then the environment wasn't so bad after all and normal selective pressures for adaptation should have been the norm. Hyperspeciation falls flat.

The flood model also fails to explain why nearly every native mammal in Australia is a marsupial (young are delivered into a pouch to finish gestation).[16] If all rats came from a single rat-kind in the ark, one might fully expect rat species that migrated to Australia to look different from those in North America, perhaps even for one to develop a pouch and not the other. But why would almost every mammal migrating to Australia develop a pouch, while almost

---

16. Non-marsupial mammals in Australia include the odd egg-laying monotremes (e.g., platypus, spiny anteater) and placental mammals introduced by humans (rabbits, cats, dogs, sheep, etc.).

all mammals in every other part of the world did not? If Australian mammals share the same pouch-bearing ancestor, it makes perfect sense why diverging species would retain pouches.[17] Young-earth evolutionists, on the other hand, are left with incredible, just-so stories where marsupials, by virtue of having traveling pouches, could travel faster and farther, migrating over land bridges that were then submerged before *any* placental mammals could cross.[18] (Somehow, marsupial moles and koalas beat out placental deer and wolves over these bridges.) Or they must defend stories that animals crossing the equator experienced environmental pressures that caused creatures as diverse as mice and kangaroos *all* to become marsupial (macroevolution mixed with magic).[19]

Changes Only through Loss of Information

When a person goes on an antibiotic for a bacterial infection, most of the bacteria are killed, but mutations may exist in a small number that make them resistant to the drug. The surviving bacteria can then reproduce to give rise to a new drug-resistant strain. Over time, the original drug becomes ineffective at combatting the infection. So-called superbugs are simply the offspring of those drug-resistant survivors.

Conventional scientists argue this is standard evolution in action, as successive genetic modifications result in new ways to dodge each new drug. Young-earth evolutionists insist otherwise. The genetic changes are argued to be neutral at best, swapping existing genes with a different type of bacteria to avoid succumbing to a drug (no new information), or are negative changes, where the mutation that evades the drug weakens the bacteria in other important ways. As an example, if a drug targets a particular protein on the bacteria, a mutation may eliminate the production of that protein. The protein had a function, however, so its loss weakens the overall fitness of the bacteria. It only lives on because all its stronger relatives were killed off. Rather than superbugs, they are sickly bugs—but at least they are ignored by the drug.[20]

If this explanation for drug resistance is normative, then each successive antibiotic should result in surviving populations of bacteria that are weaker than their parents. Each mutation will have turned off yet another

---

17. Darrel Falk provides a good description of why the rise of marsupials in Australia fits an evolutionary model well but fails to fit with a young-earth model. Falk, *Coming to Peace with Science: Bridging the Worlds Between Faith and Biology*, 157–58.
18. Taylor, "How did animals spread all over the world from where the ark landed?," 146.
19. Ashcraft, "Marsupial evolution and post-flood migration."
20. Purdom, "Antibiotic resistance of bacteria: An example of evolution in action?"

useful function or diverted still more energy away from normal metabolism to produce some agent that evades the effects of the next drug. Over time, it should get easier and easier to kill the weakened, mutated bacteria.[21]

Efforts to fight disease-causing bacteria have demonstrated the exact opposite. Bacteria such as those that generate staph infections have proven increasingly difficult to kill, with an apparently inexhaustible capacity to develop robust strains resistant to the latest antibiotic. This is only possible if the genetic code of the bacteria is changing in ways other than by damage.

Experiments with Intensive Selective Breeding Are Fast—but Not That Fast

Young-earth arguments for rapid speciation after the ark invariably draw on examples of fast morphological changes observed by selective breeding of *domesticated* animals.[22] These are inadequate examples, however, because thousands of years of domestication has introduced unusual genetic plasticity into these species relative to nondomesticated forms. A genetic foundation that permits a wider variety of shape, size, or appearance is possible because human caretakers keep them safe, fed, and in close proximity to mates. The rate of changes observed in nondomesticated animals is more appropriate for assessing young-earth claims of widespread, rapid adaptation.

It just so happens that a fascinating study of nondomesticated animals has been going on for sixty years in Russia. In 1959, Dmitry Belyayev, later joined by Lyudmila Trut, began selectively breeding wild foxes for friendly behavioral traits to better understand the genetics of domestication.[23] In each generation, only the friendliest 10 percent of the pups were selected to continue breeding. Some developments were remarkably fast, with fear and aggression diminishing in a few generations and some foxes allowing themselves to be handled by humans. A few generations more, a small number began to wag their tails. Still more generations and fur color began to become more varied. Thirty years into the experiment, vocalizations began to change and body forms began to retain juvenile features—such as floppy ears and shorter snouts—into adulthood. After more than fifty generations, characteristics

21. Reduced viability as functions are lost is explicitly claimed in Gish, *Evolution*, 33; Sarfati, *Refuting Evolution 2*, 92.
22. Purdom and Hodge, 'What are "kinds" in genesis?'; Tomkins, "Mechanisms of adaptation in biology: genetic diversity."
23. Dugatkin and Trut, *How to Tame a Fox (and Build a Dog): Visionary Scientists and a Siberian Tale of Jump-Started Evolution*; Jones, "A Soviet scientist created the only tame foxes in the world."

included an active desire for human companionship and longer and more frequent mating seasons. Scientists have already begun studies to sort out the accompanying genetic and physiological changes that have produced these adaptations.

So what does this mean for rapid speciation after the flood? The fox domestication study has applied *intensive* selection pressure for over sixty years and roughly the same number of generations. Remarkable changes have been observed, but at the same time, the current generation is still quite recognizable as foxes. The changes required to turn a fox ancestor into the equivalent of a wolf, dingo, coyote, jackal, or dog is much, much greater. The proposed "saltational" young-earth model (superfast punctuated-equilibrium), with dramatic changes taking place over the course of a few generations in response to the flood-altered landscape, is not supported by experimental evidence.[24]

THE TEN- TO TWENTY-YEAR LAG

The careful reader may have noticed that young-earth arguments used in this chapter conflict with young-earth arguments used in earlier chapters. This represents a common occurrence in young-earth reasoning. Anytime new evidence is offered for evolution or when new theories are developed for how a particular transition occurred, young-earth proponents may be counted on to reject the interpretations of the data and come up with reasons why the theories are wrong. As evidence builds for those interpretations and theories to the point where they are increasingly difficult to deny, the young-earth arguments adapt to accept much of the interpretations, but in a young-earth framework.

Examples are myriad. The geologic column was rejected outright, but then later accepted with explanations for how the flood produced it. Radioactive dating was rejected completely, followed by acceptance under particular conditions where radiometric dates match biblical dates. Punctuated equilibrium, a hypothesis that organisms did not change much over time until environmental changes forced rapid change, was long mocked as a "chicken hatching from a dinosaur egg," yet it is now embraced as an explanation for why little speciation occurred before the flood but was rapid after. All mechanisms capable of producing beneficial mutations

---

24. Wise, "Step-down saltational intrabaraminic diversification."

were dismissed, but then accepted as a viable means of diversifying organisms after the flood.

This suggests two things. First, the evidence for evolution must be steadily growing, or the young-earth arguments would not have to continually adapt to accept so much of what evolutionists contend. Second, the ten- to twenty-year lag between when evolutionists make an argument and when young-earth proponents accept it should make us realize that what is rejected today will more than likely be accepted and incorporated into the latest young-earth model at a later time. Christians would be better off not wasting so much time, energy, and resources fighting something they will inevitably embrace a few years or decades later.

ONE STEP FORWARD, THREE STEPS BACK

Few realize just how much of traditional Christian understanding has been abandoned or upended by the young-earth mission. I will conclude this chapter with a summary of what has been sacrificed.

Turning Good into Evil

Romans 1:20 tells us that God's character has been manifest in the physical world continuously since the creation. Psalm 104 speaks of God providing food for his creatures—including carnivores—and calls it good. Psalm 19:1 tells us that God's material world declares his glory. Nature is indeed cursed, but nature itself reflects its Author still today.

The young-earth version teaches that the only character of God reflected in nature is his wrath, carnivory is apart from God's will (Psalm 104 must have a cryptic meaning), and the material world declares the corruption of sin rather than the glory of God. In short, good is turned into evil.[25]

God's Sovereignty Diminished

Scripture tells us that God is sovereign over all, including what we refer to, perhaps naively, as natural evil. We often wish to give God a pass when a hurricane devastates a coast or when an earthquake levels a town. Yet Scripture tells us that when disaster falls upon a city, God has not just allowed it, he

---

25. Martin and Vaughn, *Beyond Creation Science*, 204–5, equate this view with a form of Gnosticism.

has caused it (Amos 3:6).[26] God is sovereign! Blaming animal death or natural disasters on man's sin as a way to excuse God from responsibility effectively declares that sin is more powerful than God. God did not want to introduce natural evil or animal death, but sin made him do it.

"Fine-Tuning" Abandoned

The fine-tuning argument says there are a large number of physical constants, ranging from the magnitude of nuclear forces in atoms to the strength of gravity exerted by matter, that are so finely tuned for life, it speaks strongly of intentionality. Tweak any number of these constants a wee bit up or down, and stars do not form, carbon does not join to produce complex molecules, water becomes opaque to sunlight, and the earth drifts too far or too close to the sun for life to thrive. The universe bears evidence of being carefully engineered.

By insisting that radioactive-decay rates, the speed of light, or heat-dissipation rates were radically different at times in the past, young-earth advocates unwittingly declare that the universe is *not* finely tuned. Physical constants are said to have varied wildly during the creation week and during the flood and yet the natural realm continued to function just fine (although perhaps traumatically during the flood). Young-earth advocates will still speak fondly of fine-tuning, but their arguments actively undermine it.

Return to the Gods of Mesopotamia

The ancient gods of Mesopotamia, like the gods of the Greeks and Romans, were factious and capricious. Nature was a reflection of those gods, chaotic and unpredictable as squabbles in the heavens spilled over into the human experience. The biblical writers described a very different version of God and his relationship with the material world. Nature was not chaotic, but an intentional creation fashioned to reflect the character of a benevolent, omnipotent God.

The modern young-earth view is reverting increasingly to the belief system of Israel's ancient neighbors. Nature is unpredictable, with wild swings possible for physical parameters we falsely think of as constants. The study of nature cannot be trusted to reveal an accurate story without knowing the answer in advance. Myriad natural processes (tree-ring growth, sediment layering, radionuclide decay, plate movement, fossil placement, genetic

---

26. Isaiah 45:6–7 likewise speaks of God "causing well-being and creating calamity."

structure, cosmic energy distribution, and many others) were divinely manipulated to falsely align with conventional expectations for great age and evolution. We cannot even be confident that, in human experience, goats will give birth to other goats.

A PARTING OBSERVATION

A frequently employed young-earth cartoon shows two men, each viewing the earth through a lens in the middle of a book; one book is the Holy Bible and one is a book of human wisdom (permission to reprint was denied).[27] There is great irony in this depiction, for it is far more accurate than most realize. To see the things that young-earth advocates insist they see in both the Bible and in nature, a large hole must first be cut from the Bible, and Scripture removed to make room for the young-earth lens.

---

27. Ham, *The Lie: Evolution*, 473; Hodge, "Don't creationists believe in some 'wacky' things?," 204; Lacey, book review of *Inside the Nye Ham Debate*.

13

WHAT ABOUT INTELLIGENT DESIGN?

Any thorough discussion of science and creation at this time in our culture has to at least touch on Intelligent Design (also referred to as ID). Intelligent Design, in its modern formulation, is a relatively recent movement that owes much of its popularity to the *Discovery Institute*, an ID think tank, and to the writings of Michael Behe, William Dembski, and Stephen Meyer.[1] The movement gained considerable public attention as a result of attempts to have Intelligent Design taught in public schools as an alternative to evolution. So what is Intelligent Design, and how is it unique?

For an adequate understanding of what ID is, we need to back up a few centuries. Evidence of design in nature was a common topic in the late 1600s and on through the next century, with advocates including eminent scientists such as Isaac Newton. These discussions led to William Paley's seminal work, *Natural Theology or Evidences of the Existence and Attributes of the Deity*, published in 1802. Paley advanced a teleological argument for the existence of God, arguing that when we study natural systems such as planetary motion or the anatomy of the human body, we see evidence of intricate and complex structures working in harmony to such an extent that they bear evidence of being *designed*. He offered the now famous example of finding a watch lying in the grass, and asking, after seeing its intricate inner workings, whether it made more sense to think the watch came about by some accident of nature or by the purposeful creation of a designer.

---

1. Best-known examples include *Darwin's Black Box* by Michael Behe, *The Design Inference: Eliminating Chance Through Small Probabilities* by William Dembski, and *Signature in the Cell* by Stephen Meyer.

The modern Intelligent Design movement expands on Paley's argument in an attempt to add scientific rigor. In other words, the complexity of nature does not just appeal to the human spirit as bearing evidence of intentional design. Rather, scientific methods can be applied to demonstrate that the best explanation for what we see in living organisms is creation by a supernatural intelligence, with at least some original forms created by means that preclude naturalistic explanations. The identity of the designer is intentionally left open in an attempt to make Intelligent Design a strictly scientific position.

Objective evidence of design is cited in terms of *specified complexity* and *irreducible complexity*. The idea behind specified complexity is that complex patterns may occur by random processes in nature, but a complexity that requires an exact pattern to govern a very specific purpose requires intelligence.[2] The specified complexity found in DNA is thus considered scientifically defensible evidence that intelligence was required in its construction.

Irreducible complexity refers to the belief that natural processes may be able to increase the complexity of an existing piece of biological machinery, but the simplest organelle in even a single-celled organism is still far too complex to have been created by purely natural processes. An often-cited example is the flagellum on bacteria such as *E. coli*.[3] The flagellum is a hooked filament that spins and allows the bacteria to swim. The flagellum has multiple parts that are required in order to function. Take away any part and the function ceases. It is argued that the individual parts have no function on their own, so they could not have independently evolved to give rise to the flagellum. It might be possible for evolutionary adaptation to occur in an existing flagellum, but creating the initial organ requires creation all-at-once by an external agent.

The last observation warrants additional comment, for many mistakenly think that ID is an alternative to evolution. Just as ID is not limited to a particular theological version of the designer, it is also not specific about how much evolution is disavowed. The ID umbrella includes those who reject all forms of evolution and those who only require an initial miraculous insertion of DNA to get the evolutionary process started. The only aspect of evolution that ID universally rejects is a natural transition from nonlife to life.

---

2. Others refer to the same concept as *imposed design*, e.g., Collins, *Science and Faith, Friends or Foes?*, 287.
3. Behe, *Darwin's Black Box, The Biochemical Challenge to Evolution*, 70–72.

I believe that many Intelligent Design advocates are well-intentioned Christian believers, but I find the claims that (1) intelligence in creation can be *scientifically* demonstrated, and (2) complex biological structures require miraculous creation, to be fraught with both theological and scientific pitfalls.[4]

THEOLOGICAL PITFALLS

Faith Supplanted

At a philosophical or intuitive level, the Intelligent Design argument should resonate in the heart of every Christian. Scripture tells us, after all, that the heavens declare the glory of God (Ps. 19:1). Romans 1:20 further tells us that God's attributes and divine nature are manifest in his physical creation, enough so that it leaves the unbeliever without excuse. The Bible seems to assure us that, indeed, nature reflects and proclaims its Author.

But we get an incomplete picture if we stop here, for other verses speak of the critical role of faith. Hebrews 11:1–3 reminds us that it is only by faith that we understand the world was made by the word of God. The writer of Hebrews is not contradicting what we find in Romans or the Psalms. The evidence is indeed present for all to observe, but if God has not touched the eyes of your heart, you will not see it. Why else would so many atheists insist that evidence of God in nature is entirely absent?

It may be helpful to consider an analogy using a famous illustration shown in Figure 43. When seeing this drawing for the first time, people tend to see either an old woman with a big nose *or* a young aristocratic woman looking away. Most do not see the second image without being told it is there. Some even require that aspects of the second image be highlighted before they can see it. The two images are always there, but it usually requires external input before the second woman consciously registers in the mind. In a related fashion, the evidence of God is manifest in creation for all to see, but if God does not prompt the heart to look for it, it will not be recognized.[5]

---

4. None of this critique challenges the existence or action of the supernatural (e.g., efficacy of prayer, reality of heaven and hell, resurrection of Christ, miracles). The critique applies only to claims that God's natural creation required miraculous interventions to operate properly.
5. I recognize that this is essentially the same argument young-earth advocates make, claiming that you only see the evidence for a young earth if you believe the Bible. I can only refer readers back through the pages of this book to assess the value of that claim.

By making evidence of design a scientific argument, ID advocates are essentially saying that God's prompting is no longer necessary. We can now apply spiritually neutral methods of science to demonstrate beyond reasonable doubt that life was created by God (or the more nebulous "designer"). ID, ironically, supplants faith with science.

Figure 43—Illustration by W.E. Hill.[6]

Irreducible Complexity: God in a Shrinking Box

One striking difference between William Paley's version of Intelligent Design and the modern rendering is *where* in nature we find evidence of God's authorship. Paley's argument is that it is essentially everywhere. When we observe any system within the natural realm, it is so complex and all the parts work so well together that it speaks to us of being intentionally made

---

6. Hill, "My wife and my mother-in-law."

that way. The modern ID movement turns this upside down. Evidence of a designer is not found in the totality of creation, but in things we observe that seem to be impossible to have formed by natural means.

Irreducible complexity draws our attention to the complexity of DNA or of particular organs with claims that there is no way for the various parts to have come together in a stepwise fashion by natural mechanisms. The only logical explanation is that they were created supernaturally by an intelligent designer.

There are at least two problems with this reasoning. The first is that Scripture is far more supportive of the old Intelligent Design argument than the new. Psalm 19:1 and Romans 1:20 both appear to speak of *all* of nature as bearing witness of its Author, not just the little pieces that we don't fully understand.

The second problem is that if evidence of God is found primarily in pieces of nature that are beyond our current comprehension, then evidence for God is—almost by definition—continuously shrinking. As each new discovery sheds light on how natural phenomena work, the supposed evidence of God's handiwork diminishes.

This is not a new problem. Consider Isaac Newton, whom I mentioned earlier as a proto-ID advocate. In the 1600s, Newton discovered that the elliptical orbits of the planets about the sun could be explained by the gravitational attraction between the sun and each planet. Realizing that the planets also tugged on each other, however, Newton was convinced that, over time, the regular orbits became unstable and required divine intervention to realign. He even suggested that God had made the solar system with the need for periodic supernatural adjustment as evidence of his existence, foreshadowing modern ID claims. Less than a generation later, Pierre-Simon Laplace, using advances in mathematical methods, was able to demonstrate that while the passing tug of one planet on another indeed alters the orbits, variations stay within a stable range.[7] No divine intervention was required, leading Laplace to claim, when asked why he left out God from his descriptions, that he "had no need of that hypothesis."[8]

If that example seems too long ago and too unrelated to the complexity of life, consider a more recent example following the discovery of DNA. While it was recognized that mutations in DNA were the key to bringing about

---

7. Planetary orbits within our solar system are not eternally stable, but are stable over a time span of many millions of years: https://en.wikipedia.org/wiki/Stability_of_the_Solar_System.

8. There is disagreement on Laplace's exact words. At the very least, he argued that *intervention* by God was not a helpful or necessary hypothesis.

generational changes in body plan and function, little was initially known about how beneficial mutations could arise. Damages by radiation or environmental stressors were the only known mechanisms for introducing changes, which led almost universally to *decreased* viability. The seeming impossibility of producing an improved function through mutation was believed by many Christians to be a compelling argument for the special creation of each species.

Discoveries within the last few decades, however, have been revolutionary. Mutations do not require radiation damage or toxins, but happen routinely during cell division, ranging from point changes of a single base pair to duplication of the entire genome. Duplicated stretches of DNA are ripe for alterations that could give rise to a new function without causing harm to an existing one. Beneficial mutations are no longer hypothesized, but have actually been observed in controlled laboratory experiments. In Chapter 9, an example was given where specific mutations observed in *E. coli* gave rise to a novel function that the original parent population did not have. Whether one calls this real evolution or not, it is still an example of something that was once claimed impossible by natural means but has now been demonstrated to naturally occur.

This tendency to attribute what we do not understand to divine action is what is pejoratively referred to as *God of the gaps*. ID advocates insist that this label is inappropriately applied to them, but only because they are convinced that, *this* time, nature *really* cannot explain whatever system has been declared to be impossible by natural mechanisms. Yet others through history have been equally convinced this was true for their own pet systems, right up until (or some time after) unequivocal natural explanations were discovered.

In the case of the purportedly irreducibly complex bacterial flagellum, it has already been shown that a subset of the DNA that codes for the flagellum works just fine coding for a different function.[9] But it should not even matter. Why are we confining the evidence of God to a shrinking box in the first place? We would do well to take advice from Dietrich Bonhoeffer, a German pastor and martyr during WWII:

> How wrong it is to use God as a stop-gap for the incompleteness of our
> knowledge. If in fact the frontiers of knowledge are being pushed further
> and further back (and that is bound to be the case), then God is being

---

9. Kenneth Miller, "The flagellum unspun: The collapse of 'irreducible complexity.'"

WHAT ABOUT INTELLIGENT DESIGN?   263

pushed back with them, and is therefore continually in retreat. We are to find God in what we know, not in what we don't know.[10]

Irreducible Complexity (Again): God as Inefficient Engineer

It is worth revisiting irreducible complexity from another perspective. This perspective can be introduced by the question, "How good was God at crafting his natural creation?" Or, similarly, "Did God fashion his natural creation so well that everything works within the natural laws he established, or does his creation need periodic supernatural tweaking to ensure that it behaves as divinely intended?"

This is not a question about whether miracles such as parting the sea or raising the dead are possible. It is a question of whether nature requires miracles to properly function. Isaac Newton again serves as a convenient representative for the ID position. His view, shared in principle by modern ID advocates, was that God did not create the world to fully operate within the bounds of his own natural laws, but included designed imperfections—shortcomings that required divine intervention to fix—that would point humanity's attention to the existence of a supernatural caretaker.

Consider the theological implications here. If, according to Romans 1:20, God's character is manifest in his natural creation, what we see in the ID version of God's character is *inefficiency*. Gottfried Leibniz, a contemporary of Newton, expressed this criticism in letters written to (or about) Newton:

> If God had to remedy the defects of His creation, this was surely to demean His craftsmanship.[11]

and

> When God works miracles, he does it not to meet the wants of nature but the needs of grace. Anyone who thinks differently must have a very mean notion of the wisdom and power of God.[12]

A more worthy and more biblical view of God is as the *best* Engineer, crafting nature to work seamlessly, responding to his directives and creative

---

10. Bonhoeffer, *Letters and Papers from Prison*, 310–12.
11. Brooke, *Science and Religion: Some Historical Perspectives*, 199.
12. Pojman and Rea, *Philosophy of Religion: An Anthology*, 609; Brewster, *Memoirs of the Life, Writings, and Discoveries of Sir Isaac Newton*, 285.

will without requiring suspension of his own natural laws. On this score, I will side with Leibniz, believing God to be a far more efficient designer than ID would suggest.

Specified Complexity: God on a Short Leash

The basic claim of specified complexity is that complex information-bearing systems are hallmarks of intelligence. As such, the incredible complexity of DNA and its vast storehouse of information is said to be clear evidence of intelligent creation. If the argument ended there, and if it was not advanced as a scientific argument, I would be inclined to agree. The heavens and DNA *do* speak to me of the glory of an awesome and intelligent God.

The argument for specified complexity does not stop there, however, but goes on to claim that systems with specified complexity could not have come about by natural mechanisms. I will suggest that this is nonsensical. What is to prevent the designer of the universe from calling on his creation to produce systems with specified complexity by entirely (divinely ordained) natural means? The ID equation that evidence of intelligence equals evidence of miraculous origin is effectively telling God what his limits are—God, but on a short leash.

Interventionist Design

All the previous arguments point to a conclusion that the modern ID movement is not really about whether nature bears evidence of *intelligence*, but whether it bears unmistakable evidence of miraculous *interventions*. Scientist and theologian Denis Lamoureux aptly declares that ID should really be known as *Interventionistic* Design.[13]

SCIENTIFIC PITFALL: AN UNTESTABLE HYPOTHESIS

If I have not said it loudly or frequently enough, recognition of design in life is not a bad thing. The problem is in trying to nail down that recognition *scientifically*. Take love as an analogy. I love my wife. I will argue with great conviction that my love is not merely a physiochemically induced sensation, but something far deeper and meaningful. I insist there is a spiritual or nonmaterial dimension that makes it genuine. But now ask me to scientifically demonstrate the spiritual roots of love. What experiment can I formulate

---

13. Lamoureux, *Evolution: Scripture and Nature Say Yes!*, 64.

that will test my hypothesis? I can offer evidence that is consistent with my claim, such as sharing my income, desiring her company, overlooking idiosyncrasies, and, if such an occasion were to arise, sacrificing my own safety in her protection. But there is no scientific test by which I can confidently distinguish natural and spiritual causes for my feelings and behavior. My confidence in the more-than-biology genuineness of my love for my wife derives wholly from my faith in the existence of phenomena that are not confined to the natural realm—things not testable by scientific means.

When I look at life, I unequivocally recognize design. Now ask me to provide scientific evidence of that design. *Specified-complexity* arguments claim that if it is highly complex and highly specific in its function, intelligence must have been used in its creation. For this to be a scientific statement and not just a philosophical position, we must be able to come up with ways of testing it as a hypothesis. Note that we are not asking whether the statement is true or not, but whether it is a claim that can be tested by naturalistic methods.

We need to be able to devise an experiment or set of observations that will support or disprove our hypothesis. Suppose we mix a cocktail of chemicals we think were present before life began and watch to see if a functioning DNA strand will form. When no DNA forms after years of observation, will we have proven intelligence must be required to make DNA? No. We may have simply mixed the wrong collection of ingredients, or we didn't wait long enough, or perhaps we simply were not lucky enough to be in the right place at the right time to witness a highly improbable event.

But what if we actually did see DNA form? Would this *disprove* the hypothesis that intelligence was required? Again, the answer is *no*. We would have proven that natural processes could in fact generate a complex DNA molecule, but the results would tell us nothing about whether an intelligent designer created the natural processes that gave rise to our observation. In other words, there is no experiment that can be conducted that will actually test the hypothesis that intelligence is required to create complex biological machinery with a specific function.

The argument for *irreducible complexity* can be reworded to say that if we cannot conceive of a possible way in which an organ or a biological process could have formed without external, intelligent manipulation, then it must have been generated by an intelligent designer. The truth of this statement is equally impossible to test using naturalistic methods, and boils down to the ability of an individual to imagine how something could have occurred by natural processes. If we cannot so imagine, then God.

ID advocates object to this as an oversimplification, because the arguments for irreducible complexity are based on robust statistical measures of probability for forming a complex organ or biological process (such as the multistep blood-clotting phenomenon), not just on the ability of the investigator to imagine how such a system could develop naturally. However, the statistical arguments wrongly assume that our understanding of all relevant biological systems is complete. As an example, when genetic mutations were first considered as an underlying cause of evolutionary adaptation, the mechanisms of mutation were poorly understood and the probability of any mutation producing a substantial improvement in an organism seemed statistically impossible. Now that mutations are understood far better, mutations leading to improved function are considered quite probable.

The idea that divine intervention is required to account for what we cannot explain by natural means is exactly analogous to the inherently flawed argument Richard Dawkins has employed in an attempt to use science *against* God. In *The Blind Watchmaker*, Dawkins's premise is that if we *can* understand the process by which life developed, then God does not exist (or was at least off doing something else while life formed).[14] But if we currently do or do not understand how something could have occurred by natural means, the only thing this tells us is that we currently do or do not understand how it could have occurred by natural means. Comprehending the process does not send God to the unemployment line, and failure to comprehend usually only means we do not have enough information yet.

OF BABIES AND BATHWATER

Though I believe Intelligent Design represents flawed theology and a poor understanding of what qualifies as science, it does not follow that advocates perform *only* pseudoscience, nor does it follow that notions of intelligence should be banned from scientific discussion. The proverbial admonition against throwing out the baby with the bathwater is fitting. Efforts to purge universities and editorial boards of all who even consider the possibility that intelligence may be behind the design of earth's myriad life-forms represent a blight on our supposed commitment to academic freedom and

14. Dawkins, *The Blind Watchmaker: Why the Evidence of Evolution Reveals a Universe Without Design*, 147.

the encouragement to go where the data lead.[15] If those engaging in the witch hunt for Intelligent Design sympathizers were consistent in ridding us of poor logic, they would likewise excommunicate people like Richard Dawkins who use equally bad logic in a vain effort to prove there is *no* intelligence responsible for natural processes. The hypocrisy is an outgrowth of an a priori commitment to a philosophical position of materialism, not a noble commitment to the scientific method. Truth never needs to fear the open discussion of ideas.

---

15. Notable examples of censoring otherwise good scientists within academia include the cases of Guillermo Gonzalez, an astronomy professor at Iowa State who lost his job (denied tenure) in 2007 due to his advocacy of Intelligent Design, and Richard Sternberg, who was forced out of his editorial position at the Smithsonian Institution in 2004 for *allowing* a peer-reviewed publication of a pro–Intelligent Design article in the *Proceedings of the Biological Society of Washington*: Brumfiel, "Darwin sceptic says views cost tenure"; Powell, "Editor explains reasons for 'Intelligent Design' article."

14

OPENING DOORS

It is undoubtedly true that upon arrival in heaven, those present will each find that at least some aspect of their theology was not entirely correct. All those whom God blessed with his written Word must certainly share a common faith in its authority and inspiration, in the centrality of Christ as Lord and Savior, and in the truth of Scripture's promises and commands, yet there are details that all will have missed in one way or another. It is very likely that the great host giving glory to God will include some who while on earth were on opposite sides of disagreements over the proper mode of baptism, the timing and nature of the rapture, or the proper practice of some of the gifts of the Spirit.

Given that we all fall short of perfect understanding, how important is it to get it exactly right on the question of origins? If uncertain, and aware that many insist that getting it wrong on origins is getting it wrong on the whole of Scripture, is it not safer to err on the side of literalism? There are, of course, some decisions that carry weightier consequences than others, but there are no doctrinal issues for which we can say it is *safe* to err. There are many things I may get wrong without jeopardizing my salvation, but each will have a consequence in this life that I would have better done without. Such consequences may be a limited experience or appreciation of God, a diminished witness to those around me, or relational hardships that could have been avoided.

CONSEQUENCES

If the best interpretation of Genesis 1 and 2 is consistent with what modern science now tells us about the age of the universe and the adaptive development of life over time, what could be the consequences of rejecting it?

Diminished View of God's Artistry

One consequence will be a failure to recognize and be awed by the magnificence of God's creativity when we see it. With each new fossil discovery, we should be captivated by and enjoy the incredible artistry manifest in the ability to bring life from nonlife and to create new creatures from old. We should wonder at God's pleasure in giving us tools to understand a past that no human was present to witness. Instead, each new find is met with reactions that may range from disinterest to disdain. Disdain of his creation!

Diminished View of God's Righteousness

The second follows the first. As each new scientific discovery is revealed that fits the evolutionary model, there will be a growing sense that God's creation does not adequately reflect his authorship. God appears to be allowing his natural creation to tell a very convincing story that is entirely wrong. This cannot help but influence our view of God's character. We will be forced to rationalize the righteousness of a God who designed his natural creation to intentionally lead astray all but those willing to deny the story it yields.

Diminished Witness

A third consequence is the most sobering. When talking with questioning materialists, we will unwittingly become an obstacle in their path to faith. They will be looking at God's workmanship while denying the Creator, and we will insist that to acknowledge the Creator they must deny his workmanship! Can there be a more ineffectual witness? How much better to simply open the door to show how the very work they see carries the signature of its Author!

A BETTER WAY

Consider again the story at the beginning of this book. Imagine what a difference it would have made to Riley if Doug had been equipped to show her how much deeper Genesis 1 is than a mere sequence of days, how Scripture and science both speak of a beginning to the universe and of the earth bringing forth life, the incredible artistry of life adapted through time, that nature continues to proclaim the glory of its Author, and that God delights in giving us amazing tools to explore the wonders of his creation long before humans walked the earth. I feel incredibly blessed to have students enter my office on the verge of giving up their faith and see the spark of spiritual life visibly reappear in their eyes through these conversations.

So what if you see the merits of the arguments laid out in this book, but still favor a more literalist view of the creation story? Let me suggest a page out of the playbook of Bradley Summers, a personal friend who served as a campus minister for many years before becoming a missionary in Europe.[1] Brad has the heart of an evangelist, enjoying nothing more than talking with nonbelievers about Christ. Personally, he leans toward a young earth. So what does he do when reaching out to a skeptic who raises the science objections? The abbreviated form of his answer is, "Here are four views Christians take on origins—let's talk about Jesus."

I look forward to the day when the church at large no longer tethers the work of Christ to the rejection of good science, opening once-closed doors to talk to people about Jesus. I long to see the church encouraging its youth to embrace careers in the sciences, free to explore the mysteries of God's creation, unfettered by cultural biases masquerading as biblical doctrine. I wish for a church with greater unity, sharing in the worship of the God who created all, even if disagreeing over some of the details of what that process may have looked like.

I pray that Doug, bringing a message more in the spirit of my friend Bradley, would make another visit to Riley.

---

1.   Real name has been changed due to the sensitive nature of his mission work.

BIBLIOGRAPHY

Alexander, Andrew. 1964. "Human origins and genetics." *The Clergy Review* 49:344–53.

Andrews, Roy Chapman. 1921. "A remarkable case of external hind limbs in a humpback whale." *American Museum Novitates*, no. 9 (June 3).

Anonymous. 1983. "To make a snake." *Creation* 5(4):9.

Aquinas, Thomas. A.D. 1265–1274. *Summa Theologica*. Translated by the Fathers of the English Dominican Province, 2nd ed. 1920. Part 1, Quest. 70, Art. 1, http://www.newadvent.org/summa.

Ashcraft, Chris. Undated. "Marsupial evolution and post-flood migration." *NW Creation Network*, http://nwcreation.net/marsupials.html.

Augustine. A.D. 394 est. *The Literal Meaning of Genesis*, Vol. 1. Translated and annotated by John Hammond Taylor. 1982. New York: Newman Press.

Baldwin, John Templeton. 2000. *Creation, Catastrophe, and Calvary: Why a Global Flood Is Vital to the Doctrine of Atonement*. Hagerstown, MD: Review & Herald Publishing.

Barnes, L. G., M. Kimura, H. Furusawa, and H. Sawamura. 1994. "Classification and distribution of Oligocene Aetiocetidae (Mammalia; Cetacea; Mysticeti) from western North America and Japan." *The Island Arc* 3:392–431.

Barrick, William D. 2016. "Old Testament evidence for a literal, historical Adam and Eve." In *Searching for Adam: Genesis and the Truth About Man's Origin* (Terry Mortenson, ed.). Green Forest, AR: Master Books, 17–52.

Bates, Gary. 2008. "That quote!: About the missing transitional fossils." *Creation Ministries International*, https://creation.com/that-quote-about-the-missing-transitional-fossils.

Batten, Don. 2014. "Natural Selection." Chap. 1 in *Evolution's Achilles' Heels*. Powder Springs, GA: Creation Book Publishers.

Baumgartel, Friedrich, and Johannes Behm. 1965. "λαρδοα. λαρδοπγμϛστz, σκληροκαρδια." In *Theological Dictionary of the New Testament*, Vol. 3 (Gerhard Kittel and Geoffrey W. Bromiley, eds.). Grand Rapids: Eerdmans, 605–14.

Bechly, Günter, and Stephen C. Meyer. 2017. "The fossil record and universal common ancestry." In *Theistic Evolution: A Scientific, Philosophical, and Theological Critique* (J. P. Moreland, S. C. Meyer, C. Shaw, A. K. Gauger, and W. Grudem, eds.). Wheaton, IL: Crossway, 332–61.

Behe, Michael. 1998. *Darwin's Black Box, The Biochemical Challenge to Evolution*. New York: Touchstone.

Benson, Joseph. 1846. *The New Testament of Our Lord and Saviour Jesus Christ, Vol 1: Matthew to the Acts of the Apostles*. New York: G. Lane & C. B. Tippett.

Bergman, Jerry. 2000. "Why abiogenesis is impossible." *Creation Research Society Quarterly* 36(4):195–207.

Blievernicht, Eric. undated. "Transitional Fossils?" *Revolution Against Evolution*, https://www.rae.org/essay-links/FAQ01.

Blocher, Henri. 1984. *In the Beginning, The Opening Chapters of Genesis.* Downers Grove, IL: InterVarsity Press.

Blount, Z. D., C. Z. Borland, and R. E. Lenski. 2008. Historical contingency and the evolution of a key innovation in an experimental population of *Escherichia coli*. *Proceedings of the National Academy of Sciences* 105:7899–906.

Bojowald, Martin. 2008. "Follow the bouncing universe." *Scientific American* 299(4):44–51.

Bonhoeffer, Dietrich. 1944. *Letters and Papers from Prison*. Translated by Reginald H. Fuller, edited by Eberhard Bethge. 1953. Basingstoke, UK: Macmillan.

Botelho, J. F., D. Smith-Paredes, S. Soto-Acuña, J. Mpodozis, V. Palma, and A. O. Vargas. 2015. "Skeletal plasticity in response to embryonic muscular activity underlies the development and evolution of the perching digit of birds." *Scientific Reports* 5:9840.

Bower, Bruce. 2005. "Human fossils are oldest yet." *Science News* 167:141.

Brand, Leonard. 2007. "Wholistic [sic] geology: Geology before, during, and after the biblical flood." *Origins* 61:7–34.

Branson, Robert D. 2016. "Science, the Bible, and human anatomy." *Perspectives on Science and Christian Faith* 68:229–36.

Brewster, David. 1855. *Memoirs of the Life, Writings, and Discoveries of Sir Isaac Newton, Vol. 2.* Edinburgh: T. Constable and Co. (Reprinted 2017. London: Forgotten Books).

Broderick, James. 1964. *Galileo: The Man, His Work, His Misfortunes.* New York: Harper & Row.

Brooke, John Hedley. 1991. *Science and Religion: Some Historical Perspectives.* New York: Cambridge University Press.

Brown, P., T. Sutikna, M. J. Morwood, R. P. Soejono, Jatmiko, E. W. Saptomo, and R. A. Due. 2004. "A new small-bodied hominin from the Late Pleistocene of Flores, Indonesia." Nature 431:1055–61.

Brown, Walt. 2008. *In the Beginning: Compelling Evidence for Creation and the Flood,* 8th ed. Center for Scientific Creation.

Brumfiel, Geoff. 2007. "Darwin sceptic says views cost tenure." *Nature* 447:364.

Budge, E. A. Wallis. 1904. *The Gods of the Egyptians, Or Studies in Egyptian Mythology, Vol 2.* London: Methuen & Co.

Burke, Ann C., and Alan Feduccia. 1997. "Developmental patterns and the identification of homologies in the avian hand." *Science* 278:666–68.

Callaway, Ewen. 2011. "First aboriginal genome sequenced." *Nature, News* (Sept. 22), http://www.nature.com/news/2011/110922/full/news.2011.551.html.

Calvin, John. 1554. *Commentary on Genesis,* Vol. 1, Article 24. Translated and edited by John King. Calvin Translation Society edition of 1965, https://www.iclnet.org/pub/resources/text/m.sion/calvgene.htm.

————. 1559. *Institutes of the Christian Religion*. Translated by Ford Lewis, edited by John T. McNeill. 1960. Philadelphia: Westminster John Knox, 1.13.1.

Carroll, Robert L. 1988. *Vertebrate Paleontology and Evolution*. New York: W. H. Freeman.

Catchpoole, David, and Carl Wieland. 2001. "Speedy species surprise." *Creation* 23(2):13–15.

Chang, J. T. 1999. "Recent common ancestors of all present-day individuals." *Advances in Applied Probability* 31:1002–1026.

Chen, Sidi, Yong E. Zhang, and Manyuan Long. 2010. "New genes in *Drosophila* quickly become essential." *Science* 330:1682–85.

Chicago Statement on Biblical Hermeneutics. 1982. International Council on Biblical Inerrancy.

Chicago Statement on Biblical Inerrancy. 1978. International Council on Biblical Inerrancy.

Collins, C. John. 2003. *Science and Faith: Friends or Foes?* Wheaton, IL: Crossway Publishers.

————. 2006. *Genesis 1–4: A Linguistic, Literary, and Theological Commentary*. Phillipsburg, NJ: P&R Publishing.

————. 2011. *Did Adam and Eve Really Exist? Who They Were and Why You Should Care*. Wheaton, IL: Crossway Books.

————. 2018. *Reading Genesis Well: Navigating History, Poetry, Science, and Truth in Genesis 1–11*. Grand Rapids: Zondervan.

Collins, Francis S. 2006. *The Language of God, A Scientist Presents Evidence for Belief*. New York: Free Press.

Copan, Paul, and Douglas Jacoby. 2018. *Origins: The Ancient Impact and Modern Implications of Genesis 1–11*. New York: Morgan James Publishing.

Cosner, Lita. 2013. "What distinguishes origins and operational science?" *Creation Ministries International, Feedback Archive* (Sept. 22), https://creation.com/origins-vs-operational-science.

Cowen, Ron. 2004. "Wrenching findings: Homing in on dark energy." *Science News* 165:132.

Coyne, Jerry A. 2016. *Faith vs. Fact: Why Science and Religion Are Incompatible*. London: Penguin Books.

Creation Ministries International. 2010. *Creation Evangelism: Sharing Your Faith* (DVD).

Criswell, Daniel. 2009. "Speciation and the animals on the ark." *Acts & Facts* 38(4):10.

Cuffey, Clifford. 2000. "The fossil record; evolution or 'scientific creation.'" New Orleans Geological Society, *NOGS Log* 40(6):17–33.

Davidson, Gregg. 2015. "Genetics, the Nephilim, and the historicity of Adam." *Perspectives on Science and Christian Faith* 67(1):24–34.

————. 2017. "The fossil record (evolutionary creation view)." In *Dictionary of Christianity and Science* (P. Copan, T. Longman III, C. L. Reese, and M. G. Strauss, eds.). Grand Rapids: Zondervan, 287–90.

Davidson, Gregg, and Ken Wolgemuth. 2010. "Christian geologists on Noah's flood: Biblical and scientific shortcomings of Flood Geology." *BioLogos scholarly essay*, https://biologos.org/files/modules/davidson_wolgemuth_scholarly_essay.pdf.

———. 2012. "How old is the earth? What God's creation professes." *The Christian Research Journal* 35:54–57.

———. 2018. "Testing and verifying old-age evidence: Lake Suigetsu varves, tree rings, and carbon-14." *Perspectives in Science and Christian Faith* 70:75–89.

Davis, Edward B., and Elizabeth Chmielewski. 2008. "Galileo and the Garden of Eden: Historical reflections on creationist hermeneutics." In *Nature and Scripture in the Abrahamic Religions: 1700–Present* (Scott Mandelbrote and Jitse Meer, eds.). Boston: Brill, 449–76.

Dawkins, Richard. 1996. *The Blind Watchmaker: Why the Evidence of Evolution Reveals a Universe Without Design*, 2nd ed. New York: W.W. Norton & Company.

Dembski, William A. 2006. *The Design Inference: Eliminating Chance through Small Probabilities*. New York: Cambridge University Press.

Deméré, T. A., M. R. McGowen, A. Berta, and J. Gatesy. 2008. "Morphological and molecular evidence for a stepwise evolutionary transition from teeth to baleen in Mysticete whales." *Systematic Biology* 57:15–37.

Détroit, F., A. S. Mijares, J. Corny, G. Daver, C. Zanolli, E. Dizon, E. Robles, R. Grün, and P. J. Piper. 2019. "A new species of Homo from the Late Pleistocene of the Philippines." *Nature* 568:181–186.

Dodd, M. S., D. Papineau, T. Grenne, J. F. Slack, M. Rittner, F. Pirajno, J. O'Neil, and C. T. S. Little. 2017. "Evidence for early life in Earth's oldest hydrothermal vent precipitates." *Nature* 543:60–64.

Douglas, A. Vibert. 1956. "Forty minutes with Einstein." *Journal of the Royal Astronomical Society of Canada* 50:100.

Duff, Joel. 2016. "Are ruminants derived from a common ancestor? Ruminating on the meaning of Noahic 'kinds.'" *Naturalis Historia* blog. https://thenaturalhistorian.com/2016/01/05/are-ruminants-derived-from-a-common-ancestor-ruminating-on-the-meaning-of-noahic-kinds/.

———. 2017. "Tiny plants—big impact: Pollen, spores, and plant fossils." In *The Grand Canyon: Monument to an Ancient Earth* (C. Hill, G. Davidson, T. Helble, W. Ranney, eds.). Grand Rapids: Kregel Publications, 145–51.

Duffy, S., C. L. Burch, and P. E. Turner. 2007. "Evolution of host specificity drives reproductive isolation among RNA viruses." *Evolution* 61:2614–22.

Dugatkin, Lee Alan, and Lyudmila Trut. 2017. *How to Tame a Fox (and Build a Dog): Visionary Scientists and a Siberian Tale of Jump-Started Evolution*. Chicago: University of Chicago Press.

Eddington, Arthur S. 1930. "On the instability of Einstein's spherical world." *Monthly Notices of the Royal Astronomical Society* 90:668–78.

———. 1931. "The end of the world: From the standpoint of mathematical physics." *Nature* 127:447–54.

Edward, Brian. 2009. "Literary forms and biblical interpretation." *Answers in Depth* 4:60–65.

Eldredge, Niles, and Stephen Jay Gould. 1972. "Punctuated equilibria: an alternative to phyletic gradualism." In *Models in Palaeobiology* (T. J. M. Schopf, ed.). San Francisco: Freeman, Cooper & Co, 82–115.

Etinger, Judah. 2003. *Foolish Faith.* Green Forest, AR: Master Books.

Fagan, Brian M. 1990. *The Journey from Eden: The Peopling of Our World.* London: Thames and Hudson.

Falk, Darrel R. 2004. *Coming to Peace with Science: Bridging the Worlds Between Faith and Biology.* Downers Grove, IL: InterVarsity Press.

Farrell, John. 2005. *The Day Without Yesterday: Lemaître, Einstein, and the Birth of Modern Cosmology.* New York: Basic Books.

Frair, Wayne. 2000. "Baraminology: Classification of created organisms." *Creation Research Science Quarterly* 37:82–91.

Garner, Paul. 2009. *The New Creationism: Building Scientific Theory on a Biblical Foundation.* Carlisle, PA: EP Books.

Garvey, Jon. 2010. "Adam and MRCA studies." *The Hump of the Camel* blog, Nov. 8, 2010, https://zenodo.org/record/1336742.

Geisler, J. H., M. W. Colbert, and J. L. Carew. 2014. "A new fossil species supports an early origin for toothed whale echolocation." *Nature* 508:383–86.

Gill, Christopher. 2007. "Galen and the Stoics: Mortal enemies or blood brothers?" *Phronesis* 52:88–120.

Gingerich, P. D., M. ul-Haq, I. S. Zalmout, I. H. Khan, and M. S. Malkani. 2001. "Origin of whales from early artiodactyls: hands and feet of Eocene Protocetidae from Pakistan." *Science* 293:2239–42.

Gingerich, P. D., M. ul-Haq, W. von Koenigswald, W. J. Sanders, B. H. Smith, and I. S. Zalmout. 2009. "New protocetid whale from the middle Eocene of Pakistan: birth on land, precocial development, and sexual dimorphism." *PLoS ONE* 4:e4366, 20p.

Gish, Duane. 1995. *Evolution: The Fossils Still Say No!* El Cajon, CA: Institute for Creation Research.

Gould, Stephen Jay. 1977. "Evolution's Erratic Pace." *Natural History* 86(5):12–16.

———. 1980. "Is a new and general theory of evolution emerging?" *Paleobiology* 6(1):119–30.

———. 1992. "Impeaching a self-appointed judge (review of Phillip Johnson's *Darwin on Trial*)." *Scientific American* 267:118–21.Gould, Stephen Jay, and Niles Eldredge. 1993. "Punctuated equilibrium comes of age." *Nature* 366:223–27.

Gramling, Carolyn. 2019. "Newfound fossils in China highlight a dizzying diversity of Cambrian life." *Science News* 195(8):14.

Grant, Andrew. 2013. "Planck refines cosmic history." *Science News* (Dec. 28):21.

Gravel, S., and M. Steel. 2015. "The existence and abundance of ghost ancestors in biparental populations." *Theoretical Population Biology* 101:47–53.

Green, Richard E., et al., 2010. "A draft sequence of the Neandertal genome." *Science* 328:710–22.

Greenwood, Kyle. 2015. *Scripture and Cosmology: Reading the Bible Between the Ancient World and Modern Science.* Downers Grove, IL: IVP Academic.

Gregory, T. R. 2005. *Animal Genome Size Database*, http://www.genomesize.com.

Gross, Charles G. 1995. "Aristotle on the brain." *The Neuroscientist* 1:245–50.

Grudem, Wayne. 1995. *Systematic Theology*. Grand Rapids: Zondervan.

Haarsma, Deborah B. 2017. "Evolutionary Creation." In *Four Views on Creation, Evolution, and Intelligent Design*. Grand Rapids: Zondervan.

Haarsma, Deborah B., and Loren D. Haarsma. 2005. *Origins: Christian Perspectives on Creation, Evolution, and Intelligent Design*. Grand Rapids: Faith Alive.

Hall, A. R., P. D. Scanlan, and A. Buckling. 2011. "Bacteria-phage coevolution and the emergence of generalist pathogens." *The American Naturalist* 177:44–53.

Hallam, A. 1983. *Great Geological Controversies*. Oxford: Oxford University Press.

Ham, Ken. 1999. *Creation Evangelism for the New Millennium*. Green Forest, AR: Master Books.

———. 2012. *The Lie: Evolution*, revised ed. Green Forest, AR: Master Books.

———. 2006. "What really happened to the dinosaurs?" In *The New Answers Book 1* (Ken Ham, ed.), Green Forest, AR: Master Books, 149–77.

Ham, Ken, and Jason Lisle. 2006. "Is There Really a God?" In *The New Answers Book 1* (Ken Ham, ed.). Green Forest, AR: Master Books, 7–24.

Hebert, Jake. 2016. "Deep core dating and circular reasoning." *Acts and Facts* 45(3).

Hebert, Jake, Andrew A. Snelling, and Timothy L. Clarey. 2016. "Do varves, tree-rings, and radiocarbon measurements prove an old Earth? Refuting a popular argument by old-earth geologists Gregg Davidson and Ken Wolgemuth." *Answers Research Journal* 9:339–61.

Henke, Kevin R. 2010. "Dr. Humphreys' young-earth helium diffusion 'dates': Numerous fallacies based on bad assumptions and questionable data." *The TalkOrigins Archive*, http://www.talkorigins.org/faqs/helium/zircons.html.

Herper, Matthew. 2017. "Illumina promises to sequence human genome for $100— but not quite yet." *Forbes Magazine* (Jan 9), https://www.forbes.com/sites/matthewherper/2017/01/09/illumina-promises-to-sequence-human-genome-for-100-but-not-quite-yet/#58638841386d.

Hieser, Michael S. 2015. *The Unseen Realm: Recovering the Supernatural Worldview of the Bible*. Bellingham, WA: Lexham Press.

Hill, Carol. 2019. *A Worldview Approach to Science and Scripture*. Grand Rapids: Kregel Publications.

Hill, Elly William. 1915. "My wife and my mother-in-law." *Puck* 78:11.

Hodge, Bodie. 2006. "Don't Creationists Believe in Some 'Wacky' Things?" In *The New Answers Book 1* (Ken Ham, ed.). Green Forest, AR: Master Books, 198–206.

Hoffmeier, James K. 2015. "Genesis 1–11 as history and theology." In *Genesis: History, Fiction, or Neither?* (Charles Halton, ed.). Grand Rapids: Zondervan, 23–58.

Hopson, James A. 1987. "The mammal-like reptiles: A study of transitional fossils." *American Biology Teacher* 49:16–26.

Hubble, Edwin. 1929. "A relation between distance and radial velocity among extra-galactic nebulae." *Proceedings of the National Academy of Sciences* 15:168–73.

Hublin, Jean-Jacques. 2000. "An evolutionary odyssey. Review of *The Human Career: Human Biological and Cultural Origins*, 2nd ed. by Richard G. Klein." *Nature* 403:363–64.

Humphreys, Russell D. 2011. "Earth's magnetic field is decaying steadily—with a little rhythm." *Creation Research Society Quarterly* 47:193–201.

Huse, Scott M. 1983. *The Collapse of Evolution*. Grand Rapids: Baker Book House.

———. 1997. *The Collapse of Evolution*, 3rd ed. Grand Rapids: Baker Book House.

Jacobs, G. S., G. Hudjashov, L. Saag, P. Kusuma, C. C. Darusallam, D. J. Lawson, M. Mondal, L. Pagani, F. X. Ricaut, M. Stoneking, M. Metspalu, H. Sudoyo, J. S. Lansing, and M. P. Cox. 2019. "Multiple deeply divergent Denisovan ancestries in Papuans." *Cell* 177: 1010-21.E32.

Jappah, Daniel. 2007. *Evolution: A Grand Monument to Human Stupidity*. Morrisville, NC: Lulu Press.

Jeanson, Nathaniel T., and Jeffrey P. Tomkins. 2016. "Genetics confirms the recent, supernatural creation of Adam and Eve." In *Searching for Adam: Genesis and the Truth About Man's Origen* (Terry Mortenson, ed.). Green Forest, AR: Master Books, 287–330.

Jerlström, Pierre. 2000. "Jumping wallaby genes and post-flood speciation." *Journal of Creation* 14:9–10.

Johns, Warren H. 2016. "Scriptural geology, then and now." *Answers Research Journal* 9:317–37.

Johnson, Phillip. 1997. "What is Darwinism? Why science clings to a fractured paradigm." *Christian Research Journal* (Spring): 20–26.

Jones, Lucy. 2016. "A Soviet scientist created the only tame foxes in the world." *BBC News* (Sept. 13), http://www.bbc.com/earth/story/20160912-a-soviet-scientist-created-the-only-tame-foxes-in-the-world.

Kaku, Michio. 1996. "What happened before the Big Bang?" *Astronomy* 24(5):34–41.

Kelly, Douglas F. 1997. *Creation and Change: Genesis 1.1–2.4 in the Light of Changing Scientific Paradigms*. Scotland: Christian Focus Publications.

Kemp, Kenneth W. 2011. "Science, theology, and monogenesis." *American Catholic Philosophical Quarterly* 85(2):217–36.

Kennedy, Elaine. 2000. "Solnhofen limestone: Home of archaeopteryx." *Geoscience Research Institute, Geoscience Reports* 30:1–4.

Kline, Meredith. 1996. "Space and time in the Genesis cosmogony." *Perspectives on Science and Christian Faith* 48:2–15.

Krause, J., Q. Fu, J. M. Good, B. Viola, M. V. Shunkov, A. P. Derevianko, and S. Pääbo. 2010. "The complete mitochondrial DNA genome of an unknown hominin from southern Siberia." *Nature* 464 (7290):894–97.

Kulikovsky, Andrew. 2002. "Evenings and mornings." *Journal of Creation* 16(2):83.

Lacey, Troy. 2014. Book review of *Inside the Nye Ham Debate*. Answers in Genesis, https://answersingenesis.org/reviews/books/book-review-inside-the-nye-ham-debate.

Lambert, O., G. Bianucci, R. Salas-Gismondi, C. D. Celma, E. Steurbaut, M. Urbina, and C. de Muizon. 2019. "An amphibious whale from the Middle Eocene of Peru reveals early South Pacific dispersal of quadrupedal cetaceans." *Current Biology* 29:1352–59.

Lamont, Ann. 1991. "Louis Pasteur, outstanding scientist and opponent of evolution (1822–1895)." *Creation* 14:16–19.

Lamoureux, Denis O. 2010. "Evolutionary creation: Moving beyond the evolution versus creation debate." *Christian Higher Education* 9:28–48.

———. 2016. *Evolution: Scripture and Nature Say Yes!* Grand Rapids: Zondervan.

Leisola, Matti. 2017. "Evolution: A story without a mechanism." In *Theistic Evolution: A Scientific, Philosophical, and Theological Critique* (J. P. Moreland, S. C. Meyer, C. Shaw, A. K. Gauger, and W. Grudem, eds.). Wheaton, IL: Crossway, 139–63.

Lennox, John C. 2011. *God and Stephen Hawking: Whose Design Is It Anyway?* Oxford: Lion Books.

Lents, Nathan H. 2018. *Human Errors: A Panorama of Our Glitches, From Pointless Bones to Broken Genes.* New York: Houghton Mifflin Harcourt.

Levin, Harold. 1999. *The Earth Through Time,* 6th ed. New York: Saunders College Publishing.

Lightner, Jean K. 2012. "Mammalian ark kinds." *Answers Research Journal* 5:151–204.

Lisle, Jason. 2006. *Taking Back Astronomy.* Green Forest, AR: Master Books.

———. 2008. "Can Creationists Be 'Real' Scientists?" In *The New Answers Book 2* (Ken Ham, ed.). Green Forest, AR: Master Books, 143–48.

Luo, Z. X., P. Chen, G. Li, and M. Chen. 2007. "A new eutriconodont mammal and evolutionary development in early mammals." *Nature* 446:288–93.

Luskin, Casey. 2017. "Missing transitions: human origins and the fossil record." In *Theistic Evolution: A Scientific, Philosophical, and Theological Critique* (J. P. More-land, S. C. Meyer, C. Shaw, A. K. Gauger, and W. Grudem, eds.). Wheaton, IL: Crossway, 289–327.

Luther's Works, Table Talk, vol. 54, no. 4638. 1967. Edited by T. G. Tappert and H. T. Lehmann. Philadelphia: Fortress Press.

Marsh, Frank Lewis. 1941. *Fundamental Biology.* Unknown binding.

Martin, Robert A. 2004. *Missing Links: Evolutionary Concepts and Transitions Through Time.* Sudbery, MA: Jones and Bartlett Publishers.

Martin, Timothy P., and Jeffrey L Vaughn. 2007. *Beyond Creation Science,* 3rd ed. Whitehall, MT: Apocalyptic Vision Press.

Marx, Felix G., Olivier Lambert, and Mark D. Uhen. 2016. *Cetacean Paleobiology.* Hoboken, NJ: Wiley Blackwell.

Mayor, Adrienne. 2011. *The First Fossil Hunters: Dinosaurs, Mammoths, and Myth in Greek and Roman Times.* Princeton, NJ: Princeton University Press.

McArthur, John. 2002. "Creation: Believe it or not." *The Master's Seminary Journal* 13:5–32.

McCabe, Robert V. 2008. "A critique of the Framework Interpretation of the Creation week." In *Coming to Grips with Genesis* (Terry Mortenson, ed.). Green Forest, AR: New Leaf Publishing Group, 211–50.

McDougall, I., F. H. Brown, and J. G. Fleagle. 2005. "Stratigraphic placement and age of modern humans from Kibish, Ethiopia." *Nature* 433:733–36.

McKinney, Frank. 1999. "The age of things found in the earth." In *Evolution: Investigating the Evidence* (J. Scotchmorr and D. Springer, eds.). *Paleontological Society Special Publication* 9:39–57.

McKinnon, Malcolm. 1997. *Bateman New Zealand Historical Atlas*. Auckland: David Bateman Publishing.

McKinnon, Malcolm (ed.). 1997. *Bateman New Zealand Historical Atlas*. David Bateman in association with Historical Branch, Dept. of Internal Affairs.

Menton, David. 2013. "Are there transitional forms in the fossil record?" In *The New Answers Book 4* (Ken Ham, ed.). Green Forest, AR: Master Books, 163–72.

Menton, David, Georgia Purdom, and John Upchurch. 2013. "Cavemen … really?" In *The New Answers Book 4* (Ken Ham, ed.). Green Forest, AR: Master Books, 77–86.

Meyer, J. R., D. T. Dobias, J. S. Weitz, J. E. Barrick, R. T. Quick, and R. E. Lenski. 2012. "Repeatability and contingency in the evolution of a key innovation in Phage Lambda." *Science* 335 (2012):428–32.

Meyer, Stephen C. 2010. *Signature in the Cell: DNA and the Evidence for Intelligent Design*. San Francisco: HarperOne.

Miller, Johnny V., and John M. Soden. 2012. *In the Beginning … We Misunderstood: Interpreting Genesis 1 in Its Original Context*. Grand Rapids: Kregel Publications.

Miller, Keith (ed.). 2003. *Perspectives on an Evolving Creation*. Grand Rapids: Eerdmans.

Miller, Keith B. 2014. "The fossil record of the Cambrian 'Explosion': Resolving the tree of life." *Perspectives on Science and Christian Faith* 66:67–82.

———. 1999. *Finding Darwin's God: A Scientist's Search for Common Ground Between God and Evolution*. New York: Cliff Street Books.

Miller, Kenneth R. 2004. "The flagellum unspun: The collapse of 'irreducible complexity.'" In *Debating Design* (William A. Dembski and Michael Ruse, eds.). Cambridge: Cambridge University Press, 81–97.

Mitton, Simon. 2011. *Fred Hoyle: A Life in Science*. New York, NY: Cambridge University Press.

Monastersky, Richard. 1998. "Feathered dinosaurs found in China." *Science News* 153:404.

Morris, Henry M. 1970. *Biblical Cosmology and Modern Science*. Grand Rapids: Baker.

———. (ed.). 1974. *Scientific Creationism*, 1st ed. Green Forest, AR: Master Books.

———. (ed.). 1985. *Scientific Creationism*, 2nd ed. Green Forest, AR: Master Books.

———. 1999. "Creation Evangelism." *Acts and Facts* 28(10):a–d.

———. 2001. "The microwave of evolution." *Back to Genesis* 152 (Aug.):a–d.

Morris, Henry M., and Henry M. Morris III. 1996. *Many Infallible Proofs*, revised and expanded. Green Forest, AR: Master Books.

Morris, John D. 2008. "Creation evangelism." *Acts and Facts*. 37(11):3.

———. 2008. "Sunlight before the sun." *Acts and Facts* 37(1):14.

———. 2010. "Earth's magnetic field." *Acts and Facts* 39(8):16.

Mortenson, Terry. 2006. "Why shouldn't Christians accept millions of years?" In *The New Answers Book 1* (Ken Ham, ed.). Green Forest, AR: Master Books, 25–30.

———. 2008. "Where did the idea of 'millions of years' come from?" In *The New Answers Book 2* (Ken Ham, ed.). Green Forest, AR: Master Books, 111–22.

———. 2016. "Adam, morality, the Gospel, and the authority of Scripture." In *Searching for Adam: Genesis and the Truth About Man's Origin* (Terry Mortenson, ed.). Green Forest, AR: Master Books, 459–502.

———. 2016. "When was Adam created?" In *Searching for Adam: Genesis and the Truth About Man's Origin* (Terry Mortenson, ed.). Green Forest, AR: Master Books, 139–64.

Morton, Glenn. 2001. "The geologic column and its implications for the flood." *TalkOrigins Archives*, http://www.talkorigins.org/faqs/geocolumn/.

Müller, R. D., M. Sdrolias, C. Gaina, and W. R. Roest. 2008. "Age, spreading rates and spreading symmetry of the world's ocean crust." *Geochemistry, Geophysics, Geosystems*, 9:Q04006.

Nadis, Steve. 2005. "Making multiverses." *Astronomy* 33(10):34–39.

National Academy of Sciences. 2008. *Science, Evolution, and Creationism*. Washington, DC: National Academies Press.

Nedin, Chris. 2002. "All about *Archaeopteryx*." *TalkOrigins Archive*, www.talkorigins.org/faqs/archaeopteryx/info.html.

Nielsen, J.T., A. Guffanti, and S. Sarkar. 2016. "Marginal evidence for cosmic acceleration from Type 1a supernovae." *Nature* 6:35596.

Oard, Michael J. 2006. "Where does the Ice Age fit?" In *The New Answers Book 1*. Green Forest, AR: Master Books, 207–19.

———. 2009. "Do varves contradict biblical history?" In *Rock Solid Answers: The Biblical Truth Behind 14 Geological Questions* (Michael J. Oard and John K. Reed, eds.). Green Forest, AR: Master Books, 125–48.

———. 2009. "Landslides win in a landslide over ancient 'Ice Ages.'" In *Rock Solid Answers: The Biblical Truth Behind 14 Geological Questions* (Michael J. Oard and John K. Reed, eds.). Green Forest, AR: Master Books, 111–24.

———. 2010. "The geological column is a general flood order with many exceptions." *Journal of Creation* 24:78–82.

Ogawa, R., and T. A. Kamiya. 1957. "Case of the Cachalot [sperm whale] with protruded rudimentary hind limb." *Scientific Reports of the Whales Research Institute* No. 12, 197–208.

Opderbeck, David. 2010. "A 'historical' Adam?" *BioLogos*, April 15, https://biologos.org/blogs/archive/a-historical-adam.

Origen. A.D. 184–253. *De Principiis, Book 4, Entry 16*, Translated by Frederick Crombie. 1885. (A. Roberts, J. Donaldson, and A. C. Coxe, eds., revised by K. Knight). Buffalo, NY: Christian Literature Publishing Co.

———. A.D. 240 est. *Homilies on Jeremiah and 1 Kings 28*. Translated by John Clark Smith. 1998. *The Fathers of the Patristic Church Series, Book 97*. Washington, DC: The Catholic University of America Press.

Otis, John M. 2013. *Theistic Evolution: A Sinful Compromise*. Triumphant Publications Ministries.

Pääbo, Svante. 2015. *Neanderthal Man: In Search of Lost Genomes*. New York: Basic Books.

Packer, J. I. 1993. *God Has Spoken: Revelation and the Bible*, 3rd ed. Grand Rapids: Baker.

Paley, William. 1802. *Natural Theology or Evidences of the Existence and Attributes of the Deity*. London: Wilks and Taylor.

Palmer, Jason. 2011. "Nobel physics prize honours accelerating universe find." *BBC News* (Oct. 4), http://www.bbc.com/news/science-environment-15165371.

Patterson, Roger. 2007. *Evolution Exposed: Biology*. Petersburg, KY: Answers in Genesis.

———. 2011. *Evolution Exposed: Earth Science*. Petersburg, KY: Answers in Genesis.

Pearce, E., C. Stringer, and R. Dunbar. 2013. "New Insights into differences in brain organization between Neanderthals and anatomically modern humans." *Proceedings of the Royal Society B* 280:20130168.

Peredo, C. M., N. D. Pyenson, C. D. Marshall, and M. D. Uhen. 2018. "Tooth loss precedes the origin of baleen in whales." *Current Biology* 28, 1–9

Perkins, Sid. 2007. "Catching evolution in the act." *Science News* 171:190.

———. 2008. "Seafloor chemistry: Life's building blocks made inorganically." *Science News* 173(5):6.

Peters, E. K. 1996. *No Stone Unturned: Reasoning About Rocks and Fossils*. New York: W. H. Freeman and Company.

Pojman, Louis P., and Michael Rea. 2012. *Philosophy of Religion: An Anthology*, 6th ed. Boston, MA: Wadsworth.

Powell, Michael. 2005. "Editor explains reasons for 'Intelligent Design' article." *Washington Post* (Aug. 19):A19.

Prothero, Donald R. 2007. *Evolution: What the Fossils Say and Why It Matters*. New York: Columbia University Press.

Purdom, Georgia. 2007. "Antibiotic resistance of bacteria: An example of evolution in action?" *Answers Magazine* (Sept. 19):74–76.

Purdom, Georgia, and Bodie Hodge. 2009. "What are 'kinds' in Genesis?" In *The New Answers Book 3* (Ken Ham, ed.). Green Forest, AR: Master Books, 37–46.

Qiang, J., P. J. Currie, M.A. Norrell, and J. Shu-An. 1998. "Two feathered dinosaurs from northeastern China." *Nature* 393:753–61.

Rana, Fazale. 2001. "Pseudogenes and the origin of humanity: A response to the Venema critique of the RTB Human Origins Model, Part 6." *Reasons to Believe* (Jan. 11), https://reasons.org/explore/publications/tnrtb/read/tnrtb/2011/01/12/pseudogenes-and-the-origin-of-humanity-a-response-to-the-venema-critique-of-the-rtb-human-origins-model-part-6.

Raup, David M. 1979. "Conflicts between Darwin and paleontology." *Field Museum of Natural History Bulletin* 50:22.

Reed, J. K., P. Klevberg, C. Bennett, J. Akridge, C. R. Froede Jr., and T. Lott. 2004. "Beyond Scientific Creationism." *Creation Research Science Quarterly* 41(3):216–30.

Reed, John K. 2000. *Plain Talk About Genesis*. Los Alamos, NM: Deo Volente Publishing.

Richter, Daniel, et al., 2017. "The age of the hominin fossils from Jebel Irhoud, Morocco, and the origins of the Middle Stone Age." *Nature* 546:293–96.

Ridley, Mark. 1981. "Who Doubts Evolution?" *New Scientist* 90:830–32.

Rohde, D. L. T., S. Olson, and J. T. Chang. 2004. "Modelling the recent common ancestry of all living humans." *Nature* 431:562–66.

Romanes, George John. 1910. *Darwin, and After Darwin, Vol 1*. Chicago: Open Court Publishing Company.

Rosen, Meghan. 2017. "Tiny fossils could be oldest signs of life." *Science News* (Apr. 1):6.

Ross, Hugh. 1991. *The Fingerprint of God: Recent Scientific Discoveries Reveal the Unmistakable Identity of the Creator*. Orange, CA: Promise Publishing Co.

———. 1998. *The Genesis Question: Scientific Advances and the Accuracy of Genesis*. Colorado Springs: NavPress.

Ross, Marcus. 2010. "Those not-so-dry bones." In *A Pocket Guide to Dinosaurs*. Petersburg, KY: Answers in Genesis, 83–85.

———. 2017. "The fossil record (young-earth creation view)." In *Dictionary of Christianity and Science* (P. Copan, T. Longman III, C. L. Reese, and M. G. Strauss, eds.). Grand Rapids: Zondervan, 290–94.

Russell, Emmet. 1967. "Genealogy of Jesus Christ." In *The Zondervan Pictorial Bible Dictionary* (M. C. Tenney, ed.). Grand Rapids: Zondervan.

Sailhamer, John H. 1990. "Genesis." In *The Expositor's Bible Commentary, Volume 2: Genesis–Numbers* (F. E. Gaebelein, ed.). Grand Rapids: Zondervan, 75–79.

Sample, Ian. 2011. "'Oldest bird' *Archaeopteryx* knocked off its perch in controversial new study." *The Guardian* (July 27), https://www.theguardian.com/science/2011/jul/27/oldest-bird-archaeopteryx-study.

Sankaran, A. V. 2002. "The controversy over early-Archaean microfossils." *Current Science* 83:15–17.

Sarfati, Jonathan. 1997. "How did all the animals fit on Noah's ark?" *Creation* 19(2):16–19.

———. 1999. "The non-evolution of the horse: Special creation or evolved rock badger?" *Creation* 21(3):28–31.

———. 1999. *Refuting Evolution*. Green Forest, AR: Master Books.

———. 2002. *Refuting Evolution 2*. Green Forest, AR: Master Books.

Schopf, J., and B. Packer. 1987. "Early Archean (3.3-billion to 3.5-billion-year-old) microfossils from Warrawoona Group, Australia." *Science* 237:70–73.

Schweitzer, Mary H., et al., 2009. "Biomolecular characterization and protein sequences of the Campanian hadrosaur *B. canadensis*." *Science* 324:626–31.

Schweitzer, Mary H., Jennifer L. Wittmeyer, and John R. Horner. 2005. "Gender-specific reproductive tissue in ratites and *Tyrannosaurus rex*." *Science* 308:1456–60.

Senter, Phil. 2011. "The defeat of flood geology by flood geology." *Reports of the National Center for Science Education* 31(3).

Service, Robert F. 2017. "'I don't care what they say about me': Paleontologist stares down critics in her hunt for dinosaur proteins." *Science, News* (Sept. 13), http://www.sciencemag.org/news/2017/09/i-don-t-care-what-they-say-about-me-paleontologist-stares-down-critics-her-hunt/.

———. 2017. "Scientists retrieve 80-million-year-old dinosaur protein in 'milestone' paper." *Science*, News (Jan. 31), http://www.sciencemag.org/news/2017/01/scientists-retrieve-80-million-year-old-dinosaur-protein-milestone-paper/.

Short, Kevin. 2017. "Phenomenological language and semantic naïveté." *Answers Research Journal* 10:115–20.

Slipher, V. M. 1915. "Spectrographic observations of nebulae." *Popular Astronomy* 23:21–24.

Slon, V., F. et al., 2018. "The genome of the offspring of a Neanderthal mother and a Denisovan father." *Nature* 561:113–16.

Snelling, Andrew A. 2006. "Can catastrophic plate tectonics explain flood geology?" In *The New Answers Book* (Ken Ham, ed.). Green Forest, AR: Master Books, 186–97.

———. 2008. "Doesn't the order of fossils in the rock record favor long ages?" In *The New Answers Book 2* (Ken Ham, ed.). Green Forest, AR: Master Books, 341–54.

———. 2010. "Order in the fossil record." *Answers Magazine* (Nov. 3):64–68.

———. 2015. "Hawaii's volcanic origins—instant paradise." *Answers Magazine* (Oct. 20):56–59.

Snelling, Andrew A., David Menton, Danny R. Faulkner, and Georgia Purdom. 2013. "What are some of the best evidences in science of a young creation?" In *The New Answers Book 4* (Ken Ham, ed.). Green Forest, AR: Master Books, 111–30.

Snoke, David. 2006. *A Biblical Case for an Old Earth.* Grand Rapids: Baker Books.

Soderblom, David R. 2010. "The ages of stars." *Annual Review of Astronomy and Astrophysics* 48:581–629.

Stearley, Ralph. 2013. "The Cambrian Explosion: How much bang for the buck?" *Perspectives on Science and Christian Faith*, 65:245–57.

———. 2017. "Fossils of the Grand Canyon and Grand Staircase." In *The Grand Canyon: Monument to an Ancient Earth* (C. Hill, G. Davidson, T. Helble, W. Ranney, eds.). Grand Rapids: Kregel Publications, 131–43.

Stott, J. R. W. 1972. *Understanding the Bible.* London: Scripture Union.

Struthers, John. 1881. "On the bones, articulations, and muscles of the rudimentary hind-limb of the Greenland right-whale (*Balaena mysticetus*)." *Journal of Anatomy and Physiology* 15:141–321.

Sunderland, Luther. 1988. *Darwin's Enigma: Fossils and Other Problems.* El Cajon, CA: Master Books.

Sutera, Raymond. 2000. "Origin of whales and the power of independent evidence." *Reports of the National Center for Science Education* 20(5):33–41.

Swamidass, S. Joshua. 2015. "The overlooked science of genealogical ancestry." *Perspectives on Science and Christian Faith* 70(1):19–35.

———. 2019. *The Genealogical Adam and Eve: The Surprising Science of Universal Ancestry*. Downers Grove, IL: InterVarsity Press.

Takizawa, T., K. J. Meaburn, and T. Misteli. 2008. "The meaning of gene positioning." *Cell* 135:9–13.

Tattersall, Ian. 2009. *The Fossil Trail, 2nd ed.* Oxford: Oxford University Press.

Taylor, Paul F. 2006. "How did animals spread all over the world from where the ark landed?" In *The New Answers Book 1* (Ken Ham, ed.). Green Forest, AR: Master Books, 141–48.

Thewissen, J. G. M. 2014. *The Walking Whales: From Land to Water in Eight Million Years*. Oakland: University of California Press.

Thomas, Brian. 2011. "Archaeopteryx is a bird … again." *Institute for Creation Research* (Nov. 8), http://www.icr.org/article/6429.

Tomkins, Jeffrey T. 2012. "Mechanisms of adaptation in biology: genetic diversity." *Acts and Facts* 41(5).

Turner, G. 1981. "The development of the atmosphere." In *The Evolving Earth* (L. R. M. Cocks, ed.). London: British Museum, 121–36.

Tyler, Sheena. 2017. "Evidence from embryology challenges evolutionary theory." In *Theistic Evolution: A Scientific, Philosophical, and Theological Critique* (J. P. Moreland, S. C. Meyer, C. Shaw, A. K. Gauger, and W. Grudem, eds.). Wheaton, IL: Crossway, 289–327.

Uhen, Mark D. 2010. "The origin(s) of whales." *Annual Review of Earth and Planetary Sciences* 38:189–219.

Vail, Tom (ed.). 2003. *Grand Canyon: A Different View*. Green Forest, AR: Master Books.

Vail, Tom, Michael Oard, Dennis Bokovoy, and John Hergenrather. 2008. *Your Guide to the Grand Canyon: A Different Perspective*. Green Forest, AR: Master Books.

van Bavel, Tarsicius. 1990. "The Creator and the integrity of the Creation." *Augustinian Studies* 21:1–33.

Vaterlaus, Gary. 2010. "Underneath a solid sky." In *Demolishing Supposed Bible Contradictions*, vol. 1 (Ken Ham, ed.). Green Forest, AR: Master Books, 30–32.

Venema, Dennis R., and Scot McKnight. 2017. *Adam and the Genome: Reading Scripture after Genetic Science*. Grand Rapids: Brazos Press.

Wade, Andrew D., and Andrew J. Nelson. 2013. "Evisceration and excerebration in the Egyptian mummification tradition." *Journal of Archaeological Science* 40:4198–206.

Wagner, Günter P., and Jacques A. Gauthier. 1999. "1, 2, 3 = 2, 3, 4: A solution to the problem of the homology of the digits in the avian hand." *Proceedings of the National Academy of Sciences* 96:5111–16.

Walton, John H., and D. Brent Sandy. 2013. *The Lost World of Scripture: Ancient Literary Culture and Biblical Authority*. Downers Grove, IL: InterVarsity Press.

Whitcomb, John C., and Henry M. Morris. 1961. *The Genesis Flood: The Biblical Record and Its Scientific Implications.* Phillipsburg, NJ: P&R Publishing.

White, A. J. Monty. 2006. "Hasn't evolution been proven true?" In *The New Answers Book 1* (Ken Ham, ed.). Green Forest, AR: Master Books, 283–95.

White, Robert. 1980. "Calvin and Copernicus: The problem reconsidered." *Calvin Theological Journal* 15:233–43.

Whitmore, John. 2006. "Difficulties with a flood model for the Green River formation." *Journal of Creation* 20(1):81–85.

Wiechert, Uwe H. 2002. "Earth's early atmosphere." *Science* 298:2341–42.

Wieland, Carl. 1996. "Seeing back to front: Are evolutionists right when they say our eyes are wired the wrong way?" *Creation* 18(2):38–40.

———. 1997. "Beetle bloopers: Even a defect can be an advantage sometimes." *Creation* 19(3):30.

———. 1997. "Speciation conference brings good news for creationists." *Journal of Creation* 11(2):135–36.

———. 1998. "The strange tale of the leg on the whale." *Creation* 20(3):10–13.

———. 2012. "Jesus on the age of the earth." *Creation* 34(2):51–54.

Wilcox, David L. 2016. "A proposed model for the evolutionary creation of human beings: from the image of God to the origin of sin." *Perspectives on Science and Christian Faith* 68(1):22–43.

———. 2019. "Updating human origins." *Perspectives on Science and Christian Faith* 71(1):37–49.

Wildschuttea, J. H., Z. H. Williams, M. Montesion, R. P. Subramanian, J. M. Kidd, and J. M. Coffin. 2016. "Discovery of unfixed endogenous retrovirus insertions in diverse human populations." *Proceedings of the National Academy of Sciences* 113(16):E2326–34.

Williams, Alexander. 2001. "Kingdom of the plants: Defying evolution." *Creation* 24:46–48.

Wise, Kurt P. 2002. *Faith, Form, and Time: What the Bible Teaches and Science Confirms About Creation and the Age of the Universe.* Nashville: Broadman & Holman Publishers.

———. 2017. "Step-down saltational intrabaraminic diversification." *Journal of Creation Theology and Science Series B: Life Sciences* 7:8–9.

Wise, Kurt P., and Sheila A. Richardson. 2004. *Something from Nothing: Understanding What You Believe About Creation and Why.* Nashville: Broadman & Holman Publishers.

Wolff, Hans Walter. 1974. *Anthropology of the Old Testament.* Translated by Margaret Kohl. Philadelphia: Fortress Press.

Wood, Bernard, and Paul Constantino. 2004. "Human Origins: Life at the top of the tree." In *Assembling the Tree of Life* (J. Cracraft and M. J. Donoghue, eds.). New York: Oxford University Press, 517–35.

Woodmorappe, John. 1996. *Noah's Ark: A Feasibility Study.* El Cajon, CA: Institute for Creation Research.

Yeoman, Barry. 2006. "Schweitzer's dangerous discovery." *Discover Magazine* (Apr. 27), http://discovermagazine.com/2006/apr/dinosaur-dna.

Young, Davis A. 1988. "The contemporary relevance of Augustine's view of creation." *Perspectives on Science and Christian Faith* 40:42–45.

Young, Davis A., and Ralph F. Stearley. 2008. *The Bible, Rocks and Time: Geological Evidence for the Age of the Earth.* Downers Grove, IL: IVP Academic.

Young, Edward J. 1964. *Studies in Genesis One.* Phillipsburg, NJ: P&R Publishing.

Younker, Randall W., and Richard M. Davidson. 2015. "The myth of the solid heavenly dome: Another look at the Hebrew רָקִיעַ (*raqia*)." In *The Genesis Creation Account and Its Reverberations in the Old Testament* (Gerald A. Klingbeil, ed.). Berrien Springs, MI: Andrews University Press, 31–56.

NAME (NONBIBLICAL) INDEX

SUBJECT INDEX

T

U

V

W

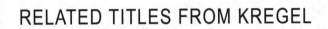

RELATED TITLES FROM KREGEL

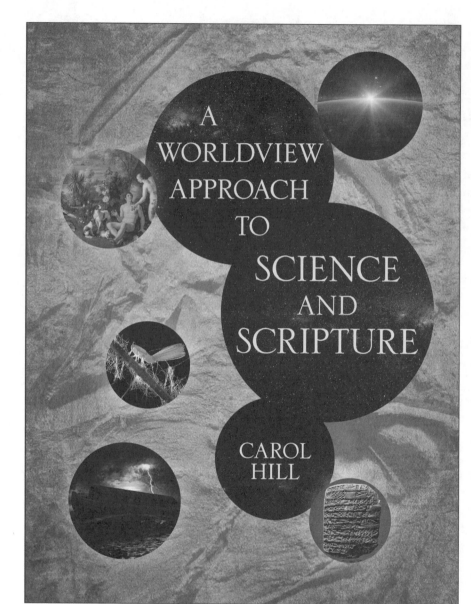

A
WORLDVIEW
APPROACH
TO
SCIENCE
AND
SCRIPTURE

CAROL
HILL

The *Grand Canyon*
MONUMENT TO AN
ANCIENT EARTH

CAN NOAH'S FLOOD
EXPLAIN THE GRAND CANYON?

Carol Hill, Gregg Davidson,
Tim Helble, & Wayne Ranney, editors

IN THE BEGINNING...
WE MISUNDERSTOOD

*Interpreting Genesis 1
in Its Original Context*

JOHNNY V. MILLER | JOHN M. SODEN